Zukunftsfähige Unternehmensführung in Forschung und Praxis

Reihe herausgegeben von

S. Kaiser, Neubiberg, Deutschland

Die Reihe „Zukunftsfähige Unternehmensführung in Forschung und Praxis" beinhaltet ausgewählte Schriften, die sich mit Theorien, Konzepten und Instrumenten für fortschrittsfähige Organisationen beschäftigen. Das Themenspektrum wird dabei durch die drei Eckpunkte, Personal-Organisation-Strategie, aufgespannt. Das Fundament der Schriftenreihe bilden wissenschaftlich fundierte Dissertationsschriften mit Anspruch auf Praxisrelevanz. Angereichert wird die Reihe durch für wertvoll erachtete Sammelbände aus Wissenschaft und Praxis. Die Verfasser wollen sowohl die Wissenschaft als auch die Führungspraxis mit Interesse an zukunftsfähiger Unternehmensführung ansprechen.

Reihe herausgegeben von
Prof. Dr. Stephan Kaiser
Universität der Bundeswehr München

Weitere Bände in der Reihe http://www.springer.com/series/13620

Maximilian Eberl

Organizational Routines Meet Experimental Psychology

The Role of Implicit Learning in the Modification of Organizational Routines

With a foreword by Prof. Dr. Stephan Kaiser

Springer Gabler

Maximilian Eberl
Neubiberg, Germany

Dissertation Universität der Bundeswehr München, Neubiberg, 2018

ISSN 2570-0219 ISSN 2570-0227 (electronic)
Zukunftsfähige Unternehmensführung in Forschung und Praxis
ISBN 978-3-658-23561-1 ISBN 978-3-658-23562-8 (eBook)
https://doi.org/10.1007/978-3-658-23562-8

Library of Congress Control Number: 2018955149

Springer Gabler

This Springer Gabler imprint is published by the registered company Springer Fachmedien Wiesbaden GmbH part of Springer Nature
The registered company address is: Abraham-Lincoln-Str. 46, 65189 Wiesbaden, Germany

Foreword

To date, the research on organizational routines is a relatively advanced field of study, as we know that organizational routines increase organizational efficiency. However, we also know that organizational routines need to evolve and new organizational members need to acquire them. In this context, the distinction between so-called ostensive and performative aspects has shown to be of particular interest. Looking at the performative aspects shows the importance of the individual in exercising the routine. Empirical observation shows that the exercise of the routine can deviate from the organizationally and formally desired way (ostensive aspect). One reason for this deviance could be that employees did not properly learn or understand the organizational routine.

The present work takes this as a starting point and wishes to explain whether a deeper understanding of implicit learning and related theories and processes might fill the gap between the ostensive and performative aspects of practicing organizational routines. Therefore, the author, Maximilian Eberl, follows the idea to link organizational routine research and experimental learning psychology. Concretely, he turns to a specific implicit learning paradigm and proposes to use the so-called AAT-training structure to investigate to what extent implicit learning is supports the learning of organizational routines. Thereby, he aims at explaining the great potential of implicit learning from three different organizational perspectives (i.e. vertical, horizontal and temporal).

Maximilian Eberl has worked on a very relevant topic, both from a research and practical point of view. The high degree of interdisciplinarity, as the author integrates approaches from experimental psychology, shows the great level of innovation of the work. It is desirable for the present work that practitioners and researchers who deal with the phenomenon of organizational routines pick up these ideas. Eberl's work provides a valuable foundation for understanding the role of implicit learning in the execution of organizational routines. Thus, the work and its author make an important contribution to the research and practice of viable organizations and management.

Munich, July 2018 Univ.-Prof. Dr. Stephan Kaiser

Acknowledgements

Thank you…

… Werner Itzelberger, for making the integration of military and academic career possible. You provided the basis for conducting experimental research in this study and offered me an outstanding network for personal and professional development.

… Stephan Kaiser, for great supervision and support.

… to my colleagues at the chair for Human Resource Management and Organization Science at the Bundeswehr University Munich for a great collaboration and fruitful discussions.

… to the Bundeswehr staff, for helping me with any question and for participating in this experimental study.

A special dedication to my wife Carolin who supported me all along the way and to my children Anna and Eva for spending all the positive energy to me.

Munich, July 2018 Dr. Maximilian Eberl

Contents

List of tables

List of figures

Abbreviations

AAT	Approach-Avoidance Task
ANCOVA	Analysis of covariance
ANOVA	Analysis of variance
ATC	Air traffic control
BDSG	Federal Data Protection Act (*German*: Bundesdatenschutzgesetz)
BMVg	German Federal Ministry of Defence (*German*: Bundesministerium der Verteidigung)
CBM	Cognitive bias modification
CR	Conditioned reaction
DV	Dependent variable
EG	Experimental group
fMRI	Functional magnetic resonance imaging
HCL	High cognitive load
IAT	Functional magnetic resonance imaging
ICL	Increased cognitive load
IFTTT	Implicit Association Test
ISO	International Organization for Standardization
IV	Independent variable
LCL	Low cognitive load
LSLT	The logical structure of linguistic theory
NIH	Not-invented-here
NS	Neutral stimulus
NTG	Non-training group
NWS	New writing style
OWS	Old writing style
PET	Positron emission tomography
PG	Placebo group
RC	Regulatory control
RT	Reaction time
SOP	Standard operating procedure
UCR	Unconditioned reaction
UCS	Unconditioned stimulus

1 Introduction

Organizational routines evolved into a central concept in organizational research and represent a fundamental idea of how organizations accomplish their work (Felin and Foss, 2009; Salvato and Rerup, 2010; Parmigiani and Howard-Grenville, 2011; Felin *et al.*, 2012). In the past decades, research on organizational routines yielded major results (e.g., Nelson and Winter, 1982; Feldman and Pentland, 2003) and strengthened the understanding of the concept. Scholars proved routines to be essential for organizations and to be an integral part of organizations (Becker, 2008; Hodgson, 2008). Although scholars are aware of the importance of this concept, to date literature lacks a commonly accepted definition of routines and suffers from numerous ambiguities as well as inconsistencies (Cohen *et al.*, 1996; Jones and Craven, 2001; Reynaud, 2005). However, Becker (2004; 2007) identified key characteristics of routines. The characteristics embodied in most definitions of routines are the recurrence, the patterned, processual and the collective social nature (Felin and Foss, 2009). These key features are also reflected in the frequently cited definition by Feldman and Pentland (2003, p. 96), that describes a routine as a "[…] *repetitive, recognizable pattern of interdependent actions, involving multiple actors*". Nevertheless, there still exist conflicting views and unsolved problems in this area of research. Different approaches to organizational routines with parallel conversations shape the field.

Researchers on routines divide into two camps: There are those taking a capability-based perspective and those taking a practice theory-based perspective. The former, mainly represented by organizational economists, are interested in the impact of routines on the firms' economic performance, and thus study routines as a black box; the latter, mainly represented by organization theorists, want to shed light on the processes inside the black box of routines (Feldman and Pentland, 2008; Parmigiani and Howard-Grenville, 2011; Dionysiou and Tsoukas, 2013). Parmigiani and Howard-Grenville (2011, p. 443) highlighted these different approaches as "[d]*istinct but complementary* […]" and characterized a combined perspective as a fruitful approach to study organizational routines. Furthermore, they emphasized the crucial role of "[…] *individual behavior, cognition and emotion* […]" (Parmigiani and Howard-Grenville, 2011, p. 444) in organizational routines as micro-level of analysis in the combined view. Viewing an organization respectively organizational routines from the capability perspective characterizes them as an input-output model that respects the collective nature of routines as a whole. On the contrary, the practice perspective views the individual actors and their motives and intentions within the organizational structure.

However, in a combined view as suggested by Parmigiani and Howard-Grenville (2011), it is required to connect the macro (capability-perspective) and micro level (practice-perspective). One approach that allows for a downward causation of the macro level into the micro level and at the same time recognizes the relationships that form the micro level (e.g., actions, skills, individuals) into the macro level is the concept of

M. Eberl, *Organizational Routines Meet Experimental Psychology*, Zukunftsfähige Unternehmensführung in Forschung und Praxis,
https://doi.org/10.1007/978-3-658-23562-8_1

methodological individualism (Schumpeter, 1908, pp. 88-100; Schumpeter, 1908 [2010], pp. 57-63; Schumpeter, 1909). Using methodological individualism allows for interpreting routines regarding individuals as the level where actions take place, and the outcome of a routine becomes tangible (Felin *et al.*, 2012). Hodgson (2008) contributed to this requirement of methodological individualism and points out that the individuals are substrate for organizational routines to grow – that means there cannot be a macro perspective without a micro-foundation. Most widely cited in respect to individual actors (i.e., the micro-level) is the ostensive-performative model of Feldman and Pentland (2003), who conceptualized routines as a cycle of the ostensive and the performative aspect.

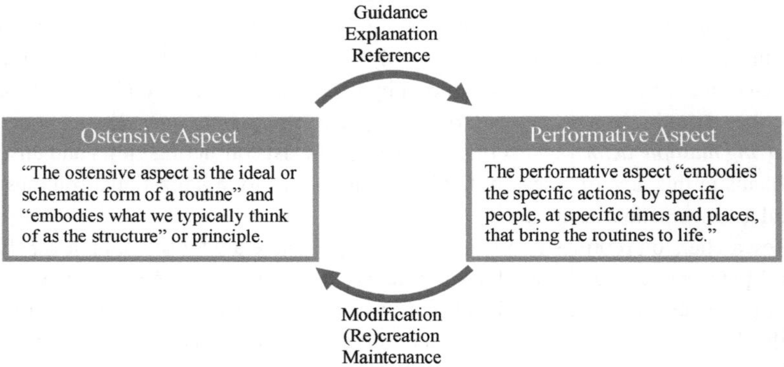

Figure 1: Visualization of the ostensive-performative distinction by Feldman and Pentland (2003, pp. 94, 101).

The ostensive aspect can be viewed as the blueprint of the organizational routine that describes the ideal schematic form of the routine and allows the organization members for guidance, explanation, and reference of what they are doing. The performative aspect "[…] *embodies the specific actions, by specific people, at specific times and places, that bring the routines to life*" (Feldman and Pentland, 2003, p. 94) and can modify, maintain or even (re)create the ostensive aspect in a feedback loop (see Figure 1). Feldman and Pentland (2003) thus viewed organizational routines as dynamic and ever-changing. That points to one of the omnipresent issues in regard to organizational routines: The misalignment of the ostensive and the performative aspect. There are different reasons why such a misalignment can arise. Two of the central issues are the need for interpretation in learning the ostensive aspect on the individual level, and the change of routines (i.e., deliberative, and non-deliberative change).

Misalignment by interpretation and learning. In more detail, the first reason for the misalignment lies in the individual actors need for interpretation and initial learning of the ostensive aspect before it can be performed. Particularly in situations when the individuals aim to perform a routine for the first time and thus have to initially interpret and learn the required information about the routine from scratch, it is likely that the performative aspect deviates substantially from the ostensive aspect. The interpretation occurs against the background of the organizational culture as well as the influence of the individual's intentional, motivational and emotional factors. Accordingly, the interpretation of routines and their underlying rules is a balancing act between the organization's expectations and the individual cognitive biases (Reynaud, 2005). The individuals' interpretative processes result in actor-specific mental models. These models determine the individual behavioral outcome of a routine (e.g., part of a routine) but also shape the overall routine performance. As there is no duplicate in humankind, the individual mental models commonly differ between the actors and so does the performative aspect of an organizational routine. Hence, the performative aspect deviates from the ostensive aspect as the organizational blueprint of the intended performance (Pentland and Feldman, 2005; Salvato and Rerup, 2010; Dionysiou and Tsoukas, 2013; Howard-Grenville *et al.*, 2016).

In applying routines, organizations seek for beneficial effects of coordination and control, regularity and reduction of uncertainty, preservation of knowledge, or economization of cognitive resources (Becker, 2004; 2005b). An actor-specific and biased interpretation of the ostensive aspect may lead to a performative aspect of the routine that varies in several respects from the intended outcome of the routine and jeopardizes the intended effects of applying routines. Viewing organizational routines as one form of organizational memory, they become a repertoire of knowledge – as mentioned, in an interpreted and eventually biased form (Miner, Ciuchta and Gong, 2008; Miller, Pentland and Choi, 2012). Routine knowledge has to be acquired before it can be brought into action.

As Senge (1990, p. 124) contributed, "[o]*rganizations learn only through individuals who learn*," and Herbert Simon (1991, p. 125) added "[a]*ll learning takes place inside individual human heads*." Learning of routine knowledge comprises both, the initial learning of the routine but also the learning that accompanies each performance of the routine. The latter, however, is on a diminishing scale and allows the organization to economize its (individual) cognitive resources over time. Rice and Cooper (2010, pp. 131-133) viewed the individual psychological processes (i.e., perception, interpretation, moderation of personal interests, and learning) also as impeding factors for the acquisition of routine knowledge and the homogenous functioning of routines in practice (see also Kogut and Zander, 1992). Because change occurs against the background of individual differences in learning and importantly in what is being learned (i.e., the interpreted knowledge), there "[…] *will always be some tension between the particular interests of individual members and the larger organizational objective or goal*" (Jaffee, 2001, p. 5; e.g., agency dilemma).

Misalignment by change. The other reason for misalignment of the ostensive and performative aspect refers to the change of routines. Becker (2005a) recognized the problem of variation respectively change in organizational routines and differentiated between two cases: Deliberative and non-deliberative change. For the first, he saw the gap in what research on routines can contribute to shape and control the preconditions of deliberative change (e.g., modeling a part of a routine). For the second type, non-deliberative change (e.g., mutation, or drift), he emphasized the "[…] *interactions of individual action and structural factors*" (Becker, 2005a, p. 258). Relating to the ostensive-performative distinction by Feldman (2003), the individual action can be located in the performative aspect and the structural factors in the ostensive aspect. Whether the change is deliberative or non-deliberative, in complex systems like organizations, change in one part of a routine takes effect on various other parts or even the complete organizational system. This effect is not always deleterious, and not always advantageous though (Nelson and Winter, 1982, p. 116).

For deliberative change initiatives, organizations may succeed in changing the structural aspect of a routine, the ostensive aspect, however, the realization of that change in the performative aspect is a different story and frequently fails. In practice, organizations then find their selves in endless iterative correction loops to bring the intended change into practice. Deliberative change of routines or its parts demand a process of relearning from the individual actor. The process of relearning can be an insuperable crux for the individual actor, as the previous actions and decisions in the routine performance already developed into associative links that proceed in a highly-automated manner without reflective decision-making. In other words, the actor is bound to the established performative aspect and cannot (or only hardly) adapt to the requirements of the changed ostensive aspect. In cases of resistance against the changed ostensive aspect, the gap between the ostensive and performative aspect might even escalate and result in the contrariwise effect as it was intended by changing the ostensive aspect. At this point, it is a smooth transition to non-deliberative change as the resistance of the individual actors can build on unconscious emotions, motivations, and intentions. Accordingly, each actor will mutate the routine differently, and in most cases, those mutations precipitate in diverging performances that increasingly drift away from the ostensive aspect (Feldman, 2000; Narduzzo, Rocco and Warglien, 2001; Becker, 2004).

Research gaps. Based on the introduced line of thought, there are several research gaps mentioned in literature that connect the points mentioned above. First and foremost, literature brought forward to examine how the level of individual action and the structural level can be aligned. As highlighted above, the alignment would allow for minimizing non-deliberative change and to foster a deliberate change of routines (Becker, 2004; 2005a; Pentland and Hærem, 2015). As yet, organizations try to enforce the compliant performance by a framework of rules and follow the misconception that such *top-downism* will result in the intended outcome of the routine. That approach even fails if the routines and rules are embodied artifacts like software. Also, incentive mechanisms (operant conditioning) frequently do not result in the intended outcome as the personal motivation, intention or emotion outweighs the incentive (Reynaud, 2005; Pentland and Feldman, 2008; Pentland and Hærem, 2015). Schulz (2008) directly connected to the gap of variation between the ostensive and performative aspect and put on the research agenda to analyze which factors could keep a routine on track.

Second, the topic of how organizational routines can be learned has its place in routine research for decades and still lacks of purposeful approaches (Geiger and Schröder, 2014). A sound understanding of the organization members' learning mechanisms for the acquisition of routines would result in the abilities to "[…] *control, design, or modify them with increased precision* […]" (Cohen and Bacdayan, 1994, p. 556).

Third, in the context of replication, it is essential be able to train and homogenously orchestrate a large number of individuals in organizations (Kogut and Zander, 1992), as well as developing an understanding of how routines carry information in the process of replication (Winter, 1990; Hodgson, 2008). So far, regarding the learning and replication of routines, organizations suffer from cost-intensive and time-consuming iterative processes to achieve the practice of a routine that is at the aspired level (Winter and Szulanski, 2001; 2002; Szulanski and Jensen, 2004). Additionally, organizations regularly fail in teaching and replicating tacit knowledge (Becker and Lazaric, 2003; Shamsie and Mannor, 2013).

Finally, the gap identified by Salvato and Rerup (2010) has substantial meaning for both issues, learning and change, regarding the misalignment of the ostensive and performative aspect. They suggested exploring routines as the link between the individual and organizational level to achieve more insights on their relationship and how the individual level can contribute to the above entities (e.g., capabilities, or strategy). Similar, Felin and colleagues (Felin and Foss, 2009; Felin *et al.*, 2012) called for an explanation of the higher level that starts at the foundations, the individuals. Contributing to this gap would allow for harmonizing the requirements arising from the individual level and those coming from the organizational level to form a goal-oriented routine that can be learned by the individual to meet the organizational intention, and that can be changed without resistance on any level.

Besides these conceptual shortcomings, there are also methodological shortcomings. Hodgson (2008) emphasized that the routine research mainly progresses by the accumulation of cases, detailed but not allowing for generalization or replication of the results. As a positive counterexample of that trend, he mentioned the laboratory study of Cohen and Bacdayan (1994), who made use of the body of knowledge in experimental psychology. Cohen and Bacdayan (1994) viewed laboratory studies as beneficial to uncover linkages between the individual and the organizational level, especially as they allow for testing hypotheses in controlled environments. Narduzzo and Warglien (2008) took the same line and suggested that organizational routines should be studied in experimental settings in laboratories. Further, they highlighted the "[…] *large body of research in experimental psychology that provides building blocks for in-depth examination of key features of routinization both at the individual and the group level*" (Narduzzo and Warglien, 2008, p. 301; see also Cohen, 1991).

Experimental psychology as methodological origin. Organizations learn through individuals who learn (Senge, 1990, p. 124). Experimental psychology covers learning as one of its well-established topics, with a long history of experimental research and a great variety of research paradigms and tools. It may, therefore, serve as a treasure chest for research on organizational routines. From a psychological point of view, learning is a cognitive process, which is subject to the duality of mind, just like any cognitive process. Psychology offers models of dual processes that divide the cognitive processes in the human mind (e.g., learning) into reflective and impulsive processes. The first are mostly explicit processes that involve reasoning and noetic decision-making, and the latter occur highly automatic with limited conscious control and thus are mostly implicit. In terms of a final common pathway, both processes interact and control human behavior. Impulsive processes predominantly control behavior under conditions of low cognitive capacity or low levels of attention (Strack and Deutsch, 2004). Learning takes place within this duality. The reflective system relies on explicit learning, which can be described as a conscious, effortful and active process that aims to memorize mainly facts (Xie, Gao and King, 2013). On the contrary, the impulsive system relies on implicit learning, which is a process that occurs effortlessly and mostly without conscious awareness. The implicitly acquired knowledge is hardly or not verbalizable (e.g., riding a bicycle, or grammar rules of someone's native language).

Learning a new task is initially a mainly reflective process, which becomes more and more impulsive due to repetition and automation. Thus, changing a well-established behavior means changing impulsive processes. Rather than taking the long and error-prone way over the reflective system via explicit learning instructions, Kaufman *et al.* (2010) proved that directly targeting the impulsive system by implicit learning is the most promising approach to change impulsive processes. Thus, in recent years, research in experimental psychology progressed in the development of training tools for implicit learning and succeeded in changing maladaptive impulsive processes in individuals, which are often crucial to the perpetuation of mental disorders such as anxiety or substance use disorders (e.g., Wiers *et al.*, 2009; 2010; 2011; Becker *et al.*, 2013; Eberl *et al.*, 2013).

There are potential points of contact between experimental psychology and routine research. As highlighted above, both, the initial implementation of a routine as well as the change of a routine require learning that finally occurs in the individual actor (Senge, 1990, p. 124; Simon, 1991). Also, organizational routines are subject to the duality of human mind. With each repetition, the balance between reflective and impulsive processing of the individual actions in routines shifts to the more automatic impulsive processing. As organizational routines also involve impulsive processes, at least in the individual actions, implicit learning may be a promising approach for routine research.

Research goals. Can implicit learning diminish the gap between the ostensive and performative aspect of an organizational routine? Following this overall question, the objective of this study is to bring together two fields of research: Organizational routines and experimental psychology – demonstrating the synergetic value of such an approach. Both fields of research will be presented in detail, carving out the obvious overlap, before implicit learning in and of organizational routines will be approached using a laboratory setting. Experimental psychology provides a great variety of both experimental study designs, allowing for replicable and generalizable results, and well-established training paradigms to assess learning processes in individuals. Thus, this study will resort to this expertise and will be the first experimental approach of this kind to meet problems of routine research on an individual level of learning, being a specialist field of experimental psychology. Using a rather young implicit learning paradigm, the Approach-Avoidance Task training (Rinck and Becker, 2007; Wiers *et al.*, 2009; Eberl *et al.*, 2013; 2014), the subjects of this study are asked to relearn a part of an organizational routine taken from the air traffic control service. That addresses a case of deliberate change as distinguished from learning a new routine and mutation or drift. Encouraged by the experimental results, this study finally aims at illustrating the great potential of implicit learning from different organizational perspectives. Those perspectives are:

- A ***vertical perspective*** that views the hierarchy of (collective) entities in organizations and seeks to contribute to an explanation of the role of impulsive processes for organizations. Within that perspective, the potential impact of implicit learning strategies in modifying impulsive processes will be discussed.
- A ***horizontal perspective*** that seeks to shed light on the role of implicit learning in the replication of organizational routines as a form of horizontal distribution of routine knowledge.
- A ***time perspective*** that focusses on the change in and of organizational routines by discussing the role of cognitive bias modification to build routines by anticipation and not by reactive evolutionary processes.

This publication is structured as follows: Chapter 2 introduces the theoretical background and divides into three sections. The first section (Chapter 2.1) develops a comprehensive understanding of organizational routines and their relation to cognate concepts. Current challenges, as well as effects of organizational routines, will be elaborated. The second section (Chapter 2.2) offers an introduction to the duality of mind and focusses on dual processing in human mind. Further, experimental psychology with the focus on learning and its different conceptions will be portrayed. The third section (Chapter 2.3) brings together the concepts of organizational routines and implicit learning as a basis to approach the research questions. Chapter 3 explains the structure and the methodological approach of the experiment and, importantly, it explains the routine modified in the experiment. Chapter 4 focusses on the presentation of the results of the experiment. It is structured along the research questions and its hypotheses. Finally, Chapter 5 begins with a recap of fundamental theoretical aspects and then interprets the results against the theoretical background to derive contributions and limitations of this experimental study.

2 Theoretical background

This interdisciplinary thesis examines the role of implicit learning in the modification of organizational routines using an experimental approach. As the application of an implicit learning paradigm is new to routine research, a profound basis of both fields that meet in this thesis is necessary to identify the boundary points of both concepts and to plan, conduct, analyze and interpret an experiment and its results. The structure of Chapter 2 reflects the interdisciplinary approach of this thesis and splits into a section on organizational routines and a section on learning, dual processing, and its theoretical background. These sections integrate into a combined view that picks-up the research goal and brings forward an approach to apply the implicit learning paradigm in organizations to diminish the misalignment between the ostensive and the performative aspect of an organizational routine.

2.1 Organizational routines

2.1.1 The quest for identity

2.1.1.1 The nature of organizational routines

The field of research on organizational routines offers various definitions and notions of the concept of routines and is influenced by many research paradigms. However, research still lacks a clear understanding of the concept and does not offer a precise delineation of related concepts, which both would strengthen the idea of routines for future work (Cohen *et al.*, 1996; Reynaud, 1998; Jones and Craven, 2001; Becker, 2004; Hodgson, 2008). That makes it necessary to acquire an extensive understanding of the nature of routines. Becker (2004; 2007) suggested to follow the concepts' historic path to the fundamental impulse of Nelson and Winter (1982) and based on this understanding to analyze the dominant characteristics of organizational routines. This study pays heed to this advice, however, expands it to gain a broader perspective on the concept. Organizational routines will be approached from the individual level by viewing habits to develop a basic understanding of automatic behaviors, to then contemplate the roots of automatic behaviors of organizations. This section focusses on the discussion of routines in *An Evolutionary Theory of Economic Change* by Nelson and Winter (1982). They drew a parallel between skills and routines, i.e., the individual level and the organization level, which is a fruitful approach to achieve an extensive understanding. Finally, fundamental characteristics of organizational routines, derived from the post-Nelson and Winter (1982) literature will be described to advance the understanding of the concept of routines.

M. Eberl, *Organizational Routines Meet Experimental Psychology*,
Zukunftsfähige Unternehmensführung in Forschung und Praxis,
https://doi.org/10.1007/978-3-658-23562-8_2

The roots of research on routines can be found in the discussion about habits[1] in the sociological publication *Economy and Society* by Max Weber (1922) and the social psychological publication *Human Nature and Conduct* by John Dewey (1922). For the first time, Weber (1922, pp. 374, 384) emphasized the far-reaching significance of habits for economics and depicted habits as potential boundary for economic actions. Dewey (1922, pp. 58-88) developed his understanding of habits at the individual level. He integrated habits not as the activity of an individual, but as the disposition of human actions. In his understanding, human beings are "[...] *creature[s] of habit, not of reason nor yet of instinct*"[2] (Dewey, 1922, p. 125). Notwithstanding, Dewey conceived habits as interwoven with cognition and emotion. Further, he highlighted that a stimulus or a particular context might cause and reinforce a habitual action as a condition of intellectual efficiency (Dewey, 1922, pp. 125-130; 173). However, Dewey was also clear on habits being "[...] *blinders that confine the eyes of mind on the road ahead* [...]" (Dewey, 1922, p. 172), in such way the "[...] *routineer's road is a ditch out of which he cannot get, directing his course so thoroughly that he no longer thinks of his path or his destination*" (Dewey, 1922, pp. 172-173).

Herbert Simon (1947), Nobel Prize laureate in economics, picked up the insights of Dewey (1922) in his research on decision-making processes in organizations. In his book *Administrative Behaviour* (Simon, 1947, pp. 88-89), he highlighted the dichotomy of habits and rational behavior. Accordingly, habits do not allow taking the time to consider various courses of action including their particular consequences in the decision-making process. In fact, he compared habits to a stimulus-response model[3] as known from behavioral psychology. Following this approach, a stimulus that could be a specific situation or similar may be sufficient to cause habitual behavior without reflection or the balancing options. Simon applied the concept of habits to the collective of individuals, which is in his understanding the organization. By doing so, he used the notion *organization routine* which was originally coined by Stene (1940, p. 1129):

> *"Organization routine is that part of any organization's activities which has become habitual because of repetition which is followed regularly without specific directions or detailed supervision by any member of the organization."*

Simon (1947, pp. 88-89) emphasized two points in Stene's definition of an *organization routine*: First, he highlighted the importance of recurrence as the constitutive element of routines. Second, he underlined the efficiency of routines that is induced by its deployment throughout the whole population "[...] *without further*

1 There are prior publications that discuss the notion of *habits* (e.g., James, 1892; McDougall, 1908; etc.), however, these publications only weakly reference to the concept of organizational routines (Becker, 2004, p. 654). Hayes and Preacher (2014) offer a comprehensive insight into the notion of *habits*.

2 *Here*: instinct in terms of emotional impulse.

3 Basic principles of this concept of behavioral psychology can be found in Becker (2004; 2007), Hodgson (2008), and Funke (1958); an overview can be found in Pavlov (1927).

conscious thought [...]" (Simon, 1947, p. 89) and without close supervision. In particular, recurrence has become a central element in many contemporary definitions of organizational routines (e.g., Feldman and Pentland, 2003; Reynaud, 2005; Dosi, Faillo and Marengo, 2008; Parmigiani and Howard-Grenville, 2011).

In the subsequent years at Carnegie Mellon University, Simon and colleagues published further influential writings on organizational theory (March and Simon, 1958; Cyert and March, 1963). These publications also cover organizational routines in decision-making processes. March and Simon (1958, pp. 141-142) referred to routines as *performance programs*; however, Cyert and March (1963, pp. 101-113) called them *standard operating procedures*. In March and Simon's (1958) book *Organizations*, bounded rationality in organizations is the fundamental concept to explain behavior in organizations, i.e., the decision-making processes that are frequently organized in performance programs. They described bounded rationality as dependent on the organizational structure and the cognitive limits of the individuals. By the fact that an individual does not have all necessary information available when making a decision and also by the fact that the individual never knows all alternatives with the involved consequences, it is subject to bounded rationality. Accordingly, it is required to simplify decision-making structures. The authors suggested organizational routines (*performance programs*) being this simplification. Triggered by a stimulus in a given situation, routines lead to behavior in compliance with predefined organizational rules (see also stimulus-response model as known from psychology). Using a defined aspiration level in the sense of a baseline, the resulting behavior of a routine becomes rateable. According to this idea, almost every behavior, notably the behavior in organizations, is the result of routines (March and Simon, 1958, pp. 47-53; 142-150; 161-171).

In *A Behavioral Theory of the Firm*, Cyert and March (1963, pp. 101-113) also described the nature of routines (*standard operating procedures*) as if-then rules. However, they discussed this kind of rules in the context of organizational learning. As a result, organizations develop routines in the process of long-run experiential learning, in which organizations (have to) react to external and internal stimuli (i.e., to adapt their routines). Routines that meet the aspiration level of an organization may be reapplied more likely than those that lead to undesired results. Following the case of undesired results, an organization will not reapply the routine that caused the undesired result, or it will adapt the routine to achieve the aspiration level.

In his doctoral thesis, written at Yale University, Sidney Winter (1964) took on the thoughts of Simon (1947; 1955) and developed an organization theory based on the ideas of evolutionary theory. He described routines as behavioral patterns that are carried out recurrently. Following Winter's theory, the only reason a routine needs to be modified is a change in the surrounding conditions of an organization or of the routine itself. Winter kept up his evolutionary theoretical perspective and published in cooperation with Richard Nelson the evolutionary-economical book *An Evolutionary Theory of*

Economic Change (Nelson and Winter, 1982). In this book, the authors "[...] *put the concept of routines center-stage* [...]" (Becker, 2004, p. 643). The publication can be seen as the first comprehensive essay on the concept of organizational routines (Raub, 1998).

In essence, for Nelson and Winter (1982) routines played a key role in advancing the understanding of behavior and change in organizations or firms, as the case may be, and thus in promoting the understanding of economic change (Nelson and Winter, 1982, p. 128). To come to this perception, they built their discussion of routines on the individual level, however not habits but individual skilled behavior. They conceived skills as an effective and objective-oriented sequence of coordinated behaviors, which can be hierarchically itemized by subskills to a more elementary level (Nelson and Winter, 1982, pp. 73, 124). Skills reduce the deliberate choice of individuals and orient their behavior to a clear-cut path of options (Nelson and Winter, 1982, p. 85). However, a novel situation may require a non-existent or poorly developed skill of an individual and accordingly may produce blundering behavior. In contrast, organizations that are missing a proper routine may not react at all and accordingly could fail in completing their business. As well as routines, skills only maintain functioning when being employed. Otherwise, they become *rusty* and need to be reacquired by the organization members, respectively the organization (Nelson and Winter, 1982, pp. 124-125).

With these explications on individual skills and their parallels to routines, Nelson and Winter's definition of routine becomes more perspicuously:

> *"Our general term for all regular and predictable behavioral patterns of firms is 'routine'."* Nelson and Winter (1982, p. 14)

In addition, Nelson and Winter (1982, pp. 14-21) suggested building the notion of routines on the analogy of genes, as known from biological evolutionary theory. They argued that both, routines and genes, share several similarities: Both are a persistent feature of their carrier in predicting its behavior and characterize the next generation in the sense of heritage, in which those that do better gain more importance over time. Based on the thoughts of Charles Darwin's (1859, pp. 77-119; 1868, pp. 1-14) evolutionary theory and the mechanism of natural selection, Nelson and Winter explicated that in the long run, only organizations with predominant routines and technologies will survive, as they can generate essential profits. For the research on organizational routines, the analogy to biological genes was the most influential contribution of *An evolutionary theory of economic change* (Becker, 2003) and can frequently be found application since then (e.g., Foss, 1993; Nelson, 1995; Hodgson, 1997; 2003; Coriat and Dosi, 1998; Pentland, Haerem and Hillison, 2010; etc.). However, Nelson and Winter (1982) did not clearly distinguish between routines being the actual organizational behavior or the behavioral disposition of an organization (Nelson and Winter, 1982, pp. 14-16; Hodgson, 2009). Accordingly, prima-facie there were inconsistent explanations of the concept of routines:

> *"It is that most of what is regular and predictable about business behavior is plausibly subsumed under the heading 'routine', especially if we understand that term to include the relatively constant dispositions and strategic heuristics that shape the approach of a firm to the nonroutine problems it faces."* (Nelson and Winter, 1982, p. 15)

Within the same sentence, routines were described as both, actual behavior as well as dispositions of behavior; a clear differentiation is missing. Nelson and Winter examined routines in several respects: They compared them to computer programs (Nelson and Winter, 1982, pp. 74, 97), thus to a mathematical-logical model based on rules. Further, they examined routines to be a kind of organizational memory (Nelson and Winter, 1982, pp. 99-107), to be the basis for truces between the organizations' individuals or groups (Nelson and Winter, 1982, pp. 107-112), or to be the target of control, replication, and imitation (Nelson and Winter, 1982, pp. 112-124). For using the notion of organizational routines in the sense of Nelson and Winter, it is essential to internalize their note on the notional flexibility of the word routine:

> *"We use ,routine' in a highly flexible way, much as 'program' (or, indeed, 'routine') is used in discussion of computer programming. It may refer to a repetitive pattern of activity in an entire organization, to an individual skill, or, as an adjective, to the smooth uneventful effectiveness of such an organizational or individual performance." (Nelson and Winter, 1982, p. 97)*[4]

In this context and with a particular regard to continuity in the behavior of organizations, Nelson and Winter (1982, pp. 96-97) position routines to be the key concept within their evolutionary framework. They localize the routine concept to be working for organizations that provide goods or services, however, malfunctioning for those producing organizations or those managing change (e.g., consultants etc.). Concluding, the publication of *An evolutionary theory of economic change* belongs to the most substantial works in the field organizational routines and attracts a significant amount of attention on the concept of routines (Becker, 2003; Parmigiani and Howard-Grenville, 2011). However, the growing number of publications on routines and related concepts entailed only a rather small conceptual progress for the understanding of routines, so that various contradictions and ambiguities can be found in the literature (Cohen *et al.*, 1996; Reynaud, 1998; Jones and Craven, 2001; Becker, 2003; 2004; 2005b). Studying the definitions of (organizational) routines that emerged after the essential impulse of Nelson and Winter (1982) yields several notional overlaps that

---

4 Skinner (1953) also indicated the "[…] *use of several different terms for different types of routines* […]" earlier, however, literature frequently ignored Nelson and Winter's note. In their evolutionary model of change, Nelson and Winter aimed to point out the resemblances among these different types of routines (Nelson and Winter, 1982, pp. 15-16).

could be recognized as fundamental characteristics[5] of routines (Becker, 2004; 2007): recurrence[6], patterns, processual nature, and collective social nature.

Recurrence. Almost all definitions comprise *recurrence* as a fundamental characteristic of organizational routines, and it can be assessed as "[…] *one of the very few points of unanimous agreement* […]" (Becker, 2005b, p. 255) in routine research. In this context, Narduzzo and Warglien (2008) draw the parallel between the individual level, based on habitual action, and the organizational level of routines. In this parallel, they assert that recurrence transforms actions into automatic reactions as a reference of past, and indicator of future behavior. In other words, routines enable organizations to strengthen their continuity and to predict its behavior. Becker (2005b) takes a linguistic avenue and identifies terminological problems with routines as a remarkably connoted term. He suggests to accept the indisputable characteristic of *recurrence* as a starting point for further research on organizational routines and to forego (new) incremental definitional and conceptual approaches to clarify the notion of routines. However, he considers the notion *routine* to be hackneyed and comes forward with the radical proposal: He distinguishes routines on the practical level (i.e., the behavioral level of action) from those on the empirical level (i.e., as "[…] *a feature of knowledge, consisting of impressions, and experiences* […]"; Becker, 2005b, p. 251). For the former, he suggests to use the term *recurrent action patterns* (see also Cohen *et al.*, 1996), and for the latter, Becker (2005b) suggests to use the term *rule*. By doing so, he expects the discussion about routines to center on the well-accepted characteristic of recurrence and accordingly to develop a fruitful understanding of routines on this common base.

Patterns. The idea of patterns is an essential element of the concept of routines that can be found in most definitions. It embodies the logical sequence and regularity of routines. However, with regard to its contents, the word *pattern* is used in different ways. Four different kinds of patterns can be found in the literature that will be discussed in the following: patterns of behavior[7], patterns of action[8], patterns of activity[9], and patterns of interaction[10]. The deviating understanding of patterns in routines can be seen as one of the several ambiguousnesses in routine research (Becker, 2004). Literature shows the synonymous use of *patterns of action* and *patterns of activity*, in some cases

---

5 There are several other overlaps, which are not discussed here in detail. However, for the sake of completeness these overlaps or characteristics should be mentioned: *self-actuating nature* and *path-dependence*.

6 Synonyms: *repetition, repetiveness, persistence* and occasionally *replication* or *regularity*.

7 Patterns of behavior: Nelson and Winter (1982, p. 15).

8 Patterns of action: Hall (1957).

9 Patterns of activity: Winter (1986); Gersick and Hackman (1990); Cohen and Bacdayan (1994); Langlois and Everett (1994); Bessant, Caffyn and Gallagher (2001); Edmondson, Bohmer and Pisano (2001, pp. 686-687); Jones and Craven (2001); Emery (2002); Zollo and Winter (2002); Lillrank (2003); Hodgson (2008; 2009).

10 Patterns of interaction: Pentland and Rueter (1994); Cohen *et al.* (1996); Jarzabkowski and Wilson (2002); Feldman and Pentland (2003); Parmigiani and Howard-Grenville (2011); Bapuji, Hora and Saeed (2012); Pentland and Hærem (2015).

even within the same publication (e.g., Pentland and Rueter, 1994). However, *patterns of behavior* can be distinguished from *patterns of action.* In its original and precise meaning, behavior is any physical activity of an organism, which in contrast to mental processes is objectively observable by others (Caspar, 2004, p. 1002; see also, VandenBos, 2015, p. 112). In contrast, an action comprises mental motives as well. According to Volpert (1974), Greif (2004, p. 391) characterized actions as intentional and goal-oriented behavior that occurs in a time-limited phase (see also Matsumoto, 2009, p. 12). In this context, Becker (2004) questioned if routines need to observable. However, in literature this question remains almost unacknowledged and, accordingly, is to some extent the reason for the distinction between *patterns of behavior* and *patterns of action* (Cohen *et al.*, 1996). Further, *patterns of interaction* can be viewed as a subset of patterns of action, and in the context of routines, they refer to social interactions (Becker, 2004). Social interactions are characterized as a symmetrical process of reciprocal stimulation and influence. This process requires two or more individuals with at least a single contact that involves a modification of behavior (Bergius, 2004, p. 452; VandenBos, 2015, p. 996).

Summing up, the closer look at the different kinds of patterns found in literature reveals a taxonomy that is fundamental to the concept of routines: Patterns of behavior, as observable activities, serve as a superordinate term. Patterns of actions respectively patterns of activities subordinate to this umbrella and are the base for patterns of (social) interaction, which are a further differentiation of patterns of action that refer to the collective, e.g., the organization as a conglomerate of individuals.

Processual nature. Based on the well-accepted fact that change is a process and that routines add to explain change (see also Nelson and Winter, 1982, p. 128), Becker (2004) clearly inferred routines to be a process. Pentland and Rueter (1994, p. 484) described routines as the "[...] *crucial nexus between structure and action* [...]", i.e., they determined routines to be the link between the organization as an object and its task of organizing, which is a systematic process of structuring. They even suggested to replace the usage of the term *routine* by the term *process*, which "[...] *can be more or less repetitive, more or less automatic, embody more or less variety, search, and so on*" (Pentland and Rueter, 1994, p. 492). In Pentland's later and seminal work in cooperation with Feldman (Feldman and Pentland, 2003), both from the Practice Theory school, they put elements of structuration theory center-stage. The model they developed bases on the processual attributes of routines and specifies routines as a source of flexibility and change. By adopting the thoughts and ontology of Latour's (1986) sociological work on power, Feldman and Pentland (2003) proposed that routines can exist both, in principle (ostensive aspect) and practice (performative aspect). These aspects connect structure and action of a firm – the first depicted by the ostensive aspect, the latter by the performative aspect – and are in a dynamic adjustment process that relates to flexibility and change (see also Pentland and Feldman, 2005).

Some authors (e.g., Piening, 2011, p. 66), assigned organizational routines more structuring elements compared to (business) processes, which distinguishes routines from individual behaviors. On the contrary, others framed routines and skills under the term business processes, because they are (structured) activities by that organizations accomplish their work (Porter, 1991; Teece, Pisano and Shuen, 1997; Ray, Barney and Muhanna, 2004).

A recent, however well-accepted understanding of routines in the processual context originates from Foss *et al.* (2012). They identified a process being the origin of a routine if it generates a reasonable standard of accomplishing a task. Accordingly, one can find the roots of routines in its processual ancestors. In a review on routines, Becker (2004) identified several processual dimensions in literature and empirical research. He pointed out three dimensions that are of importance: (a) frequency of repetition, (b) regularity of the frequency and respectively the regularity of interruptions of a routine, and (c) time pressure. (a) The frequency of repetition refers to the regularity of a routine and is an essential prerequisite for it to arise. (b) The regularity of the frequency and respectively the regularity of interruptions of a routine point to the rhythm of the routines' recurrence. Routines that often become interrupted (i.e., routines that are not executed rhythmically) will trigger the organization members to search for external alternatives to this routine (see also Zellmer-Bruhn, 2003). (c) The famous study by Weick (1990) revealed that teams resort to habitual responses in situations of time pressure.[11] Habitual responses are usually well-trained processes or so-called routines. Similar results were found in psychological research on individual routines. Betsch, Fiedler and Brinkmann (1998) and Betsch *et al.* (1999) performed computerized decision-making experiments. In these experiments, the maintenance of routines was increased in situations of time pressure. Participants fell back on adverse routinized behavior instead of searching for a superior solution. Garapin and Hollard (1999) explained such disadvantageous behavior by the requirement to coordinate and use the resources more efficiently in situations of stress. Transferred to organizational decision-making processes, Becker (2004) and also Narduzzo and Warglien (2008) determined an increased likelihood of routine choices (i.e., well-known processual and automatized solutions) in situations of time pressure (see also Cohen and Bacdayan, 1994).

Collective nature. Many scholars, regardless of which school of economic thought, had no doubt that routines are a collective phenomenon (e.g., Stene, 1940; Simon, 1947, pp. 88-89; Nelson and Winter, 1982, pp. 124-125; Weick, 1990, 1993; Grant, 1991; Hodgson, 1993; Cohen and Bacdayan, 1994; Murphy, 1994; Dosi, Nelson and Winter, 2000; Lazaric, 2000; Narduzzo, Rocco and Warglien, 2001; Cohendet and Llerena, 2003; Becker, 2004, 2005a, 2005b, 2007; Hodgson and Knudsen, 2004b; Becker and Zirpoli, 2008; Koch, 2009; Felin *et al.*, 2012; Eggers and Kaplan, 2013; Kaiser and

[11] For the sake of completeness, Weick (1990) mentioned several other sources of pressure in his study about the Tenerife air disaster, e.g., the use of a foreign language, work and rest regulations, spatial and weather conditions, staffing difficulties, technical issues, etc.

Kozica, 2013 etc.). However, the authors used different ways to embed routines into the collective of an organization or firm, as the case may be. Drawing the parallel between habits on the individual level and routines on the collective level is common in literature (e.g., Nelson and Winter, 1982; Nelson, 1995; Hodgson, 2008; Knudsen, 2008; Vromen, 2011). This parallel is certainly just a lead not an explanation for the collective nature of routines. A further indication for routines being a collective level construct can be found using a linguistic approach. Various authors employed the terms *group* (e.g., Gersick and Hackman, 1990; Grant, 1991; Hodgson and Knudsen, 2004b; Hodgson, 2008; Knudsen, 2008; Hodgson, 2009; Loch, Sengupta and Ahmad, 2013), *team* (e.g., Zellmer-Bruhn, 2003; Hodgson and Knudsen, 2004b; Salvato and Rerup, 2010) or *organization* (e.g., Langlois and Everett, 1994; Teece, Pisano and Shuen, 1997; Mintzberg, Ahlstrand and Lampel, 1998, p. 185; Vromen, 2006; Miner, Ciuchta and Gong, 2008; Wright, 2016) in their discussion of routines, others, in turn, just spoke of several involved individuals[12] (Cohen and Bacdayan, 1994; Cohen *et al.*, 1996; Feldman and Rafaeli, 2002; Feldman and Pentland, 2003; Pentland, 2010; Witt, 2010; Bapuji, Hora and Saeed, 2012).

A more explanatory approach to discuss routines as collective-level phenomenon – instead of just using collective level vocabulary – can be found in the distinction of *action* and *interaction*, the first for the individual level, the latter for the collective level (Becker, 2003; 2004). Several authors highlighted (social) interaction as a central element of organizational routines (e.g., Pentland and Rueter, 1994; Teece and Pisano, 1994; Teece, Pisano and Shuen, 1997; Dyer and Singh, 1998; Cohendet *et al.*, 1999; Emery, 2002; Zollo, Reuer and Singh, 2002; Feldman and Pentland, 2003; Vromen, 2006; Bapuji, Hora and Saeed, 2012; Felin *et al.*, 2012), which is – as previously mentioned – a process between two or more individuals (Bergius, 2004, p. 452; VandenBos, 2015, p. 996). Bapuji, Hora and Saeed (2012) stressed interaction to be a requisite element of routines to accomplish organizational tasks by multiple actors collectively. Building on an individualist foundation, Felin and Hesterly (2007) differentiated between *interactions* and *interacting individuals*; the first in terms of the relation between individuals, the latter in terms of the action between them. Coming from this knowledge-based view, routines are nested in the conglomerate of heterogeneity that is called individual-level. Thus, routines can only come into existence by utilizing the individuals' knowledge in an associated collective manner, which requires interactions in terms of relations. Teppo Felin sticked to the micro-foundational perspective embracing the role of individuals in organizations, however, he also emphasized that collective-level constructs, such as routines, can be part of this micro-foundational approach (Felin *et al.*, 2012).

Considering routines as a collective-level construct involves a distribution of the knowledge held in a routine across several individuals, organizational units, or artifacts;

[12] Also referred to as *multiple actors*, *people*, or *several members*.

that may also include a spatial or chronological distribution (Hutchins, 1991; Cohen and Bacdayan, 1994; Cohen *et al.*, 1996; Lazaric and Mangolte, 1999; Becker, 2004; Feldman and Pentland, 2008; Hansen and Vogel, 2010; Salvato and Rerup, 2010; Pentland and Hærem, 2015). The contributors to the routine are then linked through interaction, and accordingly they create a collective routine that arises "[...] *from the interplay of individual rules, interests and activities*" (Becker, 2004, p. 648). In this line of thought, Witt (2010) observed that the shared knowledge of the individuals involved in the routine does not necessarily need to be superimposable. Accordingly, there cannot be a single individual holding or performing the complete routine. The orchestration of this heterogeneity of knowledge is the challenge routines have to accomplish in order to guarantee the intended regularity and predictability they stand for (Cohendet and Llerena, 2003). In his analysis of the Tenerife air disaster, Weick (1990) noted that teamwork reduces the complexity of a given task and accordingly individual instead of collective acting may disrupt a routine. This insight underpins the importance of the collective nature to routines and its smooth functioning.

2.1.1.2 Routines and their analogies

The blurry understanding of the concept of organizational routines triggered scholars to make the concept more tangible by drawing analogies and creating metaphors. As previously mentioned, the most common ones are the comparison of routines to *genes* (Nelson and Winter, 1982, p. 14) and *rules* (Cohen *et al.*, 1996). Besides these common ones, there are several others that can be found in literature: *routines as blueprint* (Hannan and Freeman, 1977); *routines as collective behavioral dispositions* (Hodgson, 2003; Hodgson and Knudsen, 2004a; Hodgson, 2009); *routines as grammatical models* (Pentland and Rueter, 1994; Pentland, 1995); *routines as organizational habits* (Stene, 1940; Nelson and Winter, 1982); *routines as (procedural) memory* (Nelson and Winter, 1982, pp. 99-107; Cohen, 1991; Cohen and Bacdayan, 1994); *routines as scripts* (Schank and Abelson, 1977; Lord and Kernan, 1987); *routines as stimulus-response model* (Gersick and Hackman, 1990); *routines as target for control, replication and imitation* (Nelson and Winter, 1982, pp. 112-124); or *routines as truce* (Nelson and Winter, 1982, pp. 107-112). However, reviewing these analogies reveals that some analogies are very close and can be integrated. Exemplarily, the analogy of routines as rules compares in several respects to the analogies of routines as scripts or routines as a stimulus-response model. In the following section only the analogies/metaphors of routines as rules, routines as genes, routines as grammatical models, and routines as part of the procedural memory will be reviewed, as they have enduring influence for research on routines and thus cover a wide range of the historical path of our today's view on routines.

Routines as rules. The analogy of routines[13] being rules or consisting of them dates back to the *Carnegie School* and its lead figures, the organizational behaviorists Herbert A. Simon, Richard Cyert and James G. March. In their seminal book *Organizations*, March and Simon (1958, p. 141) introduced *(performance) programs* as "[…] *a highly complex and organized set of* [ex-ante] *responses* […]" to a given stimulus from the environment.[14] Much like a computer program, repetitive tasks undergo an atomization into their smallest steps and are described by explicit and conditional rules (IFTTT[15]) in the minutest details (March and Simon, 1958, p. 144). Programs, as described by March and Simon (1958, p. 145) fulfill at least two functions within organizations – and here we find common ground in the subsequent publication on routines in the light of evolutionary economics by Nelson and Winter (1982, pp. 107; 113-117) – that are control and coordination. Accordingly, by the utilization of performance programs decision processes in organizations become stable and reliable. However, the authors underlined that programs need to be linked to observable and measurable variables (March and Simon, 1958, p. 145).

In a *Behavioral theory of the firm*, Cyert and March (1963) introduced *standard operating procedures* (SOP) as a set of behavior rules. SOP "[…] *serve as the organization's primary memory* […]" (Cyert and March, 1963, p. 107), "[…] *transmit past learning* […]" (Cyert and March, 1963, p. 104) and allow to predict behavior within organizations. They change slowly, thus serve stability to organizations and guide its actions and decision-making processes (Cyert and March, 1963, pp. 103-104). However, SOP can also decay when not triggered and thereby become a shadow of their former self (Cyert and March, 1963, p. 106). Cyert and March (1963, p. 105) assigned rules – as embodied in SOP – to two levels, internal and external. The first are usually learned or trained and specific for the particular organization, the latter are more general and are also referred to as *standard industry practice*, *standard business practice*, etc., which are ubiquitous these days. In March's subsequent publications (Levitt and March, 1988; March, 1988), he shed light on why people follow rules respectively routines. Routines are described as a reservoir of rules, procedures, conventions, strategies as well as technologies, and their execution is characterized as independent of the individual actor.

More recent studies also addressed the rule-based nature of routines. In a lab experiment, using the *Target the Two* card game as known from Cohen and Bacdayan (1994), Egidi and Narduzzo (1997) explored the emergence of routinized behaviors and their underlying sets of rules, i.e. routines. In a training phase, the subjects were exposed to different starting configurations of the game that all could be solved with the same

13 Also referred to as *(performance) programs* (March and Simon, 1958), *standard operating procedures (SOP; Cyert and March, 1963)*, *rules of thumb* (Winter in Cohen *et al.*, 1996), heuristics (Narduzzo, Rocco and Warglien, 2001), or scripts (Schank and Abelson, 1977; Gioia and Poole, 1984; Ashforth and Fried, 1988).

14 Frequently, the conception of routines as (set of) rules is compared to stimulus-response model as known from psychology (e.g., Koch, 2009).

15 *If-this-then-that.*

strategy. The subjects developed a fixed set of conditional rules (IFTTT) and a routinized behavior to solve this type of starting configuration efficiently. Those routinized behaviors could also be observed in the subsequent tournament phase with different types of starting configurations, although it was suboptimal and not efficiently to use this strategy for this type of starting configuration. Egidi and Narduzzo (1997, p. 705) concluded "[...] *that players are only partially aware of the set of rules they apply, and that their knowledge of the 'logic of the game' is incomplete*".

Speaking more generally, individuals use routines mindlessly and without having a clear representation of the underlying rules. Accordingly, the individuals sometimes pursue an inadequate strategy of decision-making. In a nutshell, routinized behaviors are the outcome of routinized thinking (Egidi and Narduzzo, 1997, p. 680). In a more recent inquiry on the relation of routines and rules, routines were viewed as artifacts (software, machines, manuals, etc.) that embody normative rules. These artifacts facilitate and restrain the routine performance and thus can be seen as the link between rules and action (D'Adderio, 2008; Pentland and Feldman, 2008; D'Adderio, 2010; Quinn, 2011). Pentland and Hærem (2015), however, noted that rules are not necessarily followed, even if converted into artifacts like software.

A frequently raised objection to the conception of routines as rules comes from the camp of the of the practice theorists and puts the determinism of rules into question. Framing their thoughts on the sociological roots of Zimmerman (1970) and Giddens (1984, p. 21), Pentland and Rueter (1994, p. 507) wrote: "*Rules are resources of action, but they do not determine action*". A similar sentence can be found in Becker (2005b) who added that rules influence action by serving as an underlying mechanism for routines. However, even though rules are the underlying mechanisms of routines, they only *influence* action and do not determine action respectively the routine in practice. This view is aligned with Wittgenstein's (1953 [1958]; I.201) famous rule-following paradox:[16]

> *"This was our paradox: no course of action could be determined by a rule, because every course of action can be made out to accord with the rule."*

In his later publication *Remarks on the foundations of mathematics*, Wittgenstein (1956; I.113) underlined the incompleteness of rules and their openness to subjective interpretation and capriciousness:

> *"However many rules you give me – I give a rule which justifies my employment of your rules."*

Interestingly, Reynaud (2005) argued comparable to Wittgenstein in her in-depth discussion on the differences between routines and rules – however, she did not cite Wittgenstein once. Advancing Blau's (1955; ch. 2) conception of rules, Reynaud (2005, p. 850) asserted that rules are incomplete unless they are "[...] *applied in the light of*

---

[16] Also referred to as *Kripke-Wittgenstein paradox*.

knowledge, of information contained in the other rules, as well as custom, and practice, and context." This idea shifts the focus on a distinction between formal rules and applied rules. Formal rules reside on a general level and can best be compared to grammatical rules[17] that are complete in their entity. In contrast, applied rules are incomplete, as described before. They are abstract as they are awaiting interpretation in specific contexts and thus adapt to diverse situations of decision-making.[18] Derived from this distinction, Reynaud (2005) regarded routines to be an interpretation mechanism to manage the incompleteness of rules in application. It becomes obvious that "[…] *rules are explicit, while routines are more often implicit*" (Reynaud, 2005, p. 866) and that rules usually do not provide solution but a theoretical approach to solve a problem. Also, Spender (2002) remarked that rules regularly prove as insufficient as they are on a general level, ceteris paribus among specific requirements of situational context.

Other researchers brought in cognate thoughts on routines and rules. Becker (2005b) also differentiated between a level of representation (formal or explicit) and a level of action – knowledge of the former does not allow to deduce the resulting action clearly. Lawson (1997, p. 162) took the same line by stating: "[…] *any action that results can never be reduced simply to the sets of rules by which it was conditioned.*" Furthermore, what we can observe as the performance of a rule is always mediated by human agency, he added. Burns and Scapens (2000) took a different approach in their framework: Referring to institutionalization, they developed an of idea interacting rules and routines that in the long-term facilitate change in organizations. In this framework, formal rules incorporate existing routines, as well as organizational principles and values. By integrating actor-specific properties, the repeatedly performed rules advance existing routines or form new routines, which may become institutionalized in the form of revised or new rules.

One of the recent approaches to link organizational routines with rules came from Geiger and Schröder (2014), who developed a rule-based understanding of routines (see Figure 2). They clearly distinguished between rules and routines. Organizational rules are referred to Cyert's and March's (1963) SOP and should best be understood as normative behavioral expectations. Further, rules enable organizations to establish boundaries into an organization by having sanctioning power. At the same time, they certainly left room for interpretation. Organizational routines comprise rules on the one hand, but on the other hand also its interpretation and performance (Geiger and Schröder, 2014).

---

17 Basically, *grammatical rules* should be clearly distinguished from IFTTT-rules as they are not necessarily of conditional kind (Pentland, 2010). In the referred source, formal rules are described by a syntactical character, which meets the idea of grammatical rules. However, a thoughtful use is advised.

18 There can be found parallels to Winter's (1995) distinction between *abstract patterns of relationships* and *concrete patterns of action*.

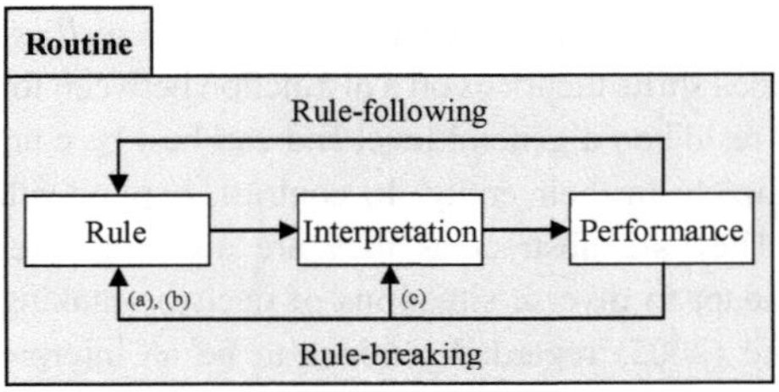

Figure 2: Routine concept by Geiger and Schröder (2014).

In Geiger's and Schröder's (2014) conception of routines, rules are the normative and stable elements of a routine. The interpretation of a rule is described with reference to Weick (1995) as sense-making of the normative reference. In contrast, the performance is described as the actual and perceptible outcome of interpreted rules. Two cases of outcome may occur: On the one hand, *rule-following* can be observed when a performance is congruent with the rule, i.e., the interpretation was correct in the sense of the normative expectation. On the other hand, in case we observe a deviating performance compared to the normative rule, it is referred to as rule-breaking (see Figure 2). The organization can react in three distinct ways to rule-breaking: (a) rule-reinforcement by sanctioning; (b) reflective questioning and change of the existing rule (see double-loop learning); and, (c) evolutionary drift of the routine as a consciously or unconsciously overlooked rule-breaking. The complete mechanism of a rule as normative expectation, its interpretation and performance describes an organizational routine in the understanding of Geiger and Schröder (2014).

Concluding, the analogy of *routines as rules* originated from the roots of routine research in line with Carnegie School of thought. It is at least of historical importance. From a today's perspective and having the illustrated concerns in mind, rules in the sense of March and Simon (1958) and Cyert and March (1963) can best be thought of as cognitive regularities. This insight is an enlargement for the routine concept, which covers the potential complexity of routines appropriately (Cohen, 1991; Delmestri, 1998; Becker, 2004).

Routines as genes. The starting point for the analogy of *routines as genes* can be seen in individual habits, which are the closest generative dispositional factors of human behavior that compare to biological genes in the socioeconomic domain. However, to come into existence routines require two or more individuals and accordingly should be conceived as meta-habits within a social structure of habituated individuals (Hodgson, 2008; 2009). Having this connection established and in mind, a closer look to the analogy of routines as genes becomes more comprehensible.

Nelson and Winter (1982, pp. 9, 11, 14, 17, 142) as the originators of this analogy borrowed their ideas for an evolutionary and anti-orthodox theory of the firm from biology, more precisely from Charles Darwin. They coined the analogy of *routines as biological genes*, or in a broader sense of *organizational genetics* on the body of thought of Darwin's evolutionary theory. For the sake of developing a better understanding of organizational routines and the organization *per se*, they underline to utilize any adjuvant idea from biology, even though it has to be modified to serve the objective. Distinguishing between *potential* behavior and *actual* behavior of an organization, they described routines to be the part of the organism[19] that determines the potential behavior, whereas the actual behavior is also affected by the organism's environment. This point of view emphasizes the emergence of routines, their relative persistence, and their embeddedness into a hardly controllable evolutionary process an organization undergoes within its lifecycle.

As in biology, the evolutionary process of a routine is driven by the three core Darwinian principles of *variation*, *selection*, and *inheritance* (Darwin, 1859; 1868; Nelson and Winter, 1982, p. 14; Knudsen, 2008; Hansen and Vogel, 2010). In accordance to this analogy, routines "[...] *change over time, in both desired and undesired ways* [...]" (Winter, 1975, p. 102).[20] Parmigiani and Howard-Grenville (2011) added that routines seen as genes can lead to both, change and rigidity. More precisely, desired changes of routines are often incremental and difficult, but mutation, i.e. unintentional change, is likely to happen, so that routines adapt to environmental needs in an evolutionary adjustment process. Nelson and Winter (1982, p. 18) introduced the concept of *search* as the counterpart of mutation as known from evolutionary biology. Modified or even new routines may emerge from existing routines by search. This evolutionary process is framed by the organizations' search policy, which also determines the likelihood of the distribution of the modified or newly developed routine within the organization. Commonly, mutation is a negatively embossed notion. However, Nelson and Winter (1982, p. 116) did not only conclude that routines mutate, importantly, they also concluded that these mutations are *not always* deleterious.

To some extent, the analogy of routines as genes has been criticized substantially. Cohen *et al.* (1996) considered this analogy to be weak, as routines emerge, diffuse, and configure continuously throughout the life cycle of an organization. Genes, in contrast, change slowly with the alternation of numerous generations, which leads to a developmental retardation of the current genetic material concerning organisms' needs and its environment. Similar arguments can be found in Hodgson (2003; 2008) who perceived the analogy of genes as beneficial despite its shortcomings. He recognized the similar way routines, and genes store information; furthermore, both can be seen as "[...] *generative, rule-like structures and potentialities*" (Hodgson, 2008, p. 19). However, he also emphasized the differences between routines and genes: Routines have a shorter longevity and do not replicate in a biological manner "[...] *from generation to*

---

[19] *Here*: the organization.

[20] Although, this work was published in 1975 and discussed (behavioral) routines as genes, Nelson and Winter (1982) proved to be the first comprehensive and most seminal publication on organizational routines as genes.

generation but also within the life of socio-economic units" (Hodgson, 2003, p. 366). Another point brought up by Hodgson (2008) is the question whether routines are a generative structure itself or the output of such structure, however, being both turns out to be controversial.

Also, Winter (1995) as one of the originators of this analogy addressed the differences between routines and genes. He noted "[...] *firms do not have a natural life span, and not all ultimately die. Neither can they be regarded as having a natural size. Some may be big, some small*" (Winter, 1995, p. 69). Further, he highlighted the capability of organizations to actively change their routines whereas organisms stuck with their set of genes during their life span. In an ontological analysis, Vromen (2006) discussed the analogy of routines as genes and concluded that this analogy is misleading and it may be over-simplified in several respects. Similar to Hodgson (2003; 2008) and unlike to Nelson and Winter (1982, p. 14), Vromen (2006) criticized neither genes nor routines determine (organizational) behavior but are potentialities of behavior. In this respect, genes are best conceived as basic constituents of routines. He also related to the dead versus live routines discussion (see also Chapter 2.1.1.3) and underlined that the evolutionary perspective by Nelson and Winter (1982) excludes conscious and deliberate choice of actors and individuals. Vromen (2006, p. 558) argued that "[...] *individuals are functionally connected with each other are a crucial part of the functioning of routines* [...]", which leads the individuals to make deliberate choices instead of automatic and mindless decisions.

Promoting the approach of routines as patterns of action, Pentland, Haerem and Hillison (2010, p. 935) at the same time assessed the routines as genes analogy as too simplistic for empirical research and downgrade it to "[...] *nothing more than a metaphor.*" They questioned whether it is up to date for organization theorists to stick to the genetic approach to routines, when "[...] *molecular biologists have abandoned the Central Dogma of the genotype/phenotype* [...]" (Pentland, Haerem and Hillison, 2010, p. 935). In biology, the fundamental logic of an "[...] *relationship between the complexity of an organism and the number of coding sequences on its genomes* [...]" (Rose, 2007, p. 145) was proofed wrong. Thus, a couple of assumptions Nelson and Winter (1982) built their evolutionary theory on are no longer valid in biology, however, are still used in organization theory. In an earlier publication, also Winter (1987) recognized the limitations of this analogy at a more general level and emphasized that the evolutionary theory was not developed for particular cases of biology nor economy. Following this line of thoughts, evolutionary theory should be understood as a conceptual framework that offers an ontological and beneficial overlap for both domains.

Despite its shortcomings, this evolutionary theoretical analogy can be found in many studies on organizational routines (e.g., Adler, Goldoftas and Levine, 1999; Knott, 2001;

2003; Gilbert, 2005; Phillips, 2005; Aime *et al.*, 2010).[21] However, one should keep in mind the words by Knudsen (2008) who remarked "[…] *there is no straightforward analogy between the details of biological genes and the details of habits and routines* […]" and at the same time that we can find common ground in the principles of biological and economic evolution, which can be a breeding ground for future research and our understanding of evolutionary economics.

Routines as grammatical models. Salancik and Leblebici (1988) introduced a perspective on organizational transactions that builds on *generative grammar* as known from Noam Chomsky (1955; 1956; 1957) who developed this concept and thus brought about the linguistic revolution.[22] Pentland and Rueter (1994) transferred the above thoughts of generative grammar to the concept of organizational routines. They analyzed data from a software company's service hotline and found a sequential structure in the service encounters that did not fit in the traditional view of organizational routines, because there were numerous exceptions, in many cases interruptions, a low analyzability of solution determination, and an extensive deliberation in the decisions. According to their newly developed understanding of routines as grammars of action, individuals perform routines by choosing a sequence of actions from a repertoire of possible actions. By doing so, routines become responsive and flexible sequences deliberately build by actors in dependency on the requirements of the routine's context, similar to grammar in linguistics – inexhaustibly adaptive.

Pentland and Rueter (1994) and Pentland (1995) adopted the terms and also the hierarchical structure known from linguistics to the concept of organizational routines (see Table 1; Chomsky, 1956). *Moves* are the smallest element of a routine and can be compared to single *words* of a language. Using the grammatical correct combination of moves produce subroutines, which correspond to phrases (*not* sentences) in language. The combination of phrases brings up complete sentences, respectively the combination of subroutines creates specific instances of a routine, called performances. An organizational routine refers to the entity of a language as the set of all grammatically possible sentences that can be expressed in a language (e.g., Mandarin or Spanish). In principle, a routine represents all possible performances to accomplish a task. Thus, it is rather a set of patterns that adapts to the particular situation than a single pattern.

This conception shifted the focus from mindless repetition of routines to a mindful choice of actions (see also Chapter 2.1.1.3) and strengthened the role of individuals by allowing them to compose each performance according to the specific context. Routines become *effortful accomplishments* that acknowledge both, structure and agency. The complexity of the context and the interactional nature of routines makes them "[…] *unlikely to unfold the same way every time*" (Pentland and Rueter, 1994, p. 488). Thus,

21 For an overview of these studies, see Parmigiani and Howard-Grenville (2011, pp. 431-433, 441).

22 The publications from 1956 and 1957 are distillations of Chomsky's work *The logical structure of linguistic theory* (LSLT; 919 pages). LSLT originates from his junior research fellowship at Harvard University (1951-1955) in preparation for his doctoral dissertation and was first published in 1975.

the occurrence of variety in routines is a fundamental part of this conception and the major advantage mentioned by Pentland and Rueter (1994). Furthermore, grammatical models allow to map the layered character of routines respectively subroutines and to connect separated events in a sequence of events. Finally, from a perspective of control, grammatical models enable an organization to identify normatively correct performances of a routine from others. Pentland and Rueter (1994) regarded the reduced consideration of the actor's experience as one of the weak spots of their analogy. Obviously, experience is involved in the actor's choice of actions, however, cannot be visualized in the grammatical model (see Table 1).

Behavioral entity	**Grammatical counterpart**
Organizational Routine The set of possible performances for a particular task, described in part by a grammar. Example: customer service.	*Language* The set of possible sentences in a particular language, described in part by a grammar. Example: English.
Performance A single, complete repetition of a routine. Example: A particular customer service encounter.	*Sentence* A single, complete expression in language. Example: 'The dog is barking.'
Subroutine Intermediate part of a routine that acts as a building block. Examples: Answering the phone, authorizing a credit card.	*Syntactic constituent* Intermediate part of a sentence that acts as a building block. Examples: Noun phrase ('the dog'), verb phrase ('is barking').
Move Unitary act of the routine. Examples: Greet customer, transfer customer.	*Word* Unitary element of a language. Examples: 'dog', 'barking'.

Table 1: Analogies between behavioral and grammatical entities (Pentland and Rueter, 1994, p. 490).

The analogy found its way into subsequent conceptions of routines, in particular into the work of Martha Feldman and colleagues (2000; 2003) who built on the importance of syntax to processes in organizations and advances the idea of grammar from a practice theoretical perspective of organizational routines. She emphasized that also the underlying rules of grammar may change and that the repertoire of actions to choose from may be enlarged by the creation of new elements, both actor-driven (Feldman, 2000). There is no noteworthy criticism to find in literature, however the opposite. Exemplarily, Bénédicte Reynaud (2005) called the newly created understanding presented in this analogy *pioneering work* and spotlights it in her work.

Routines as procedural memory. Michael Cohen (1991) laid the cornerstone of this analogy by connecting ideas of psychology with insights of organization theory. He found fertile ground in interweaving both domains and introduced the results of the psychologists Singley and Anderson (1989) on different forms of memory as well as the ideas of the economic sociologist Stinchcombe (1990) on organizational learning, uncertainties, skills, and routines. Singley and Anderson (1989, pp. 197-200) presented the distinction between declarative memory[23] (know-that) and procedural memory (know-how), which is fundamental to this analogy.[24] Procedural memory is a relatively automatic and inarticulate kind of memory that stores motor activities and cognitive skills. In contrast, declarative memory stores explicit content that is accessible by conscious awareness, i.e., facts, events, propositions and images (Squire, 1987, p. 242). Compared to the declarative memory, the procedural memory typically has a lower rate of decay – however, it is also more complex to access and to transfer.

In an experimental study based on the insights of Cohen (1991), Cohen and Bacdayan (1994, p. 554) revealed "[…] *organizational routines as interlocking, reciprocally-triggered sequences of skilled actions.*" Thus, the organization conflates individual skilled actions. At least in parts, these individual skilled actions are stored in the procedural memories of individuals. The interlinking of these distributed routine chunks creates a multi-actor-routine, i.e., an *organizational routine*. Accordingly, organizational routines can be seen as the procedural memory of organizations. Due to the roots on the individual level, organizational routines comprise tacit knowledge[25] and thus are difficult to replicate. As highlighted by the authors, routines tend to misfire at times and deliver a suboptimal performance, which Cohen and Bacdayan (1994) attributed to the relatively automatic recall of behavior stored in the procedural memory.[26] As routines reside "[…] *partially in the 'organizational unconscious'* […]" (Cohen and Bacdayan, 1994, p. 556), i.e., the individual procedural memories, it is hard to observe and analyze them. For this reason, Cohen and Bacdayan (1994) suggested making more use of laboratory research designs in future. However, just a few researchers followed this call.

Egidi (1996) and Egidi and Narduzzo (1997) replicated Cohen's and Bacdayan's (1994) experiment and found that routines cannot be memorized completely because of their variety and number. However, missing routine chunks can be reconstructed from prior (eventually unconscious) experience and give rise to the emergence of new routines. In addition, they found that the procedural knowledge of routines acquired in the experiment is strongly affected by path-dependence, which can lead to suboptimal performances of a routine.

Besides the replication of the original experiment mentioned above, Cohen and Bacdayan (1994) got widely cited with this analogy (e.g., Zollo, Reuer and Singh, 2002; Jarzabkowski, 2004; Pentland and Feldman, 2005; Rerup and Feldman, 2011; Felin *et al.*, 2012). Lazaric and Denis (2005) used this analogy to analyze how to create and

[23] Also referred to as *explicit memory*.
[24] Lazaric (2008, pp. 206-209) gave a compact overview about the distinction between declarative and procedural memory.
[25] Also referred to as *tacit knowing*. The term was originally coined by Michael Polanyi (1958, pp. 90-99; 1966, pp. 4-25) and describes that "[…] *we can know more than we can tell* […]" (Polanyi, 1966, p. 4). Common examples for actions involving tacit knowledge are riding a bicycle or identifying a particular face out of thousands.
[26] *Here*, it is referred to Luchins' (1942) *Einstellung effect*.

change a procedural memory in organizations. In their case study of a French meat-processing firm, they found that hierarchical pressures do not guarantee the memorization process, however, for a successful memorization process (in both, procedural and declarative memory) they found confidence toward the management as the key element. In a subsequent publication, Lazaric (2008) used the distinction between procedural and declarative memory to analyze the underlying cognitive micro-mechanisms of routines to explain what drives emergence and change in organizational routines. She highlighted that organizations do not only have to memorize and preserve knowledge (*here*: primarily declarative knowledge), but also have to be able to forget it. Regarding procedural knowledge, individuals' emotions and motivations were identified as drivers of change in organizational routines, as they are conceived as distributed across individuals.

Also, Feldman and Pentland (2003) related to the analogy of procedural memory. In their conception, organizational routines consist of an ostensive and a performative aspect. The ostensive aspect is the ideal schematic form of a routine that can be compared to a "[...] *socially distributed stock of knowledge* [...]" (Feldman and Pentland, 2003, p. 101) throughout the organization. That aspect may also comprise tacit knowledge, which is stored in the procedural memory. On the other hand, the performative aspect embodies the specific enactment of the routine in person, time, and place – that means it significantly integrates tacit knowledge and thus contributes to the procedural memory of an organization. These aspects are interdepended in a circular flowing relation and mutually constitutive. With this conception, Feldman and Pentland (2003) contributed one of the major impulses to routine research (Becker, 2008), building i.a. on the distinction between declarative and procedural memory.

2.1.1.3 Dead vs. live routines: From a static to a dynamic understanding

The dichotomous discussion on routines as being *dead* versus *live*[27], *mindlessness* versus *mindfulness*, *automatic* versus *effortful*, or in a broader sense *static* versus *dynamic* accompanies routine research for several decades now and divides literature into two camps (Becker, 2004; Reynaud, 2005). Organizational behavior literature tends to portray routines as dead, mindless, automatic, habitual, static or rigid. However, literature influenced by sociology paints a different picture of routines being live, mindful, effortful, sense-making, dynamic or flexible.[28]

The term ***dead routines*** was brought up by Cohen (2007) with reference to Dewey's (1922, p. 71) *dead habits* to bring the discussion about the mindless nature of routines to an extreme. The idea of a mindless execution of routines traces back to Ashforth and Fried (1988) and was followed by many others (Biddle, 1990; Gersick and Hackman,

27 These terms will be used to structure this section as they deliver "[...] *a powerful message about the nature of routines and the role of agency in routines, which has been lacking in earlier routines literature*" (D'Adderio, 2010, p. 11).

28 Exceptions can be found in both camps.

1990; Cohen, 1991; Louis and Sutton, 1991; Kilduff, 1992; Postrel and Rumelt, 1992; Nelson, 1995; Dosi, Nelson and Winter, 2000; Lazaric, 2000; Knott, 2001; Reynaud, 2005). However, even before the in routine literature frequently cited publication by Ashforth and Fried (1988), scholars used the term *mindlessness* to describe the non-deliberative and script-following nature of routines. There are several works with similar thoughts available (Stene, 1940; Simon, 1947, pp. 88-89; March and Simon, 1958, p. 142; Weiss and Ilgen, 1985; Winter, 1986; Waller, 1988). From the perspective of this stream of research, routines are static patterns of (inter-)actions which are performed mindlessly and can be stored unequivocally (Pentland and Feldman, 2008). The carrying out of these patterns gets triggered by a clearly specified event or action (Winter, 1986; Geiger and Koch, 2008). Kilduff (1992, p. 135) pointed out that "[...] *group members do not consciously* [...]" choose a routine when facing a task, they rather automatically perform a routine that builds on a shared understanding. This point was picked up by Lazaric (2000) who anchored routines in cognitive and social automatisms that result in actors following the patterns without further deliberation. Interpreting routines as automatic repetition of low-skill action on a subconscious level contributes to the idea of routines as a construct to economize the individuals and organizational cognitive resources (Becker, 2004).

Live routines as the counterpart of dead routines were first mentioned by Pentland and Feldman (2008) with reference to Cohen (2007) and accordingly Dewey (1922). With live routines, Pentland and Feldman (2008) took up the idea of viewing routines as generative systems that may produce new actions or patterns of action with each performance of the routine. In fundamental respects, this view is corresponding to Pentland's and Rueter's (1994) earlier publication on routines as grammars of action, in which they developed the popular interpretation of routines being rather *effortful accomplishments* than mindless repetition. Based on these thoughts, but also on Giddens' (1984, p. 60) thought of *practical consciousness,* as a substantial element of structuration theory, many researchers joined the idea of routines as a mindful, sense-making, dynamic and flexible construct (Pentland, 1995; Weick, 1995, p. 103; Costello, 2000, p. 15; Feldman, 2000, 2003; Perren and Grant, 2000; Edmondson, Bohmer and Pisano, 2001; Feldman and Pentland, 2003; Howard-Grenville, 2005; Reynaud, 2005; Levinthal and Rerup, 2006; Burns and Scapens, 2008; Geiger and Koch, 2008; Greenhalgh, 2008; Bruns, 2009; Brown and Lewis, 2011; Burns and Quinn, 2011; Goh, Gao and Agarwal, 2011; Rerup and Feldman, 2011; Bresman, 2012; Cacciatori, 2012; Turner and Rindova, 2012; Pentland and Hærem, 2015). Giddens (1984, p. 86) referred to routinized social behavior and not explicitly to routines.

However, organizational routines have *interactions*, which are an elementary element of social behavior, as a constituent feature, which are an elementary element of social behavior. These interactions, as Schegloff (1982, p. 89) discussed, are effortful achievements. Two significant contributions that support the idea of mindful patterns of action and routines as effortful accomplishments come from the same decade, it is

Weick and Roberts (1993) and Pentland and Rueter (1994). Weick and Roberts (1993) built on the cognitive body of thought by Solomon Asch (1952) and the idea of mind by Gilbert Ryle (1949) to develop a concept of *collective mind* that is determined by *heedful interrelating* in patterns of activities in groups. Also, Weick and Roberts (1993) did not directly relate to (organizational) routines. However, there are several parallels to the routine discussion, not at least in their three examples[29] for heedful interrelating.

In contrast, Pentland and Rueter (1994) directly contributed to the routine discussion, however, took a different approach with their grammatical model of organizational routines.[30] As explained above, they describe routines as grammars of action, i.e., an individual actor has to choose from a repertoire of mutually accepted actions in accordance with an underlying grammatical system to accomplish a task without leaving a set of possible patterns. That turns a routine performance into a deliberative and effortful accomplishment. The combination and recombination of actions from the organizational repertoire allow for variation in the routine performance within the boundaries of a grammatical model. Martha Feldman (2000) found common ground in the idea of Pentland and Rueter (1994) that routines allow for variation and thus are effortful accomplishments. She expanded that view in the sense that the accomplishment is ongoing and can be seen as emergent. From her perspective, variation and particularly change is more than choosing from a set of possible actions. Accordingly, routines can be thought of as "[…] *flows of connected ideas, actions, and outcomes. Ideas produce actions, actions produce outcomes, and outcomes produce new ideas*" (Feldman, 2000, p. 613). This perspective is close to the teleological change model by van de Ven and Poole (1995) but with the addition that Feldman related change to both, consensus and conflict. By doing so, she embraced the role individual agency to shape "[…] *routines as a richer phenomenon*" (Feldman, 2000, p. 613) in which the internal dynamics and individuals define the potential for change and thus highlight the temporal structure of *the* routine.

In a subsequent and often-cited publication, Martha Feldman and Brian Pentland (2003) brought together their ideas to advance routines as a live and flexible concept of how organizations get things done. In their introduced ontology, derived from the body of thought of Giddens (1984) and Bourdieu (1977; 1990) as well as the language used by Latour (1986), Feldman and Pentland (2003) constructed routines of two interrelated parts: On the one hand there is an abstract and ideal form of the routine that embodies structure, the so-called *ostensive aspect*, and on the other hand, there is the actual performance of a routine that embodies agency, the so-called *performative aspect*. The ostensive aspect may exist in various forms. It may be codified in norms or artifacts but may also have the form of procedural or tacit knowledge. It is likely to be distributed throughout the organization and to comprise the subjective understandings of the

29 They chose one example from the laboratory and two examples from aircraft carriers.

30 Here, only Pentland and Rueter (1994) are referenced as they are the originators of the analogy of routines as grammars of action. Another important publication in this analogy was Pentland (1995).

organizations' individuals. Further, the ostensive aspect can never define a specific performance of a routine but rather the abstract form of it. That is because it is impossible to specify a pattern of behavior fully. Building on Wittgenstein's (1953 [1958]; I.201; 1956; I.113) arguments, the interpretation of the rules describing the pattern also require rules, and so on and so forth – accordingly, a clear interpretation is not possible (see also Feldman and Pentland, 2008).

On the contrary, the performative aspect "[...] *are the specific actions taken by specific people at specific times when they are engaged in an organizational routine*" (Feldman and Pentland, 2003, pp. 101-102). In this context, Feldman and Pentland referred to routines as *effortful accomplishments* (Pentland and Rueter, 1994), to the *improvisational nature of practices and routines* (Bourdieu, 1977; Suchman, 1983; Bourdieu, 1990; Hutchins, 1991; Weick and Roberts, 1993; Orlikowski, 2000) and to the individuals' engagement in terms of *reflective self-monitoring* (Giddens, 1984), which can be seen as the three main ingredients of the performative thought on routines. As said before, the ostensive and the performative aspect are interrelated, and both cannot be treated and understood separately but need to be understood as a unit in which change in one aspect inevitably leads to change in the other aspect as well. Taking a closer look at the ostensive aspect and its relation to the performative aspect, the ostensive aspect gives agents *guidance*, *explanation*, and *reference* in their performance of a routine (see Figure 1, p. 3).[31] The countermove form the performative to the ostensive aspect allows to feed back the outcome of a performed routine to its ideal schematic form by *(re)creating*, *maintaining* and *modifying* it. Adopting this mechanism reveals organizational routines' potential for endogenous change and their capacity to generate variety. Thus routines become a dynamic and ever-changing organizational feature (Feldman and Pentland, 2003).

There can be found various authors in today's literature who share this view: Geiger and Koch (2008) concluded that routines are rather complex practices than mindless patterns of action. Also, Cacciatori (2012) referred to Feldman and Pentland (2003) to describe routines on the basis of structuration and practice theory as "[...] *effortful accomplishments of mindful individuals* [...]" (Cacciatori, 2012, p. 1559) and not as mindless and fixed responses to a trigger situation. However, Becker *et al.* (2005) remarked that the nature of a specific routine determines the role of mindfulness can have. In a recent paper by Pentland and Hærem (2015), the authors summed up many of the thoughts shown above and once again illustrate the mindful, non-automatic and variation producing nature of organizational routines that made Feldman's and Pentland's (2003) concept of routines so widely accepted.

[31] Feldman and Pentland (2003, pp. 106-107) used the terms of *guiding*, *accounting*, and *referring* to describe the relation between ostensive and performative.

2.1.2 Organizational routines: Macro-concepts and micro-foundations

Several authors embedded organizational routines into a hierarchy of higher and lower level concepts, such as firm strategy, dynamic and organizational capabilities, individual skills, competencies, or experiences (e.g., Andersen, 2003; Salvato and Rerup, 2010; Eggers and Kaplan, 2013). This section will explore some of the relationships between these levels to establish an understanding of the embeddedness of routines into the organization and to shed light on the emergence and constraints of routines. Starting from a macro perspective, routines will be portrayed as the building blocks of capabilities. Subsequently, the micro perspective focuses on the individual level and finally links it to the organization as a collective entity.

2.1.2.1 Routines as building blocks of capabilities

In an extensive review of the routine literature, Parmigiani and Howard-Grenville (2011) identified two major camps in the routine domain: on the one hand, there are organization theorists, on the other hand, there are organizational economists. The first camp views organizational routines from the practice perspective and is mainly interested in the internal dynamics of a routine, i.e., in opening the *black box* and analyzing the internal structure of the routine to find out how the routine operates. The latter group views routines from a performance and outcome-oriented perspective and focuses on the purpose and motivation for executing an organizational routine. This section adopts the capabilities perspective and aims to illustrate how the concept of organizational routines contributes to building capabilities.

Nelson and Winter (1982) can be seen as the originators of the capabilities perspective as they introduced a "[…] *firm-specific, path-dependent view of routines that highlights their complexity and underpins their effect on performance differences*" (Parmigiani and Howard-Grenville, 2011, p. 416). There are many definitions of organizational capabilities available, nearly as much as authors on this topic. Accordingly, a terminological fuzziness surrounds the concept (Collis, 1994; Winter, 2000).[32] One of the first definitions arose from *An evolutionary theory of economic change* by Nelson and Winter (1982, p. 52) who conceived a capability being "[…] *the range of things a firm can do at any time* […]". This definition is still vague and in the following the authors used routines and capabilities interchangeably (Nelson and Winter, 1982, pp. 73, 124-125). However, in a subsequent section of the book, Nelson and Winter (1982, p. 142) highlighted that the application of a particular set of routines characterizes a capability.

[32] In the introduction of Dosi, Nelson and Winter (2000), the terminological issues of the capability concept were discussed in detail.

Nevertheless, to specify the notion of capability more precisely, it is necessary to elaborate the relationships between routines and capabilities sufficiently. Capabilities[33] can be subdivided into five dimensions: (1) strategic capabilities[34]; (2) organizational capabilities (s.s.)[35]; (3) functional capabilities[36]; (4) market and demand capabilities; and (5) dynamic capabilities (Carlsson and Eliasson, 1994; Collis, 1994; Hauknes, 2000). In this study, the term (organizational) capability encompasses the first four dimensions as routine literature did not differentiate between these dimensions sufficiently. However, dynamic capabilities were frequently mentioned separately and accordingly their interplay with routines will be portrayed with an additional focus. As mentioned earlier, organizational routines are regularly located within a hierarchy of other concepts. Various authors described comparable hierarchical levels in their publications (e.g., Andersen, 2003; Salvato and Rerup, 2010; Eggers and Kaplan, 2013): Individual level concepts (cognition, emotion, social context, skills, competencies etc.) form the basis for routines. These routines are the building blocks for dynamic and organizational capabilities. The concepts of dynamic and organizational capabilities will be illustrated in more detail in the following, to be capable of drawing conclusions on the relationship of routines and capabilities.

Dynamic capabilities are in most cases referred to Teece and colleagues (Teece and Pisano, 1994; Teece, Pisano and Shuen, 1997) and are a higher-level construct that enables organizations to adapt lower level entities (e.g., routines, organizational capabilities) to a dynamically changing environment. In essence, this conception is similar to what Nelson and Winter (1982, pp. 17-18, 126-128) called higher-order routine. Some authors regarded dynamic capabilities as an extension of the resource-based view, which is rather static than dynamic (Barney, 1991; Barreto, 2010). Teece, Pisano and Shuen (1997, p. 516) described dynamic capabilities "[...] *as the firm's ability to integrate, build and reconfigure internal and external competences to address rapidly changing environments*". Teece and colleagues built on the thoughts of Leonard-Barton (1992) on how knowledge of organizations can be both, essential for innovation but also hindering. This paradox may turn *core capabilities*[37] into *core rigidities* and thus jeopardizes an organization's competitive advantage. More recent definitional approaches are in line with the definition above, however, add additional points.

Zollo and Winter (2002) highlighted the aspects of patterns and collectivity. That is similar to definitional approaches of routines, however, on a higher-level. They defined

---

33 In several cases, the term *organizational capabilities* was applied in describing all kinds of capabilities that refer to organizations in contrast to individual capabilities. That may lead to confusion in the context of organizational capabilities in the sense of integrative or coordinating capabilities (2).

34 Also referred to as *selective capabilities*.

35 Also referred to as *integrative* or *coordinating capabilities*.

36 Also referred to as *technical capabilities*.

37 Here, it is also referred to Prahalad and Hamel (1990) and their concept of core competencies, which is an essential cornerstone of the dynamic capability approach.

a dynamic capability as "[…] *learned and stable pattern of collective activity through which the organization systematically generates and modifies its operating routines in pursuit of improved effectiveness*" (Zollo and Winter, 2002, p. 340). In a prominently staffed chapter of Helfat *et al.* (2007) – including i.a. Sidney G. Winter, David J. Teece, Sydney Finkelstein, and Margaret A. Peteraf – the authors emphasized the variety of forms of dynamic capabilities and defined them "[…] *as the capacity of an organization to purposefully create, extend, or modify its resource base*" (Helfat *et al.*, 2007, p. 1). According to their conception, a dynamic capability serves three functions in an organization that not necessarily have to be present as a triple: (a) identification of the need/opportunity for change; (b) formulation of a response to (a); and (c) implementation of relevant actions. These functions reveal an inherently patterned structure of dynamic capabilities that distinguishes them from ad hoc problem-solving, notwithstanding that both may change lower level entities (Eisenhardt and Martin, 2000; Winter, 2003).

Eisenhardt and Martin (2000), however, took the view that dynamic capabilities consist of simple rules in high-velocity markets and resemble routines in moderately dynamic markets. They argued that dynamic capabilities "[…] *are the organizational and strategic routines by which firms achieve new resource configurations as markets emerge, collide, split, evolve, and die*" (Eisenhardt and Martin, 2000, p. 1107). The authors noted their definition being close to the understanding of other authors (e.g., Kogut and Zander, 1992; Amit and Schoemaker, 1993; Cockburn, Henderson and Stern, 2000) and highlighted dynamic capabilities being specific organizational and strategic processes (e.g., innovation processes, alliancing). In another definition, Zahra, Sapienza and Davidsson (2006, p. 924) aligned to Winter (2003) and viewed "[…] *dynamic capabilities as the abilities to reconfigure a firm's resources and routines in the manner envisioned and deemed appropriate by the firm's principal decision-maker(s).*" This definition revealed the roots of dynamic capabilities in the behavioral theory of March and Simon (1958), as bounded rational decision-makers take decisions under uncertainty. Further, it linked the concept to evolutionary theory (Nelson and Winter, 1982) and the resource-based view.

There was a clear distinction between dynamic capabilities and organizational capabilities by Zahra, Sapienza and Davidsson (2006). However, they remarked that this is usually not the case in the literature. In contrast, the role of dynamic capabilities – to change lower level entities such as routines and organizational capabilities – is comparatively unambiguous. Interestingly, Zahra and colleagues drew the conclusion that a dynamic capability does not necessarily need to reside above organizational capabilities and routines. In fact, they may also be nested inside organizational capabilities or routines. Although the concept is still not unambiguously characterized (Salvato, 2003), in a review of 40 articles about dynamic capabilities Barreto (2010) found that they are often characterized by processes and routines. Further, he highlighted the definition of Zollo and Winter (2002; see above) because it is close to early definitions of organizational routines. Zollo and Winter (2002) recognized the function of a dynamic capability as an altering mechanism of operational routines. As routines affect an organization's performance, dynamic capabilities indirectly influence performance outcomes too. Certainly, the routines and capabilities created by the organization's dynamic capabilities may differ and hence their achievable performance level (Zott, 2003; Zahra, Sapienza and Davidsson, 2006).

Organizational capabilities are the hierarchical level below dynamic capabilities, and moreover, they typically operate on the firm-level to execute essential functional activities (e.g., production, distribution, marketing etc.; Helfat and Peteraf, 2003; Salvato and Rerup, 2010). Certainly, the distinction of the level of routines and organizational capabilities, as well as the relation between them, is not clear-cut (Abell, Felin and Foss, 2008). In a publication on firm strategy and competitive advantage, Grant (1991) emphasized organizational capabilities not just being the assemblage of team resources. He rather viewed an organizational capability as "[…] *a routine, or a number of interacting routines*" and noted that they differ in their complexity (Grant, 1991, pp. 122-123). The coordination between individuals and other resources is substantial to capabilities, he argued (see also Cohen *et al.*, 1996), and further, the repetition of coordinated and patterned processes reflects what usually is understood by the term routines as described by Nelson and Winter (1982). The latter characterized capabilities as mechanisms to select and to schedule routines to achieve a particular outcome (Nelson and Winter, 1982, p. 100) and as dependent on individual skilled behavior that might become rusty when not exercised repetitiously (Nelson and Winter, 1982, p. 124). Winter (2000; 2003) kept this view in subsequent publications. According to this view, an "[…] *organizational capability is a high-level routine (or collection of routines) that, together with its implementing input flows, confers upon an organization's management a set of decision options for producing significant outputs of a particular type*" (Winter, 2000, p. 983; 2003, p. 992). Felin *et al.* (2012) analyzed this definition and highlight routines, experience, learning and other resources being inputs to capabilities. Thereby, routines become metaphorically speaking *building blocks of capabilities*.

The conception of routines being the building blocks of organizational capabilities is rife can be found in various publications (e.g., Dosi, Nelson and Winter, 2000; Winter, 2000; Andersen, 2003; Helfat and Peteraf, 2003; Dosi, Faillo and Marengo, 2008; Salvato and Rerup, 2010; Eggers and Kaplan, 2013). Routines are the crucial building blocks of organizational capabilities, however, not the only ones (Dosi, Nelson and Winter, 2000; Narduzzo, Rocco and Warglien, 2001). As an example for other components of capabilities, Dosi, Nelson and Winter (2000) named databases, which are neither routines nor individual skills. Additionally, for capabilities applies the same as for routines, the tacit knowledge involved in lower level constructs (routines, individual skills) restricts the degree to which they can be codified (Grant, 1991; cf. Zollo and Winter, 2002). Nonetheless, Levinthal (2001) considered routines as powerful enhancements of capabilities to integrate complementary behavior of individual actors into an organization's outcome (see also Narduzzo, Rocco and Warglien, 2001). Dosi, Faillo and Marengo (2008) also regarded routines being a major building block of organizational capabilities and suggest using them as the unit of analysis for organizational capabilities.

Similarly, Eggers and Kaplan (2013) followed this call and interpret organizational capabilities as assemblages of organizational routines, in which the building blocks can be taken apart and reassembled as a function of (new) interpretations. However, they noted that existing research does not sufficiently cover the assembly process itself. Their review identified cognition as being an important part of the development and deployment of organizational capabilities. Cognition contributes to the three dynamics underlying organizational capabilities: (1) constructing capability building blocks a.k.a. routines; (2) assembling routines into organizational capabilities; and (3) matching those firm-specific capabilities to external opportunities. Eggers and Kaplan (2013) underlined that the relationships of the processes above are of recursive nature. Cognition and capabilities shape each other in an iterative manner (see also Helfat and Peteraf, 2003). Cognition acts as an important mechanism that integrates knowledge and experience in the process of routine assemblage and thus alters the relationship between capabilities and performance (Eggers and Kaplan, 2013; cf. Salvato, 2009). Accordingly, cognition transforms an ordinary set of routines into an organizational capability (Gavetti, 2005; Eggers and Kaplan, 2009, 2013; Kunc and Morecroft, 2010; Benner and Tripsas, 2012). Besides cognition, experience plays an important role in the emergence of organizational capabilities.

As mentioned above, Felin and colleagues (Felin and Foss, 2010; 2011; Felin *et al.*, 2012) highlighted that experience forms the basis of routines respectively organizational capabilities. This basis was also suggested by Helfat and Lieberman (2002). They analyzed the birth of organizational capabilities in the context of a firm's market entry and found that experience has a profound influence on the capabilities a firm develops. However, differently from biological genetics, firms may escape their heritage and thus shape the subsequent performance according to their needs deliberately (Helfat and Lieberman, 2002). This deliberate process of decision-making to overcome undesired heritage exemplary shows the involvement of the policy maker's cognition and reflects its importance. Having the above points about cognition and experience as individual level constructs in mind, the following critique of Felin and Foss (2009) is particularly interesting. In a review of organizational capabilities literature, they criticized that individuals regularly become depicted as homogeneous. These homogenous individuals lead to a constant performance level that will not be affected by the fluctuation of employees or other heterogeneity factors (Kogut and Zander, 1992; Henderson and Cockburn, 1994; Felin and Hesterly, 2007). From a today's perspective about micro-foundations of organizational constructs like routines or capabilities, conceiving individuals as homogenous is hardly agreeable and substantially directs the focus for future research on these constructs to an integrated view of micro and macro levels.

As shown in this section, organizational routines are a key concept to understand both, dynamic and organizational capabilities. Parmigiani and Howard-Grenville (2011) suggested considering organizational routines as the fundament of both kinds of capabilities – organizational and dynamic capabilities. However, as Felin and Foss (2005) noted, there is a lack of a clear understanding of the routine concept. Building the definitional approaches of capabilities on such ambiguous concept may be problematic but at least to be a logically consistent approach.

2.1.2.2 Linking individuals and the collective level

Organization theory is a diffuse field of research and thus offers a wide variety of options for consistent argumentation (Jaffee, 2001, p. 1). As vague as some points are, others are unambiguous throughout literature. So, the corpus of organization theorists and sociologists agreed on the collective nature of (formal) organizations (Simmel, 1908 [2009]; e.g., Taylor, 1911, p. 70; Weber, 1922 [1978], pp. 48-49; Stene, 1940, p. 1127; March and Simon, 1958, p. 4; Cyert and March, 1963, p. 27). Besides shortcomings regarding other characteristics of organizations, many of the metaphors on the notion *organization* clearly reflect the collective nature of organizations (Morgan, 2006, pp. 5-7). Research depicted organizations as machines (e.g., Smith, 1776 [1982], pp. 19-21 etc.; Weber, 1922 [1978], pp. 973-974), organisms (e.g., Burns and Stalker, 1961, pp. 96-125; Katz and Kahn, 1978, p. 18), brains (e.g., Simon, 1947, pp. 220-244; Beer, 1972; 1979; 1985), cultures (e.g., Morgan, 2006, pp. 115-125), and so on. All of these images can be taken apart into its subunits. Machines are a construction of its parts. Organisms consist of cells. Brains cluster billions of neurons. Moreover, cultures are i.a. a conglomerate of customs, beliefs, morals, norms, and knowledge. Inevitably, this leads to the question: What is the unit of analysis to gain insights about an organization or, respectively, a routine as an organizational concept?

Geoffrey Hodgson (2007b, p. 219) suggested that all theorizing should "[…] *build from elements which are taken as given*". In respect of organizations, the action-taking individuals bring concepts (e.g., routines) to life and transform their outcome into tangible behavior. Thus, one way to approach organizational concepts may be using the sociological doctrine of methodological individualism[38] (cf. methodological holism; e.g., Durkheim, 1895 [1982], p. 138; Durkheim, 1897 [2002], p. XLIV). The roots of methodological individualism, however, can be found in economics, not in sociology.[39] It was the economist Joseph Schumpeter who first coined the German term *methodologischer Individualismus* (Schumpeter, 1908, pp. 88-100; 1908 [2010], pp. 57-

38 For an extensive review on methodological individualism, see Udehn (2001).

39 It should be noted that there are differently termed, however, in some respect comparable earlier approaches to methodological individualism (e.g., Bernard Mandeville, Adam Smith, Carl Menger).

63) and later on the English correspondent *methodological individualism* (Schumpeter, 1909).

> *"Each mass manifestation of course consists of individual manifestations and one could assume that in order to understand the first, the latter have to be examined."*[40] (Schumpeter, 1908 [2010], p. 60)

The quote implicitly mirrors that breaking down a mass manifestation to its individual manifestations is not necessarily the only way to understand these. Nevertheless, he concluded that methodological individualism enables us to produce results in a short and convenient way and thus, within a pure theory supersedes the social approach (Schumpeter, 1908, p. 95; 1908 [2010], p. 61). The results reconstructed from elementary units of mass manifestations may even be more complex compared to its source, at least in their insights. Methodological individualism as conceptualized by Schumpeter is, however, restricted to pure theory s.s. (Schumpeter, 1908, p. 96; 1908 [2010], p. 62). Schumpeter's contemporary, influencer, and teacher Max Weber picked up the concept of viewing individuals and their actions as the basic unit first in his essay *Some categories of interpretive sociology* (Weber, 1913 [1981], p. 158) and later in his posthumous published magnum opus *Wirtschaft und Gesellschaft* (Weber, 1922; 1922 [1978]) as one of the methodological principles of his sociological outline of economy and society.[41] Methodological individualism as discussed by Weber (1922; 1922 [1978]) requires a profound understanding of his concept of *verstehende* (or interpretative) sociology and in particular of social action that would go beyond the scope of this chapter. However, to offer a shorthand introductive explanation, Weber (1922 [1978], p. 4) defined sociology and social action as follows:

> *"Sociology (in the sense in which this highly ambiguous word is used here) is a science concerning itself with the interpretive understanding of social action and thereby with a causal explanation of its course and consequences. [...] Action is 'social' insofar as its subjective meaning takes account of the behavior of others and is thereby oriented in its course."*[42]

Methodological individualism in the sense of Weber is action-based and requires starting the analysis of social phenomena with the only thing that is real and present – human beings. If there is such thing as society, accordingly, it can only be the social action-taking individuals that compose society and its adherent concepts. Sociological

---

[40] German original quote: "*Jede Massenerscheinung besteht natürlich aus individuellen Erscheinungen, und so liegt der Schluß nahe, daß man die letzteren untersuchen müsse, um die ersteren zu verstehen.*" (Schumpeter, 1908, p. 93).

[41] It should be noted that Max Weber did not use the term methodological individualism, however, described it accurately.

[42] German original quote: "*Soziologie (im hier verstandenen Sinn dieses sehr vieldeutig gebrauchten Wortes) soll heißen: eine Wissenschaft, welche soziales Handeln deutend verstehen und dadurch in seinem Ablauf und seinen Wirkungen ursächlich erklären will. [...] 'Soziales' Handeln aber soll ein solches Handeln heißen, welches seinem von dem oder den Handelnden gemeinten Sinn nach auf das Verhalten anderer bezogen wird und daran in seinem Ablauf orientiert ist.*" (Weber, 1922, §1)

concepts that are not explicable within the meaning of individuals and their actions should be abandoned (Weber, 1922 [1978], pp. 13-15). He emphasized the distinctiveness of interpretative sociology against natural sciences, which adds "[...] *subjective understanding of the action of the component individuals* [...]" (Weber, 1922 [1978], p. 15) to external observation as known from natural sciences.

The doctrine of methodological individualism found its advocates in the post-Weberian phase. Frequently, literature referred to Friedrich von von Hayek (1942; 1943; 1944; 1952) and Karl Popper (1944a; 1944b; 1945) as facilitators of methodological individualism, but also to more recent interpretations, e.g., Jon Elster (1982; 1985) who takes an analytical Marxist perspective to methodological individualism (Udehn, 2001, pp. 114-121, 200-210, 310-316; Udehn, 2002; Hodgson, 2007b). Hayek's interpretation of methodological individualism is less radical than those shown above (Udehn, 2001, p. 114). Besides the human being and its action as an observable fact, he integrated the individual's interpretation of action (subjectivism) and the interaction between individual actors into his approach (von Hayek, 1942, pp. 277-278, 283; von Hayek, 1952, pp. 33-34). Karl Popper built on the thoughts of Weber and Hayek, however, at the same time, he delineated his understanding of methodological individualism from the Austrian School (Udehn, 2001, p. 209). The Popperian methodological individualism claims to reduce all collective actions and behavior to the individual-level (Popper, 1945 [1947], p. 87). In this logic, Popper even found common ground with Psychologism, even though he opposed Psychologism in some of his other writings and rather argued for the autonomy of sociology (e.g., Popper, 1945, p. 88). However, Popper (1945 [1947], p. 91) added a dash of psychological vocabulary (attitudes, decisions) in his view on methodological individualism:

> "[Methodological individualism,] *the important doctrine that all social phenomena, and especially the functioning of all social institutions, should always be understood as resulting from the decisions, actions, attitudes, etc., of human individuals, and that we should never be satisfied by an explanation in terms of so-called 'collectives' (states, nations, races, etc.).*"

This interpretation is, compared to Hayek's understanding, less radical than those of Schumpeter or Weber. Interestingly, Jon Elster – Marxist and defender of the rational choice approach – brought methodological individualism back to its strict interpretation. Similar to Weber (1922 [1978], p. 15), Elster (1989, p. 13) stated:

> *"The elementary unit of social life is the individual human action. To explain social institutions and social change is to show how they arise as the result of the action and interaction of individuals."*

With this reductionist understanding of methodological individualism (see also Elster, 1985, p. 5), he intended to build micro-foundations for Marxism using game-theory as a utility to explore and explain the *sociological black box* of social structure and social change (Elster, 1982).

To sum up preliminary, the five interpretations of methodological individualism presented above have commonalities, however, also differ in several respects. A further review of the literature would lead the reader to the insight that there is no single accepted definition of methodological individualism, especially none that is in line with Schumpeter's (1908; [1908] 2010) original meaning (Hodgson, 2007b). Viewing the conceptual development of methodological individualism raises questions: Should social phenomena be entirely reduced to individuals, or should individuals only be part of the explanation (Udehn, 2002)? Does only the individual actor and its actions matter, or also the relations among the individual actors (Hodgson, 2007a)? Hodgson (2007a) advanced the concept and suggests to leave the strict interpretation of methodological individualism behind. Further, he suggested integrating the interactive nature of social relations into the concept. Accordingly, methodological individualism should explain social phenomena "[…] *in terms of individuals and social structures*" (Hodgson, 2007b, p. 220). Adopting such broadened understanding of methodological individualism allows analyzing organizational routines as generative structures including questions on routine acquisition, replication, change, and so on (Hodgson, 2007a; b).

Routine research, for the most part, focused on the collective level and practiced downward causation (Foss *et al.*, 2012). Thus, assumptions about the underlying layer, i.e., assumptions about the individual level (e.g., homogeneity of human capital), were at least implicitly made. Felin and colleagues (Felin and Foss, 2005; 2009; 2011; Felin *et al.*, 2012) tackled these assumptions by highlighting the heterogeneity of individuals in organizations (e.g., gender, values, preferences, beliefs, knowledge, experience, etc.) and accordingly claimed an upward causation (i.e., micro-foundations) for organizational routines. Further, they viewed individuals, structure, processes and interactions at the core of routines' micro-foundations and accordingly, as emphasized in the quote below, also at the heart of methodological individualism.

> "*The notion of 'microfoundations' certainly is not new. It is traditionally allied […] with 'methodological individualism' in the philosophy of social science.*" (Felin *et al.*, 2012, p. 1352)

Several authors in the field of routines argued in the way a methodological individualist would do, however, without naming the concept methodological individualism or identifying themselves with it. Nelson and Winter (1982, p. 72) acknowledged that organizational behavior is "[…] *reducible to the behavior of individuals* […]", and in return, the individual actions influence the collective level, e.g., an organizational routine.[43] Similar, Salvato and Rerup (2010) expected individual actions to have an effect on other hierarchical levels. Hierarchy is a recurrent theme in routine research (e.g., Cohen *et al.*, 1996; Dosi, Nelson and Winter, 2000), which also

[43] Illuminating in this respect, however too far-reaching here, is Herbert Simon's (1985) article on whether studying the *Homo economicus* (omniscient and rational) or the *Homo psychologicus* (bounded rational). Although the article originates from a political context, it as well allows basic conclusions for organizations.

contributes to the micro-foundations discussion that is driven, at least partially, by the body of thought of methodological individualism. A metaphorically spoken hierarchical relation comes from Hodgson (2008, p. 18), who describes routines as "[...] *organizational meta-habits, existing on a substrate of habituated individuals in a social structure*." There are two notions in this definition that contribute to the approach of methodological individualism. First, describing individuals as the *substrate* assigns them a substantial role for organizational routines. In an ecological sense, thus individuals provide the vital substances that organizational routines and accordingly the organization in principle require for surviving (i.e., perception, actions, etc.). Secondly, social structures have a broad scope, however, can here be understood for the sake of convenience as "[...] *various aspects of a society, including culture and its related values, systems of institutions* [...], *and the relationships among various actors within the system* [...]" (Earley, 1997, p. 14).

Breaking this down to an organization leads to the insight that there are organizational analogs of the characteristics mentioned in the definition. Organizations are *social structures*, however, on a different level than in society (Aldrich and Martinez, 2010). For instance, organizations have cultures as well, so-called organizational cultures. Those base on shared assumptions, values, and beliefs (e.g., Schein, 1985 [2004], p. 17), similar to culture in society. Ultimately, the carriers of organizational assumptions, values, and beliefs are individuals that went through a learning process. Systems of intra-organizational institutions (e.g., contracts, policies, departments, or teams) and the systems of these institutions serve as another example. Institutions are also reducible to individuals who exemplary conclude a contract or are the base unit of a department or team. Moreover, there are relationships among the individual actors, but also between individuals and other levels of an organization. Having this in mind, the term *social structure* in the quote of Hodgson (2008) gives the metaphor above a profoundness that one might miss on first reading. Routine literature, especially from the micro-foundations branch, referred to those and cognate characteristics frequently. Common topics discussed in this branch are relationships and interactions, cognition and its encompassed processes learning, knowledge and memory, but also decision-making processes or bounded rationality. Some will be discussed in more detail in the following to embrace the interdependency of the collective level with the individual level in more depth.

The relationships and interactions between individuals are building blocks of routines as they are frequently understood as sequences of interlocking individual habits (e.g., Hodgson, 2008; Salvato and Rerup, 2010). Interlocking habits describe a sequence in which a habit triggers the next one (individual level) to bring a routine (collective level) into existence. Importantly, routines allow (and in some cases force) individuals in organizations to develop "[...] *a common disposition to behave and think in a particular way in a particular class of situations*" (Knudsen, 2008, p. 131). Relationships and interactions, however, enable individuals to interchange the current status of a routine, the expected next step and consequently allow to trigger the subsequent habit. Viewing relationships from this perspective makes them a premise and, at the same time, a consequence of a routine. However, as Hodgson (2008) added, an organization needs to provide individuals with an environment and with the conditions to realize this common behavior and mindset. Here, we find a fundamental interdependence between the individual and collective level.

As mentioned above, another common theme in the micro-foundations branch and an important building block for explaining organizational routines as a collective-level concept is cognition (Felin *et al.*, 2012). Cognition attributes to one of the three components of mind and encompasses "[…] *all forms of knowing and awareness, such as perceiving, conceiving, remembering, reasoning, judging, imagining, and problem solving* […, as well as] *an individual percept, idea, memory, or the like*" (VandenBos, 2015, pp. 201-202). Conceiving routines as the vehicle to orchestrate habitual instrumental actions in a goal-oriented direction requires the individual actors to undergo a cognitive process (March and Simon, 1958, p. 151). In this process, the individuals are asked to perceive and analyze the situation in order to fetch a learned and stored part of the routine from their memory that results in achieving the goal or getting closer to it (Narduzzo and Warglien, 2008). However, this connotes individual cognition as a limitation to what can be achieved by a routine (Kogut and Zander, 1992; Pentland and Rueter, 1994). Individual psychological processes, preceding the individual action in the routine performance differ among the organization members.

Preceding processes are learning routine knowledge; the perception and interpretation of a situation or cue, and also the handling of personal interests. That is to say, two or more individuals may percept other characteristics of a situation, which leads to divergent interpretations of that particular situation and accordingly to a divergent recall of their routine knowledge and the subsequent action. Additionally, that happens against the background of different personal interests (Nelson and Winter, 1982, p. 104; Lawson, 1997, p. 162; Felin and Foss, 2009; Zbaracki and Bergen, 2010). Knowing that there are other views, here it is perspicuous that "[o]*rganizations learn only through individuals who learn*" (Senge, 1990, p. 124), or in other words that "[a]*ll learning takes place inside individual human heads*" (Simon, 1991, p. 125). Consequently, an organization is only able to expand its knowledge by individuals who learn or by acquiring individuals who already learned in other environments (Simon, 1991). In both cases, the knowledge that the organization absorbs resides in the individual memories. In regard to routines, Cohen and Bacdayan (1994, p. 567) pointed to the profound ways in which "[…] *individual memories interact and shape* […]" organizational routines.

Besides this learning-based approach to the frequently asked question where the knowledge of organizational routines resides, there is a different and less radical approach to this issue that argues from the point of quality of knowledge. There are two distinct forms of knowledge, *declarative knowledge*[44] and *procedural knowledge*.[45] The first refers to facts and information that can be expressed and stored in a static memory (know-that), on the contrary, the latter refers to mental and motor skills that are hard or impossible to articulate (know-how; Singley and Anderson, 1989, pp. 197-200; see also Chapter 2.1.1.2, section: Routines as procedural memory). Declarative knowledge can be expressed and importantly it can be codified in artifacts (Hodgson, 2008). However, organizational routines also have a tacit component, and thus they also consist of knowledge that cannot be articulated or separated from the individual action (Lazaric, 2000). Cohen (2012) brings forward the argument that individuals retrieve habits from their non-declarative system with a reduced conscious and verbal access. Thus, understanding routines, as described above, as interlocking habits gives them a strong tacit character and makes it impossible to codify them completely. That proves true, especially when considering that routines are not always the formal procedure of an organization (Hodgson, 2008).

Nelson and Winter (1982, p. 104) took a firm stand on this issue by stating that *all* the knowledge of skills and routines, whether articulable or tacit, resides in the memories of the organization members.[46] Adopting this view of routine knowledge residing on the level of individual memory also leads to the insight that an organizational routine cannot be held by one individual alone. The complexity of routines usually involves specialized actors with specific knowledge to carry out their part of the routine. That entails a confined overlap of the individual knowledge parts, or in extreme cases a complete separation without any overlap (Becker, 2004). The distribution of routine knowledge across several individuals highlights the importance of micro-foundational focus in the research on organizational routines that pays attention to the individuals itself, but also to structure, processes, and interactions as suggested by Felin and colleagues (Felin and Foss, 2011; Felin *et al.*, 2012).

Summing up, organizational routines are a concept that undoubtedly includes several individuals and in most instances belongs to the collective level. The micro-foundations approach seeks to explain this collective level concept from what is real and tangible, the individuals. Feldman (2000) claimed not separate organizational routines from those who exercise the routine as this will make routines a richer phenomenon. Individual cognitive processes enable an organization to accumulate, store and retrieve routine knowledge. However, individual knowledge on its own does not allow an organization to perform a routine. Routine performance is about the goal-oriented combination of different knowledge fractions of individuals that are driven by relationships between those organization members and the interactions along a structured organizational process. Finally, it is to say, and this is very much in the tradition of methodological

44 Also referred to as explicit, conceptual, propositional, or descriptive knowledge.

45 Also referred to as implicit, or tacit knowledge.

46 It is to note that Nelson and Winter (1982, pp. 97-98) used the term *organization member* in a flexible way. However, in most cases *organization member* referred to the individual actor.

individualism, there cannot be an organizational routine without an individual, but at the same time, the "[...] *organizational whole is greater than the sum of the properties of its individual members, taken severally*" (Hodgson, 2007a, p. 111).

2.1.2.3 *Routines, emotion and motivation*[47]

Much of the research on organizational processes and routines neglected the effects of emotions, even though they influence a broad range of them (Elfenbein, 2006; Barsade and Gibson, 2007; Salvato and Rerup, 2010). In the field of organizational routines, the focus was mainly on deliberative processes (cognition), however, not on impulsive or emotion-based processes (Cohen, 2007; Winter, 2013). An emotion describes a transient "[...] *complex reaction pattern, involving experiential, behavioral, and physiological elements, by which an individual attempts to deal with a personally significant matter or event*" (VandenBos, 2015, p. 362). The relationship between emotion and motivation is complex and yet not fully clear. However, as motivation can be conceived here as the "[...] *willingness to make an effort in the pursuit of a goal* [...]" (Matsumoto, 2009, p. 319), emotions often turn out to be the driver that energizes and directs the motivation (Gaulin and McBurney, 2004, pp. 121-142).

To draw on the ostensive-performative distinction (Feldman and Pentland, 2003), the relevance of both, emotion and motivation, becomes concrete. There is the ostensive aspect, commonly referred to as the ideal schematic form of a routine, which however needs to be interpreted by the individual actors before performing their part of the routine. The process of interpretation is a balancing act between the *individual* mental model of a routine and the *organizational* ideal schematic form of it. The process involves emotional and motivational factors that shape the mental model and accordingly the performance (Howard-Grenville *et al.*, 2016). Exemplarily, the transformation of the organizational ostensive aspect into an actor's interpretation of it, relies on different perspectives on how to approach the routine enactment (Zbaracki and Bergen, 2010; Turner and Rindova, 2012), or dissentient intentions and goals for the organizational routine (Howard-Grenville, 2005; D'Adderio, 2014).[48] Accordingly, the ostensive models hold by different individuals commonly vary (Pentland and Feldman, 2005; cf. Dionysiou and Tsoukas, 2013). Even if the ostensive aspect on the organizational level and its interpretation on the individual level match, the performance of the routine may still differ from the ostensive expectation as action involves the individual's power, dispositions, emotions, and motivations (Salvato and Rerup, 2010; Feldman, 2016; Simpson and Lorino, 2016; Turner and Cacciatori, 2016). Routine literature regularly brings up the question how to overcome the misalignment of the ostensive and performative aspect, which is still not answered (Howard-Grenville *et al.*,

[47] Although recent findings from the field of neuroscience showed that cognition and emotion are interdependent (Ochsner and Gross, 2005; 2008), here, for the sake of distinctiveness a separation appears to be helpful.

[48] For an overview see Howard-Grenville and Rerup (2016).

2016). However, there are numerous references in routine literature that underline the influence of motivation and accordingly of emotion for routine research.

Already March and Simon (1958, pp. 143-144; ch. 4) discussed the role the motivation of individuals in the implementation and execution of programs (routines). Nelson and Winter (1982, p. 109) implicitly emphasized the importance of motivated individuals in routine functioning by asserting that rule enforcement mechanisms are crucial for routine performance, however also limited. Becker (2004) picked up this point in a review of the routine literature. He pointed to the fact that there is always an option to circumvent the rules describing a routine and that precise rule following may reduce or even thwart the performance of a routine. In a case study, Lazaric and Denis (2005) analyzed the introduction of ISO norms in a meat-processing firm. They found that the management and the employees negotiated the patterns that led to routine performance. On the employees' side, a confidence toward the management supported the motivation of the actors and minimized the deviation between the ostensive and performative aspect. Coming from a strong practice theoretical background, Feldman (2000) examined change in a college housing organization. She suggested not to separate the routine from the people who act in the routine, as these people think, feel, care, and are carriers of will and intention. An integrative view of patterns of action with those who perform them would enrich our understanding of the construct of organizational routines.

Concluding on the above, individuals with their emotions and motivations are not interchangeable in organizational routines. It is the individual that shapes the emergence of routines. Accordingly, the actors' motivation and commitment possibly are the major factors in preventing their intention to circumvent a routine to adapt it to their goals (Nelson and Winter, 1982, p. 108). Thus, an important task for an organization to motivate its individuals to ensure a smooth routine functioning aligned to the organizational purpose (Grant, 1991).

2.1.3 Routines and context

2.1.3.1 Replication of organizational routines

The notion of replication was broadly used in the literature on organizational routines (Foray and Steinmueller, 2001; Winter and Szulanski, 2001; Szulanski and Winter, 2002; Winter and Szulanski, 2002; Becker and Lazaric, 2003; Hodgson, 2009; Jonsson and Foss, 2011; Friesl and Larty, 2013; D'Adderio, 2014; etc.). Simplified, Winter and Szulanski (2001) or also Teece, Pisano and Shuen (1997) described replication as the transfer of business processes from one place to another. Particularly, an organization should consider those processes for replication that were successful in their application and performance as yet (e.g., superior routines). Some replicators, i.e., such organizations that replicate themselves entirely or partly, were able to replicate their proven business units or processes hundredfold throughout the world. Successful replicators are exemplarily the McDonald's Corporation, the Avis Budget Group, H & M Hennes & Mauritz AB or the Inter IKEA Holding B.V. (Love, 1995; Knott, 2003, pp. 48-66; Konlechner, 2011). In such cases, replication creates value as the different units of these organizations perform the same tasks (e.g., a McDonald's restaurant in India has basically the same function as a McDonald's restaurant in the United States: Preparing and selling meals quickly and in a consistent quality).

A successful replication can achieve several effects, e.g., competitive and first mover advantages, planning reliability, faster growth, increased profitability, or contiguousness to the key market (Galbraith, 1990; Kostova, 1999; Argote and Ingram, 2000; Winter and Szulanski, 2001, 2002; Szulanski and Winter, 2002). Hodgson mentioned the movement of employees from the source to the target of the routine and the enlistment of external knowledge resources (consultants, experts) as the two most significant mechanisms for replication (Hodgson, 2009). D'Adderio (2003) beheld the future path for replication in the mechanism to encode knowledge in artifacts, particularly software, as this allows to reconfigure the routine knowledge according to the underlying principles and thus makes replicated routines flexible in their performance. Besides those mechanisms, literature presented two strategies that may influence the success of a replication process. First, there is the template-based approach that focuses on the exact replication of a routine. A source routine serves as the template, and the goal of the replication process is to transfer this routine without deviation or modification into the target unit. Secondly, the principle-based approach considers a successful replication also possible without using a template but by transferring processual principles by developing an understanding of the causal relationships of these principles (Baden-Fuller and Winter, 2007). Konlechner and Güttel (2010) remarked that the research about replication strategies is still deficient and accordingly additional research in this area may offer new insights for routine research in general.

The replication of routines is however still a challenging process that may fail (Szulanski, 1996; Teece, Pisano and Shuen, 1997; Jensen and Szulanski, 2004; Schulz, 2008). For instance, to preserve or gain an organization's competitive advantage, it is not just necessary to replicate a routine but also to innovate it at the same time. Challenging is also the handling of the organization member's attitudes, on both sides, the source and the target unit (Szulanski and Winter, 2002). For knowledge transfer, as it is the case for the replication of organizational routines, in particular, the openness to new insights, which originate from a different unit, is crucial. The organization members in the receiving unit need to absorb the incoming knowledge sufficiently to make the replicated routine functioning in their organization. The issue of not accepting external knowledge in the receiving unit is regularly referred to as *not invented here syndrome* (Clagett, 1967; Katz and Allen, 1982). Another, mission-critical factor for the success of replication is the speed of transition of a routine from one place to another, particularly in competitive environments as imitation by competitors may be the result of a delay in that transition (Winter and Szulanski, 2001).

Replication is a transfer of knowledge that is embedded in repetitive organizational processes. As outlined in the previous sections, knowledge can be explicit (i.e., articulable) or tacit/implicit (i.e., not or not entirely articulable). Besides explicit knowledge, in most cases, routines consist of tacit elements too (Nelson and Winter, 1982, p. 104; Teece, 1982). In a broad sense, this may be human capital in general, or in a narrower sense, this can be tacit knowledge derived from experiences (e.g., particular movements, audio cues, or distribution of attention). An organization member needs to develop the tacit knowledge during or after the replication process to facilitate the functioning of a routine. That is one, however, a substantial factor that makes replication of routines a cost-intensive, challenging and protracted process (Nelson and Winter, 1982; Winter and Szulanski, 2002, p. 121), which may require an iterative approach (Szulanski and Jensen, 2004). Hodgson (2008) even took a more radical position on the role of tacit knowledge for routines. Until it is evident how the preservation and replication of tacit knowledge embedded in routines works, one cannot understand the functioning of routines in general, he criticized. However, what became clear from the study of Cohen and Bacdayan (1994) is that tacit knowledge is less subject to decay and thus a replication of this inarticulate knowledge would be beneficial in the long term.

The context-dependent nature of routines is widely acknowledged (Teece and Pisano, 1994; Dosi in Cohen *et al.*, 1996; Cohendet and Llerena, 2003; Becker, 2004; Howard-Grenville, 2005; D'Adderio, 2010, 2014; Turner and Fern, 2012; Turner and Cacciatori, 2016). Also, Feldman and Pentland (2003) highlighted the role of context in their ostensive-performative distinction. Thus, the ostensive aspect needs to be adaptive to contextual details that may vary from performance to performance (see also Feldman, 2003). Nevertheless, that context dependency of routines causes problems for the replication process and cannot be simplified as done by Hahn (McLeod and Hahn, 1949) who remarked that an identical replication of a plant with its labor force would double the output of the first plant. Uncoupling a routine from its original context weakens its bearing (Elam, 1993; Elam and Arrow, 1993). Similar, Madhok (1997, p. 47) considered "[…] *differences between home and host context erode the appropriateness and applicability* […]" of routines and decrease the value of the embedded knowledge.

In an experimental setting, Reimer, Opwis and Bornstein (2002) taught individuals to solve the Tower of Hanoi puzzle. After the subjects had established a routine to process the problem, the experimenters confronted the subjects with a comparable task in a varied context. The original routine from the Tower of Hanoi puzzle was suboptimal for this task, however, maintained by the subjects. Reimer, Opwis and Bornstein (2002) concluded that routines are subject to context and that individuals are prone to inertia (see also Einstellung effect by Luchins, 1942). As organizations are no laboratories that can control the context perfectly, there are always contextual differences between the source and the target unit. Accordingly, universal best practices or routines do not exist; they can only fit locally (Amit and Belcourt, 1999; Becker, 2004). Nonetheless, organizations should not excuse failed replication processes by that, but conceive the contextual adaptation of routines in the replication process as a challenge to gain local best solutions for a homogeneous performance across different locations. Replicating a routine into new cultural or economic contexts requires adapting the routine to the new environment to maintain its value (Hodgson, 2009).

In a canonical correlation analysis of a data set of 122 best-practice transfers in different organizations, Szulanski (1996) analyzed the correlation between transfer difficulties and its sources on an intra-organizational level (i.e., knowledge transfer barriers). He found three key obstacles hindering the knowledge transfer: (i) the recipient's lack of absorptive capacity; (ii) causal ambiguity; and (iii) difficult relationships between the source and the recipient (see also Kostova and Roth, 2002). These results point to the insight that the knowledge transfer of routines does not fail because of low motivation, as often presumed, however, because the knowledge about the replication process is missing. To overcome these issues in the replication of routines, Szulanski (1996) suggested focusing on developing closer relationships between the organization members, and on developing a deeper understanding of the methods and communication of the replication process. However, not only the replication of routines is problematic, but also the research on routine replication has its pitfalls. Most empirical studies on the replication of routines only allow limited insights and generalization, as they focused on specific routines in specific contexts.

Finally, there are two camps of researchers on replication of routines, those who think exact replication is feasible and those who contradict. The majority (Rivkin, 2001; Winter and Szulanski, 2001, 2002; Reimer, Opwis and Bornstein, 2002; Szulanski and Winter, 2002; Becker, 2004; Narduzzo and Warglien, 2008) belongs to the group that thinks that an exact replication is *not* possible, however, which does not necessarily mean it should not be the goal.[49] Hodgson (2003; 2008) emphasized the limited knowledge we have about the replication of routines and criticized that the knowledge we have is mainly an accumulation of case studies. These case studies alone may not answer the questions we have, exemplarily, to clarify if the rife hypothesis that a template-based replication is more effective than a principle-based replication. However, experiments in controlled environments could be an appropriate method to contribute to a substantial debate about replication.

2.1.3.2 Change, stability, and rigidity of routines

In routine research, much of the discussion centers around stability and change (e.g., Feldman and Pentland, 2003; Farjoun, 2010, see also Chapter 2.1.1.3). Stability is often used to highlight the structural aspects and the longevity of the patterns embodied in organizational routines. However, stability also subordinates terms like inertia or

[49] A differentiated discussion on the need for contextual adaptation in the replication process can be found in Turner and Cacciatori (2016).

rigidity. Both relate the absence of change with a negative connotation. Inertia comes from a backward-looking logic, and in contrast, rigidity embraces a forward-looking rationale. The use of the generic term change is mostly neutral and subordinates the terms variation and mutation. Change, in general, can be deliberative or non-deliberative, likewise variation, which has a more positive connotation than change, however. The notion of mutation arises from evolutionary literature and clearly refers to a non-deliberative interpretation of change. As Nelson and Winter (1982, p. 116) added, mutations "[...] *of course are not always deleterious*."

As discussed in the previous section, the innovation of routines is necessary to sustain a competitive advantage and to prevent imitation or substitution. Apparently, in part, this conflicts the stability-providing effect of routines and requires organizations to balance stability and change to allow innovation. That does not necessarily mean that stability is unfavorable. In rough and complex situations, e.g., when external conditions change rapidly, the orientation-providing effect of stable patterns, such as established routines, may be valuable (Howard-Grenville, 2005; Pentland *et al.*, 2012; Kozica, Kaiser and Friesl, 2014). Stability can even be a prerequisite for change and the other way round, together they may build a dualism (Farjoun, 2010). However, organizations occasionally hang on to routines even though they do not meet the expected performance and receive negative feedback. In the long run, this conventionalism leads to inertia (Kilduff, 1992; Rumelt, 1995; Becker, 2004). A distinct form of stability can be found in rigid routines (Schreyögg, 2013).

These routines provide an organization with a sequence of actions that is robust or even resistant to change and has the stamina to overcome critical situations, in both, the positive and negative meaning. Characteristically, every single action in this sequence is well-defined and designed to solve a specific problem. In environments requiring highly reliable processes (e.g., hospitals, air traffic control, or nuclear power plants) the implementation of rigid routines is desired. However, if rigidity is not intended deliberately, it may restrict an organization's ability to react with variation to dynamically changing environments (Felin *et al.*, 2012). Pentland and Rueter (1994, p. 506) stressed that all performances of a routine fit into a single model of that routine and argued that despite routines "[...] *have a great deal of regularity, there is always the possibility of exception, breakdown, creativity, shirking, error, and other variety-producing contingencies*." This statement points out that change in routines can be deliberative or non-deliberative and, as Becker (2005b) suggested, the differentiation is useful in explaining change of organizational routines.

Nelson and Winter (1982, pp. 116-117, 121) determined deliberate change that occurs beyond the control systems of an organization as a threat to the functioning of routines. Additionally, they expected mutation (non-deliberative change) to be present when routines replicate to another place. Putting organizational routines to the heart of their evolutionary approach of the firm implied that "[m]*odeling the firm means modeling the routines and how they change over time*" (Nelson and Winter, 1982, p. 128; see also

Hodgson, 2008). That clearly refers to a deliberative decision-making process of changing routines, which however is difficult (Pentland and Hærem, 2015). Becker (2004) viewed routines as the unit of analysis to explain economic and organizational change. He referred to the processual conception of routines by Pentland and Rueter (1994) that described routines as grammars of action.

Becker (2004) asserted that using the approach of grammars of action allows not only explaining the deliberative choices that lead to economic or organizational change but also to those explaining the change of routines themselves. Such modeling also includes some level of stability, which is contained in the underlying grammatical rules. So far, it is unclear to which extent the degree of stability prevents routines from changing. Hannan and Freeman (1989, pp. 66-90) viewed the capacity of routines to change as limited. Building on the body of thought of Nelson and Winter (1982, pp. 124-125) that routines become rusty and decay when not exercised, they expected routines to have a great portion of inertia. Change in the set of routines of an organization thus originates from survival, extinction, and the creation of specific routines. Winter (1994, p. 100) put inertia and change of routines in a nutshell: "*The prevailing organizational routines do not mark the edge of the feasible, but the point where learning stopped–or, more optimistically, the point that learning has now reached.*" Reading this quote underlines the uncertainty that accompanies organizations and scholars in the discussion of whether routines cause change or inertia.

With the ostensive-performative concept of routines, Feldman and Pentland (2003) contributed a model that described organizational routines as a source of both, stability and change. The ostensive aspect embodies structural elements and thus spends stability for the individuals that enact the routines, as well as for the organization as a whole. On the other hand, the performative aspect integrates agency into the performance of a routine and thus puts it to the test for change with each enactment. Viewing routines through this practice-theory-based lens assigns the particular aspects specific functions. The ostensive aspect offers the actors a normative goal, a template of behavior including the legitimation for this behavior, and a reference to actions in patterns that are incomprehensible for the individual actor. The performative aspect is responsible for the creation of the routine by ensuring its repetition and at the same time maintaining the functioning of a routine. Lastly and besides maintaining it, the performative aspect allows the actors to deviate from the behavioral template of the ostensive aspect. Deliberatively or non-deliberatively the actors can alter the pattern of a routine by adding or omitting actions and thus create a modified version of the ostensive aspect, which then will be put to the test with the next performance.

The popularity the ostensive-performative distinction received since its publication, per se, shows the need routine research has for an integrative model of change and stability in routines. Feldman's and Pentland's (2003) model allows mapping diverse forms of change, starting from deliberative variation and ending with non-deliberative forms like mutation. It also justices to different forms of stability, e.g., an extreme form like rigidity. Also, Becker (2004, p. 649) acknowledged "[…] *the fact that routines can be simple rule-following behavior at one point of* [sic!] *time, but involve adaptive and creative behavior at another point of* [sic!] *time*." These mechanisms explain endogenous change (deliberative and non-deliberative) arising from the agents involved in the performance of the routine. Agents change routines based on different motivations, which exemplary may be efficiency or optimization of the process on the positive end, however, which may also be personal advantages or obstruction on the negative end. Exogenous events, such as changes in the context of a routine, can also result in a deliberately or non-deliberately altered routine. The ostensive-performative distinction, however, does not allow explaining or inducing an exogenous change of a routine that individuals outside the routine deliberately seek (e.g., the management or consultants). If one interprets the creation of routines as a form of deliberative change, which builds on the experience from past routines, the findings of Pentland and Feldman (2008) revealed that managers who design artifacts and accordingly hope to create an ostensive aspect by their expectations will fail in shaping the actual routine and its performance by actors.

Rice and Cooper (2010, pp. 131-133), though, asserted that deliberate change is possible. However, they also identified impeding factors of deliberate change (e.g., limited actor processing capabilities, opponents anticipating negative consequences, inertia, or cultural and organizational biases). Further, changing an existing routine or replacing it completely with a new routine produces costs, such as an increased cognitive effort for learning and performing the altered routine, as well as costs for the risks involved in managing the emerging uncertainty associated with the new routine and the incomplete knowledge about it and its performance. In most cases, the altered routine will cause a reduced performance during the initial repetitions due to the retraining of the involved actors. For infrequently and rarely performed routines a practical and efficient choice thus may be to stick with the existing routine. Eggers and Kaplan (2013) also thought that a deliberate creation of routines induced by managers is possible. Building on the thoughts of Salvato (2009) that the mindful handling of environmental cues (internal and external) can influence the creation and variation of organizational routines, Eggers and Kaplan (2013) expected managers to be able to formalize knowledge from prior experience into a new or changed routine. A constraint to this process is, however, that managers cannot fully control the experiences an organization or its members make.

Summing up, routines incorporate both, stability and change. The first aspect, stability, is anchored in the patterned nature of organizational routines. Whether it is intended or not, stability can have positive as well as adverse consequences for an organization. On the other hand, change may occur in different forms (deliberately, non-deliberately) and accordingly named differently (e.g., variation, mutation) with the adherent connotations. The current models for change in and of organizational routines, however, do not allow to make use of deliberate exogenous change. Most studies were conceptual or built on cases that do not allow to uncover the underlying mechanisms of deliberately induced change.

2.1.4 Concluding remarks on organizational routines

This publication purposefully avoids emitting another definition of organizational routines, as the "[…] *term is used by many people in many different contexts, and, it seems, to describe many different 'things'*" (Becker, 2004, p. 664). In short: The concept is already sufficiently *blurry*. The approach to the concept of organizational routines in this publication, in contrast, rests on developing a broad understanding of the concept without restricting or dividing it to one of the major schools of thought (e.g., evolutionary economics, behavioral economics, institutional economics, capabilities approach, et cetera). Along the historical path of routines, starting from the habits literature (Dewey, 1922; Weber, 1922 [1978]; Stene, 1940), over the ideas on decision-making and rational choice by the behavioral economists from Carnegie Mellon University (Simon, 1947; March and Simon, 1958; Cyert and March, 1963), to the enduringly influential evolutionary approach on the theory of economic change by Nelson and Winter (1982), the fundamentals of routines were illustrated.

Subsequently, frequently appearing characteristics of routines that were used in the literature to describe the concept were portrayed to outline the nature of routines. The four common analogies of organizational routines introduced thereafter, help to make the concept of routines more accessible and to raise awareness for the discussion on the static vs. dynamic character of routines. Having established such broad understanding allowed embedding organizational routines in the hierarchical levels above (capabilities, dynamic capabilities) and below (individuals, actions). The horizontal view on routines in the previous section took the context and replication of routines, as well as the associated mechanisms into account and emphasized the embeddedness of organizational routines. Finally, the effects routines provoke in organizations build the focus in this section and represent the final logical step in obtaining the here intended comprehensive understanding of organizational routines in the sense of cause-and-effect. Accordingly, in the following, six effects of routines will be discussed; these are (1) coordination and control, (2) building truces, (3) regularity and reduction of uncertainty, (4) path-dependence, (5) preservation of knowledge, and (6) economizing cognitive resources.

Coordination and control. Organizational routines characteristically are patterned sequences that standardize processes in organizations and make the subsequent actions predictable (Gersick and Hackman, 1990; Cohendet and Llerena, 2003), at least in the trajectory of possible actions (Pentland and Rueter, 1994; Pentland, 1995). Standardization facilitates comparing different performances of a routine and thus allows to control its future performances or dependent routines (Becker, 2004). Several authors on routines supported the view that routines have an inherent coordinative power

(Stene, 1940; Nelson and Winter, 1982, p. 107; March and Olsen, 1989, p. 24; Grant, 1991; Coriat, 1995; Dosi, Nelson and Winter, 2000; Narduzzo, Rocco and Warglien, 2001; Reimer, Opwis and Bornstein, 2002; Reynaud, 2005; Abell, Felin and Foss, 2008; Grote *et al.*, 2008; Rerup and Feldman, 2011; Edmondson and Zuzul, 2016). As Teece, Pisano and Shuen (1997) added, the coordinative capacity of routines is firm-specific and not general in nature, which implies that the coordinative power of a specific routine does not transfer automatically in the case of routine replication. In this context, Nelson and Winter (1982, p. 107) noted "[…] *coordination is preserved, and organizational memory refreshed, by exercise* […]" only. However, the sources of this coordinative power differ among the authors (Becker, 2004).

Drawing on longitudinal data of the development and realization of a planned community in Orlando, Edmondson and Zuzul (2016) observed that "[…] *providing a structuring system that supports communication and experimentation* […]" is a facilitator for coordination and control of large and complex project routines. Grote *et al.* (2008) highlighted the capacity of routines to reduce complexity, to increase stability, and to establish shared expectations (see below for *truces*; or see Nelson and Winter, 1982, pp. 107-112) as drivers of coordinative capabilities of routines. Abell, Felin and Foss (2008, p. 490) found the coordinative power in the routines' "[…] *nature to internalize externalities* […]." Another more practical approach in explaining the coordinative effect of routines stems from its repetition that makes them well-practiced over time and provides the actors with a predictable plan that does not need to be managed. Besides offering coordination, it also saves time and energy to be applied in non-routine tasks (Simon, 1947, p. 73; Gersick and Hackman, 1990; Reimer, Opwis and Bornstein, 2002). March and Olsen (1989, p. 24) argued from the idea of the collective nature of routines and the essential interactions among the actors of a routine. Thus, "[r]*outines make it possible to coordinate many simultaneous activities in a way that makes them mutually consistent.*" Similarly, Grant (1996) noted the potentiality of routines to maintain a high-level of simultaneity and the variety of the interaction patterns of routines as arguments for the coordinative capacity of routines. Against the mainstream rationale that organizational routines reduce the need for interaction, Hoffer Gittell (2002) proposed the opposite. Adopting the traditional thoughts that routines allow organizations to prespecify actions and the combinations of actions (sequences), she, however, found routines being a coordination mechanism among the actors by facilitating their interactions. Hoffer Gittell (2002) concluded routines to contribute in reducing uncertainty (see below) by the facilitated interactions and accordingly wider shared information. Despite having different foci in the framing of the coordinative effect of routines, their conclusions are in line and acknowledge that routines are a mechanism to control and coordinate organization members' actions.

Building truces. Organizations consist of members of different intentions and interests. Some of these members are authority figures that enforce or promote their ideas by sanctioning or incentivizing. That mechanism is, however, just an expression of intra-organizational conflict and arising from motivational factors (Nelson and Winter, 1982, pp. 107-108). Nevertheless, also on the same hierarchical level, there are different interests to find that potentially result in conflicts among the actors. In both cases, organizational routines function as truces that resolve or at least diminish those conflicts. Nelson and Winter (1982, pp. 110-111) viewed the routine operation primarily as a form of establishing a truce among the supervisor and the supervised (i.e., the different hierarchical levels). Such orchestration of diverse interests of the various hierarchical levels relates the truce building effect to political factors, exemplarily to power (Burns, 2000; Lazaric and Denis, 2005). However, also on the same hierarchical level routines effect that actors' conflicts become resolved or mediated. The fundamental mechanism underlying this effect is that the actors are not surprised by the behavior of other actors and build a common basis for acting (Simon, 1947, p. 73; Coriat and Dosi, 1998; Pentland and Feldman, 2005; Burns and Scapens, 2008).

When a routine is established and operates as a truce, changing the routine becomes a disruptive break and puts the effects of the routine to the test. That might result in the revival of the already solved or muted conflict (Nelson and Winter, 1982, p. 134; Lazaric and Denis, 2005). Due to the fragmentation of conflicts Pentland and Feldman (2005) did not expect the mere existence of a routine to bring the truce into effect. Further, they thought that the scope of a single routine is limited and makes it necessary to build a network of routines to solve intra-organizational conflicts. Very much in the thought of the dynamics of the ostensive-performative cycle of routines, they conclude that truces are not conceivable as a stable condition but as an ongoing process of validation, which is highly dynamic in nature. In other words: "*This perspective suggests that truce is a relative rather than an absolute term*" (Pentland and Feldman, 2005, p. 809).

Regularity and reduction of uncertainty. A variety of authors described organizational routines as regular, repetitive and predictable patterns (Nelson and Winter, 1982; Levitt and March, 1988; Grant, 1991; Langlois and Everett, 1994; Pentland and Rueter, 1994; Dyer and Singh, 1998; Zollo, Reuer and Singh, 2002; Lillrank, 2003; Zbaracki and Bergen, 2010; Parmigiani and Howard-Grenville, 2011). These three aspects are characteristics of routines. However, at the same time regularity is an effect that stems not only from the regularity of the patterns but also from the inherent stability and the repetitive nature of routines – likewise interrelated. Of course, organizational routines also incorporate and allow change. As yet, change is often incremental (McKeown, 2001; D'Adderio, 2008), irrespective of the underlying model of organizational routines. Feldman and Pentland (2003) found change occurring in the repetitious performances in the ostensive-performative cycle – step-by-step, repetition by repetition. Over time, these deviant performances alter the ostensive aspect. Nelson and Winter (1982) described evolutionary mutation as a mechanism of change, per se incremental. Despite knowing that an exception or a breakdown of a routine is always possible, Pentland and Rueter (1994) suggested that change originates from a gradually refined vocabulary or an adapted set of grammatical rules.

Notwithstanding in these three examples, there is the potential for change, they nonetheless underlined the prevalence of stability and thus regularity in organizational routines. That said, stability is, as Becker (2004, p. 659) distilled from literature (Langlois, 1992; Postrel and Rumelt, 1992; Shapira, 1994; Tyre and Orlikowski, 1996), the "[…] *baseline against which to assess changes* […]." Because routines contain the potentialities for both, change and stability, these not necessarily equally weighted potentialities need to be equilibrated by the organization and the actors (Feldman, 2003; Howard-Grenville, 2005; Turner and Rindova, 2012). Turner and Fern (2012) found that experience plays a major role in balancing routines' stability and variability, and highlight a shift from stability-spending properties of routines for inexperienced actors to variability-spending properties for experienced actors. However, the stability that the experienced actors underwent in previous performances of the routine enables them to vary the current or future performances of the routine. Accordingly, in complex and with uncertainty afflicted situations (e.g., context change) inexperienced actors benefit from a stabilizing effect of routines that reduces uncertainty in their performance. For experienced actors, the routine gives them the necessary stability to enact a contextually adapted pattern of action in response to a contextual change (variable performance).

Such a model requires an organization that applies routines and does not only preserve them as written-down recipes, and this kind of organization has to enable the actors to perform variations (Grote *et al.*, 2008). As "[u]*ncertainty is the absence of the data or information necessary to make an informed judgment*" (Spender, 2002, p. 154), routines can contribute to reducing uncertainty on the whole continuum between inexperienced and experienced organization members. On one end of the continuum, routines allow the inexperienced actors to pick the right actions in complex and uncertain situations. Even though the actions do not perfectly adapt to the requirements of the situation, they enable the actor to deal with uncertain situations instead of stalling. On the other end of the continuum, flexible organizational routines facilitate the experienced member to adapt the standardized procedure to a specific contextual requirement and thus to maximize the performance of the routine (Howard-Grenville, 2005). Switching the perspective from the level of the actor to that of the organization as an entity reveals additional insights. From that view, routines have an inherent capacity to increase predictability by fixing particular parameters and by reducing the need for cognitive resources (Becker, 2004; 2005a). For the organization's management, these two aspects allow dealing with uncertain situations by acquiring managerial foresight for the next steps and their consequences, as well as by having available cognitive resources at all organizational levels to deal with exceptions or similar. To sum up, in the words of Hoffer Gittell (2002, p. 1424), "[…] *routines can be increasingly effective in the face of uncertainty*."

Path-dependence. In a comprehensive analysis of increasing returns in economics, Arrow (2000) traced the roots of path-dependence back to Cournot (1838 [1897]) and Veblen (1915). From there, the concept went through an extensive development and was applied in a multitude of fields (Egidi and Narduzzo, 1997), such as technological change (David, 1985; Arthur, Ermoliev and Kaniovski, 1987; Arthur, 1989; David and Greenstein, 1990; Galor and Tsiddon, 1991; Dosi and Kaniovski, 1994; Bruggeman, 2002; David, 2005), political sciences (Berman, 1998; Alexander, 2001; Greener, 2002; Hansen, 2002; Holzinger and Knill, 2002; Greener, 2005), organizational learning (March, 1991; Zhou, 1993; Egidi and Narduzzo, 1997; Rycroft and Kash, 2002; Carlile and Rebentisch, 2003), or economic and organizational change (North, 1991; Cavalcante, Kesting and Ulhøi, 2011; Schreyogg and Sydow, 2011; Pentland *et al.*, 2012). Respectively, there is no clear and concise understanding of path-dependence. Oversimplified, some scholars describe the concept with the terms *history matters*, *imprinting of organizational behaviors*, *inertia* or sometimes as *lock-in* – however, the interchangeable and mistaken use of these terms in literature emphasizes the ambiguities that surround this concept (Levi, 1997; Pierson, 2000; Vergne and Durand, 2010; Schreyogg and Sydow, 2011). Knowing that a narrow and precise conceptualization of path-dependence would postulate a separate chapter, at least a short explanation is offered here: Path-dependence describes that the choices we made in past decision-making processes influence the choices we make in the contemporary setting. The costs of reversal at certain points are (too) high, and thus a once chosen path does not allow to easily return to the initial or one of the previous points to make an alternative choice. In consequence, that means a suboptimal path may be preferable from the cost perspective as the costs for changing the chosen path to the optimal choice may exceed the losses of maintaining the suboptimal choice (Levi, 1997; Sydow, Schreyögg and Koch, 2009).

In the field of organizational routines, researchers regularly referred to the effect of path-dependence (or also inertia[50]). Already Nelson and Winter (1982, pp. 110-112, and various other sections) applied the concept to explain the mechanisms of routines as predictable and inflexible, and their effects on firm behavior, innovation, or economic change in general. In contrast, Egidi and Narduzzo (1997; see also Cohen and Bacdayan, 1994) used a card game to analyze the creation of routinized behaviors on the group level with a focus on cognitive micro-foundations of routines. The strategies the groups developed and thus the decisions they made in the past, determine their strategy and actions in a subsequent phase of the game in a suboptimal way by maintaining their routinized behavior. The subjects were tied to the prevailing patterns in a manner that prevented them from searching an optimal solution to the task. This study was a striking example of how routines can lead to path-dependence.

Pentland *et al.* (2012) described the abstract level of routines as a reservoir for conserving an organizations' history. The abstract level has different names in the literature on organizational routine, e.g., ostensive-aspect (Feldman and Pentland,

[50] In the literature about organizational routines, the term *inertia* referred to both, stability and path-dependence.

2003), dispositions (Hodgson and Knudsen, 2004b; 2010, p. 79), or organizational skills (Nelson and Winter, 1982). In their generative model of routines, Pentland *et al.* (2012, p. 1489) noted that "[…] *past actions influence current actions, and current actions can be selectively retained as part of the history.*" In short, that means the organization conserved its previous decisions in the abstract version of the routine. That understanding clearly refers the routine idea to path-dependence, as the recursive relationship of action and history is the cornerstone of path-dependence (see also the ostensive-performative cycle of Feldman and Pentland, 2003). There are several other authors of routine literature who referred to path-dependence (Levitt and March, 1988; March, 1994; Nelson, 1995; Malerba and Orsenigo, 1996; Coriat and Dosi, 1998; Amit and Belcourt, 1999; Zott, 2003; Schulz, 2008; Teece, 2009, pp. 20-21, 117). The stable patterns associated with organizational routines have positive effects like regularity or truces among the actors. However, they also lead to commonly negatively perceived effects like path-dependence (Becker, 2004; Narduzzo and Warglien, 2008).

As mentioned before, routines require balancing stability and flexibility. An overbalance on the stability side may result in rigid patterns that effect path-dependence. Once an organization depends on a path of narrowed options for current and future decision-making, the remaining portion of routine flexibility becomes inhibited and facilitates the evolvement of inertia. Part of that argument is that organizations neglect what Nelson and Winter (1982, p. 122) called *search*, and accordingly are not even aware of the existence of superior alternatives (Narduzzo and Warglien, 2008). For the progression of routine research, the explanatory power of path-dependence lies in great part in the ability to support explaining the emergence of inertia embodied in organizational routines (Pentland and Hærem, 2015). Further, path-dependence allows understanding how the repetitious carrying out of organizational routines entails lock-ins that can only be resolved by deliberate or exogenous control (Sydow, Schreyögg and Koch, 2009; Vergne and Durand, 2010; cf. Pentland *et al.*, 2012).

Preservation of knowledge. Organizational routines store context-specific operational knowledge that is remembered by doing (Nelson and Winter, 1982, pp. 97-99; Loch, Sengupta and Ahmad, 2013; Winter, 2013). As Becker and Lazaric (2003) emphasized, routines consist of two levels, the potentiality for action and their expression. The knowledge embodied in organizational routines manifests at the level of expression (performance) with the enactment of actions that reflect the knowledge in practice (Orlikowski, 2002; Feldman and Orlikowski, 2011; Radwan and Kinder, 2013). The knowledge conserved in routines can be declarative knowledge as well as procedural knowledge. The first is codifiable, and the latter is tacit in nature. Usually, routines encapsulate both at the same time (Cohen and Bacdayan, 1994; Miller, Pentland and Choi, 2012). The tacit components of routines can hardly be verbalized or codified. Retaining and circulating tacit knowledge is hardly feasible for organizations. The repeated performance of tacit knowledge in routines is one (eventually the only) option to articulate such knowledge and thus to make it accessible to others (Obstfeld, 2012).

However, by their collective nature, routines as a repository of knowledge are more than just an accumulation of individual knowledge but a form of an organizations' memory (Nelson and Winter, 1982, p. 107; Lazaric, 2013). The knowledge preserved in the organizational memory allows the organization to undergo a process of experiential learning (backward-looking logic). In this process, the internal stock of knowledge is the basis for altering existing routines (deliberately and non-deliberately) and for the creation of new routines. Subsequently, these routines become part of the organizational memory and effect preserving the knowledge for future iterations (Gavetti and Levinthal, 2000; Eggers and Kaplan, 2013).

Economizing cognitive resources. Individuals and subsequently organizations as collectives of individuals have bound cognitive resources for, e.g., information processing or decision-making (Simon, 1947; Simon, 1955; 1967; 1972; Miller, 1956; March and Simon, 1958, ch. 6; Lazaric, 2000; March, 2006). In analyzing the economizing of cognitive resources, the procedures of organizations need to be considered. That includes organizational routines in particular (Shapira, 1994). Becker (2004) and others (see Chapter 2.1.1.2, section: Routines as procedural memory; and Chapter 2.1.1.3) recognized routines to process on a subconscious level. Similar to habits on the individual level, organizational routines thus reduce the need for cognitive resources and promote efficiency (Feldman and Pentland, 2003; Wood and Neal, 2009). The routine limits the actor's and organization's options in the decision-making process and integrates past (possibly conscious) decisions into the current performance. Such freed cognitive resources allow the organization members to realize situations that require non-routine performance. However, not every organization is capable of breaking out of the *routine mode* (Gersick and Hackman, 1990). Leaving the cognitively economized path in a (complex) non-routine situation can be seen as an organizational capability. Typically, high-reliability organizations are a carrier of such a capability. At a sacrifice of cognitive resources, these organizations (e.g., air traffic control or military organizations) then switch from the routine mode to a mode of conscious processing and search (Reason, 1990, pp. 34, 57, 182, 196; Reason, 2000).

In this section, six effects of organizational routines were portrayed. It is worth noticing that not all of these effects need to be present at once or to exist at all. Organizational routines can even be dysfunctional and countervail the desired effects. However, some of the discussed effects (e.g., coordination and control, or building truces) refer to fundamental requirements of an organization to ensure its functioning and should regularly be considered as the minimum contributive effectiveness of a routine. Other effects (e.g., path-dependence, or preservation of knowledge) may lead to both, a positive or a negative result. Exemplary, path-dependence can support an organization to narrow the options in a decision-making process, but it can also lead to a lock-in with no desirable solution to exit. At times when organizational routines do not work as intended or do not effect in the desired way, the organization's managers need to recognize the need for an altered routine and need to create a new routine deliberately to escape jeopardizing the organization's existence.

When viewing one of the major challenges of routine research, the deviation between the ostensive aspect and the performative aspect, the introduced effects become more tangible and appraisable. Against the background, that the individual actor is the last instance to bring the routine into life, the effect of routines to build truces can be understood as essential to align the individuals' interpretation of the ostensive aspect. Moreover, that effect has a substantial and positive influence on the effect of coordination and control. On the one hand, it allows the social system of individuals in the organization to orchestrate itself (self-regulation on the basis of previous conflicts and established truces). On the other hand, routines and the truces they build give the management an instrument to align drifting individuals to the routine interpretation the majority of individuals acknowledges. These effects go along with the positive side effect that the demand for cognitive resources of the individuals is reduced. Taken together, these effects support the actors but also the organization as a whole to reduce uncertainty and to foster regularity in the performance of the routine (i.e., to align the ostensive and the performative aspect). However, as mentioned before, path-dependence may in some cases be positive, in others negative for the organization. Similar, the preservation of knowledge can be both, positive as well as negative for the organization.

The individual actor as the final instance in the performance of a routine, and also as the instance that interprets the ostensive aspect to transform it into action, thus might be the lever to control the organizational level concept called organizational routine (see also Chapter 2.1.2.2). Much of handling the challenge of variation between the ostensive and performative aspect has to do with the individual's motives and its ability to learn routines. At this point, it is more than consequential to access the challenge from a learning perspective. In the following chapter, the foundations for taking such perspective will be put in place.

2.2 Learning and its theoretical background

2.2.1 A brief overview of learning theory

Learning is a commonly used term in everyday life with a broad connotation. Besides the colloquial understanding, psychological literature offers a more accurate approach to learning. Anderson (1995, p. 4) put a definition that meets the understanding to be found in psychological literature precisely. He defined learning as "[…] *the process by which long-lasting changes occur in behavioral potential as a result of experience.*" Hence, learning is a process of alteration resulting in an enduring change in behavior potential. Recalling the behavior potential entails observable behavior, which serves as proof that learning has taken place. Nevertheless, learning does not need to result in an observable behavior. In those cases, the process of learning is incapable of proof.

For learning it is crucial that a long-term change of the behavior potential occurs. Thus, learning becomes distinguishable from other processes that effect a (highly) long-term or a short-term change of behavior, such as maturation or drug use (Anderson, 1995, pp. 4-5). This conception of learning shows consistency over the past decades of research on learning in the field of psychology, e.g., Hilgard and Marquis (1961, pp. 11-12), Bredenkamp and Wippich (1977, p. 23), Shuell (1986, pp. 412-414), March (1996, pp. 310-311), Okano, Hirano and Balaban (2000, pp. 12403-12404), Bergius (2004, p. 546) or Domjan, Grau and Krause (2010, p. 17). The psychology of learning repeatedly exposed two theoretical positions of central importance: behaviorism (including associationism) and cognitivism (Wittig, 2001, p. 109; Bergius, 2004, p. 546; Hasselhorn and Gold, 2009, p. 36; Gerrig, 2013, pp. 145-170). Both to be discussed in the following.

Behaviorism. In his manifest on behaviorism, Watson (1913) built on the findings of Pavlov (1927).[51] He described behaviorism as a perfectly objective, experimental branch of natural science, aiming at prediction and control of behavior, clearly delineating behaviorism from the psychology of consciousness and the method of introspection.[52] The learner's inner processes are defined to be unobservable. Hence, they are not object to research in behaviorism (Watson, 1913, pp. 158-159). *Conditioning* and *social learning*[53] are the substantial theories of learning in the scientific movement of behaviorism. Conditioning, being an associative form of learning, is subdivided into *classical* and *operant conditioning* (Myers, 2010, pp. 292-293; 317-319).

Classical conditioning describes a learning process in which the organism learns the association between two stimuli. More precisely, the organism learns the association between an unconditioned stimulus (UCS) and a neutral stimulus (NS). An UCS is a stimulus that leads to an unconditioned reaction (UCR), which is a natural reaction or a reflex without any process of learning needed (e.g., salivation). Due to the learned association between the UCS and the formerly NS, which is then called conditioned stimulus (CS), this formerly UCR reaction to the UCS now also follows the CS as a conditioned reaction (CR; Wittig, 2001, p. 110). Pavlov (1927) conducted basic experiments on classical conditioning with lasting impact (Mitchell, De Houwer and Lovibond, 2009). He conditioned dogs to react with salivation (CR) to an acoustical signal (CS), which had been followed by food (UCS) throughout the phase of conditioning. Recent research still makes use of classical conditioning. Rozin and Fallon

[51] Pavlov already conducted behavioristic experiments on classical conditioning around the turn of the century.

[52] The behavioristic movement obviously influenced subsequent economic theories and schools of thought, such as March and Simon (1958, pp. 9-10, 139-142) or Cyert and March (1963).

[53] *Also* referred to as observational learning.

(1987) explored the association between feelings of disgust and the presentation of food. Interesting studies on Pavlov's conditioning can also be found in Siegel *et al.* (1982) and respectively in Siegel and Ellsworth (1986) and Siegel (1984; 2001). They explored whether the setting of drug consumption functions as CS and therefore influences the dose tolerance of the drug user. The study was supportive of this idea. The drug (UCS) triggers a physiological reaction in the body (UCR) to metabolize the toxin. When the drug user is in the usual drug-taking environment, this serves as CS and already triggers the physiological reaction (now CR). Thus, the dose tolerance is higher in the usual drug-taking environment than in other places. That demonstrates the importance of this very basic concept to date.

Operant conditioning is a learning process, in which the likelihood of a specific behavior is manipulated by the consequences of the very (Wittig, 2001, p. 113). Classical conditioning involves learning the association between two occurrences outside of the organism's control, whereas operant conditioning depends on learning about the association between a specific behavior and its consequences (Myers, 2010, p. 304). The basic principle of operant conditioning is the *law of effect*, which was formulated by Thorndike (1898). He devised a puzzle box in which he placed a cat and encouraged it to escape with an enticing fish outside of the box. To escape the puzzle, box the cat had to press a lever. After eating the fish, the cat was put back into the initial position. This procedure was repeated 10 to 20 times. In the first trials, the cat behaved arbitrarily, and it took up to five minutes until the cat pressed the lever by chance. In successive trials, the cat became faster at pressing the lever, and finally, some of the cats needed only five seconds to open the puzzle box. Thorndike (1898, p. 13) concluded for this trial-and-error experiment that only the successful and rewarding behavioral impulse was consolidated. The cats learned to associate the lever in the box (*stimulus*) with a behavior of favorable consequences (*response*). Thorndike called this the law of effect which can be formulated as follows:

> *"A response that is followed by satisfying consequences becomes more probable and a response that is followed by dissatisfying consequences becomes less probable."* (Gerrig, 2013, p. 157)

Based on the law of effect, Skinner (1938) conducted experiments that enhanced the basic understanding of operant behavioral control (Myers, 2010, p. 305). He placed hungry rats in a box[54], where pushing a lever (in a later version the lever was replaced by a button) was rewarded with food (Skinner, 1938, p. 53; Heron and Skinner, 1940). The experiments showed that behavior was controlled by its consequences. Consequences were subdivided into *extinction, punishment*, *negative* and *positive reinforcement* (Skinner, 1938, pp. 61-66). In a subsequent study, Ferster and Skinner (1957) explored the relationship between the frequency of reinforcement and stability of behavior. The effectiveness of 20 different schedules of reinforcement was

54 *Coll.*: Skinner box.

systematically evaluated. Continuous reinforcement led to fast learning results but also to fast extinction effects when reinforcement was held off. Intermittent reinforcement was found to be most effective, as it results in the most enduring learning effects. To date, the concept of operant conditioning is in the focus of research. Scott, Scott and Goldwater (1997) improved the posture and through this the achievements of a high jumper by operant conditioning.

In an ambitious humanitarian project, Poling *et al.* (2010a; 2010b; 2011) operantly conditioned giant African pouched rats to find landmines and other explosive devices. In 2009, the rats cleared 93.400 square meters for explosive devices in Tanzania. The animals proofed to be extremely accurate (average of 0.33 false alarms per 100 square meters) and fast in detecting explosives. A metal detector search could not reveal more landmines than the rats. Mgode *et al.* (2011), as well as Mahoney *et al.* (2012), conditioned the same species of rats to find markers for tuberculosis in saliva samples. The rats were trained to show a specific behavior when results were positive. Most impressively, in only seven minutes a rat processed the same amount of saliva samples that a laboratory assistant processed over a complete work day.

Social learning is a method of learning within a social context. The learner observes the behavior of a model (individual or group) and either adapts his behavior or imitates the observed behavior conditioning (Myers, 2010, pp. 317-318). Whether this form of learning should be assigned to behaviorism is a legitimate question. Initial experiments on social learning used reinforcement as a mechanism of operant conditioning (Bandura, Ross and Ross, 1961, pp. 581-582). Bandura (1977b, p. 194) integrated the insights of these experiments in his *social learning theory*, where he already presented learning as a result of the reciprocal relationship between personal and external determinants, rather than only referring to external determinants of learning, as proposed in behaviorism. In 1986, Bandura further enhanced his social learning theory to the *social cognitive theory* by integrating cognitive factors such as expectations and self-reflection (Kihlstrom and Harackiewicz, 1990; Lerner, 1990; Zimmerman and Schunk, 2003, pp. 443-448). Hence, social learning can be regarded as a link between behaviorism and cognitivism (Lefrançois, 2006, p. 193). Thus, sometimes Bandura's theories were referred to as *cognitive behaviorism* (Madsen, 1988, pp. 481-485). Bandura and colleagues (1961; 1963a; 1963b) and Bandura (1965) conducted the most famous experiments of social learning (Myers, 2010, pp. 319-320; Gerrig, 2013, pp. 372-374).

In their study, Bandura, Ross and Ross (1963b) divided preschool children into three different groups. All groups watched a movie, in which an adult hit and kicked a doll called Bobo, yet the movie took different endings in each of the three groups. In the first group, the movie ended without any consequences for the aggressor, in the second group the aggressor was rewarded with sweets for being aggressive, while in the third group, the aggressor was admonished and reprimanded for the very same behavior. After the movie presentation, the children were guided to a different room, appointed with a Bobo doll, where they were left on their own to play. Significantly, the subjects of group one and two showed more aggressive behavior than those of group three. The children of the first two groups imitated the behavior of the adult in the movie, partially even carrying out the very same motion sequences. Control groups showed that children of all three groups behave similarly aggressive when asked to imitate the behavior they had seen in the movie. Bandura concluded that all children learned the same behavioral patterns, yet they differed in their performance. Next to the main outcome of social learning, the discrimination between the acquisition of new competencies and the performance of behavior is an important result of this study (Bandura, Ross and Ross, 1963b).

More recent studies revealed that children also imitate behavior when the role model is not reinforced and also when the role model is not a human being but a comic character (Gerrig, 2013, pp. 168-169). In today's multimedia-based world, with characters that are not always realistic images of what they represent, the importance of social learning is conceivable. It was in the year 1977 already – the year in which Bandura (1977b) published the social learning theory – that Huesmann *et al.* (2003) started a longitudinal study on the impact of the amount of violence consumed via television between the age of six and ten, and levels of aggression in adulthood. The levels of aggression were collected 15 years after the observation period using self-report and reports from the participant's social environment. A significant correlation between both dimensions of measurement was found. Anderson (2003; 2004) evaluated the relationship between playing violence glorifying computer games and the general tendency to violence of the players. Results were manifold. An increased consumption of such computer games was positively correlated with the readiness to show aggressive behavior, aggressive cognitions, aggressive mood states, reduced willingness to help others and it was regularly associated with an upholding excitation of the cardiovascular system.

In this section, the three presented forms of learning were exemplary put into the context of recent research to underline their contemporary impact. That shows the role *behaviorism* plays in today's research on learning and beyond, even though it partially opened up to cognitive influences as the social cognitive theory of learning demonstrates.

Cognitivism. Behaviorism had shaped the understanding of behavior and learning for a long time, before the above-described experiment by Bandura, Ross and Ross (1963b) introduced the cognitive revolution in psychology (Lefrançois, 2006, pp. 193-194). Even though cognitivism does not trace back to an individual founder (Schultz and Schultz, 2011, pp. 353-355), literature (e.g., Goldstein, 2008, p. 15; Fisher, 2009, p. 52) often referred to Neisser (1967). Further important milestones on the way to cognitivism were the research seminar on artificial intelligence at the Dartmouth College in the year of 1956, as well as a symposium on the information theory at the Massachusetts Institute of Technology in the same year (Miller, 2003). A critic of behaviorism and a supporter of cognitivism is the psycholinguist Noam Chomsky (Goldstein, 2008, p. 12). In his book review on the behavioristic opus, *Verbal Behavior* by Skinner (1957), Chomsky (1959) harshly criticized behaviorism. For instance, he did not regard imitation and reinforcement, but in innate biological predispositions and cognitive aspects to be the central mechanisms of infant language development. Griffiths and Schabracq (2003, pp. 181-182) cited Chomsky to emphasize that he considered behaviorism to have reached its limits, leaving the future to approaches focusing on mental processes – hence to cognitivism:

> *"Thus it is quite possible – overwhelmingly probable, one might guess – that we will always learn more about human life and human personality from novels than from scientific psychology.*[55] *The science-forming capacity is only one facet of our mental endowment. We use it where we can but are not restricted to it, fortunately."* (Chomsky, 1988, p. 159)

The influence of cognitive psychology has modified the grasp of learning processes. Shuell (1986) witnessed a variety of changes and amplifications in the 50s, 60s, and 70s of the 20th century compared to behaviorism. Thus, learning became to be an active and targeted process following rules of logic. This process also includes metacognitive processes such as planning and targeting of objectives, the active selection of stimuli, the organization of learning content and the adoption of learning strategies. Furthermore, he observed the expansion by higher-level learning processes. On the one hand this addressed the organization and instrumentalization of individual learning activities[56], and on the contrary, it referred to the awareness of one's knowledge or ignorance. Flavell and Wellman (1977) subdivided this knowledge about learning content into four categories: (a) knowledge about the task, (b) knowledge about the own abilities, strengths, and weaknesses, (c) knowledge about the value of different strategies and their efficiency (d) knowledge about the dependency on other influence factors. Shuell (1986) also emphasized the role of past knowledge. Thus, learning is a cumulative process, in which new information cannot be regarded isolated but needs to be integrated into the existing knowledge.

Another change he could observe is a new understanding of the things that were learned. Behaviorists suggest that the learner learns a new association, while cognitivists assume the acquisition of knowledge about showing a certain behavior and its purpose. Shuell (1986) concluded his observations of the transition from behaviorism to cognitivism by identifying the cognitive process analyses as a new paradigm of learning research. The new paradigm arises in the interest of researchers to measure learning efficiency and cognitive abilities. Norman (1978, p. 39) concisely expressed the keynote of research on cognitive learning:

---

[55] *Here*: In terms of Behaviorism.

[56] E.g., Brown (1978, p. 80): prediction, planning, checking and monitoring of the learning process.

> *"I do not care about simple learning*[57] [...] *that only takes 30 minutes. I want to understand real learning, the kind we all do during the course of our lives* [...]. *I want to understand the learning of complex topics."*

He perceived complex topics as topics that need weeks or years to be learned. Keeping this keynote in mind, as the standard that cognition researchers address to the process of learning and its exploration, allows to examine selected cognitive concepts. Cognitive approaches now consort with the mere behavioristic learning theories. The *gestalt theory*[58] will be given special attention. Other theories and concepts of cognitivism, such as *self-efficacy* (Bandura, 1977a) or *learning by instruction*[59] (Glaser, 1963), will not be covered here due to their extent and relevance for this study. As already mentioned, the above-introduced idea of *social learning* can also be discussed from a cognitive point of view. However, here it served as the crucial link between behaviorism and cognitivism and will not be addressed in this section.

Cognitive learning theories root in the Gestalt psychology[60] by *Max Wertheimer*, *Wolfgang Köhler* and *Kurt Koffka* (Gross, 2010, p. 225), who argued that the understanding of mental phenomena can only evolve from considering them as an organized and structured ensemble (Sternberg and Mio, 2009, pp. 92-94). In the 1920s, Wertheimer (1922; 1923) already established the sound basis for Gestalt theory. He stated his understanding of the very as follows:

> *"There are wholes, the behaviour of which is not determined by that of their individual elements, but where the part-processes are themselves determined by the intrinsic nature of the whole. It is the hope of Gestalt theory to determine the nature of such wholes."*[61] (Wertheimer, 1938, p. 2)

One of the important outcomes of Gestalt theory is the idea of insight learning as a strategy of problem-solving. In collaboration with Wolfgang Köhler, Wertheimer described several steps of insight learning: problem occurrence, trying, restructuring, insight, application, and transfer (Zervos-Kopp, 2013, p. 351). In his famous book *The Art of Thought*, Wallas (1926) similarly concludes problem-solving to be a process of several steps that are commonly known as the *four stages of creativity*: preparation, incubation, illumination, and verification. A classic experiment in Gestalt psychology and insight learning was conducted by Wertheimer (1945), targeting students and the shape of rectangles (Novick and Bassok, 2005, p. 338). Students were familiar with calculating the area of rectangles and were now asked to calculate the area of a parallelogram. To solve the problem, they had to restructure their knowledge, as they

---

57 *Here*: Behavioristic forms of learning, e.g., classical or operant conditioning.

58 Rarely referred to as *learning by seeing the reason*.

59 Also referred to as instructional design, or simplified as *teaching*.

60 Also, Gestaltism. For a comprehensive discussion about Gestalt psychology, see (Todorovic, 2011).

61 Original German quote: „Es gibt Zusammenhänge, bei denen nicht, was im Ganzen geschieht, sich daraus herleitet, wie die einzelnen Stücke sind und sich zusammensetzen, sondern umgekehrt, wo – im prägnanten Fall – sich das, was an einem Teil dieses Ganzen geschieht, bestimmt ist von den inneren Strukturgesetzen dieses Ganzen" (Wertheimer, 1925, p. 3).

merely had to shift the area of a triangle to be able to use the formula they already knew. This very insight to be able to use the hitherto existing knowledge is expressed by the following quotation from *Productive Thinking* by Wertheimer (1945, p. 48):

> *"Given the parallelogram problem, after she*[62] [...] *had been shown briefly how to get at the area of the rectangle, she said, 'I certainly don't know how to do that.' Then after a moment of silence: 'This is no good here,' pointing to the region at the left end; 'and no good here,' pointing to the region at the right. 'It's troublesome, here and here.' Hesitatingly she said: 'I could make it right here ... but ...' Suddenly she cried out, 'May I have a pair of scissors? What is bad there is just what I need here. It fits.' She took the scissors, cut the figure vertically, and placed the left end at the right."*

Based on these findings, insight became the cornerstone of Gestalt psychology (Lefrançois, 2012, p. 179). Insight is reckoned among the strongest and most effective principals of learning (Heineken and Habermann, 1994, p. 53).

Summary. Two approaches to learning psychology were introduced with its prominent theories to provide the basis for understanding implicit learning, which will be discussed in the following section. Each of the presented learning theories has had an enduring impact on psychology. However, not to forget that there are two sides to every coin. As pointed out above, Chomsky (1959) harshly criticized Skinner's behaviorism, and Tinbergen (1951, pp. 78-79), to name another example, criticized the aspiring cognitivism. He awards Gestalt theory with much furor in psychology, yet within the very same sentence, he finds fault with its little explanatory potential. Tinbergen delineated Gestaltism as a merely descriptive theory. Hence, he called upon researchers to focus on *stimuli*[63] as the most highly developed link to the psyche. Thanks to new technical developments, such as the electroencephalogram or the positron emission tomography, researchers were able to follow that call (Myers, 2010, pp. 61-62). Thereby, today it is possible to explore behavior and changes in behavior in terms of learning on a new cognitive, neuroscientific level (Gross, 2010, p. 16). Since the mid-1980s these research paradigms increasingly entered psychological research. This process becomes evident in the publication of new subject-related journals such as the *Journal of Cognitive Neuroscience* (Vol.1: 1989), *Cognitive, affective & behavioral neuroscience* (Vol.1: 2001), *Social cognitive and affective neuroscience* (Vol.1: 2006), or *Developmental Cognitive Neuroscience* (Vol.1: 2011). Following the shift of paradigm from behaviorism to cognitivism in the 1960s, the 1990s can be referred to the transition from cognitivism to neuroscience, which is still in its infancy.

[62] *Here*: A five-year-old girl.
[63] *Here*: In terms of neurobiology.

2.2.2 The duality of mind

Learning is a cognitive process and all cognitive processes are subject to the duality of mind. The fundamentals of the duality of mind originate from ancient philosophy. Plato (1993, pp. 144–152, 354–361), for instance, argued that the human soul[64] divides into *reason*, *spirit*, and *appetite*. Accordingly, it is tripartite and not dual. However, the key conclusion is the insight that human mind (or soul) is not a single system. Also, the medieval time's philosophers approached the complexity and division of the animal and the human mind and thus established another basis for today's dual-process theories (e.g., Descartes, 1633 [1985], p. 108). With Sigmund Freud's theorizing of the (dynamic) unconscious, originating in studies of mental disorders as a manifestation of unconscious mental states, the thought of the duality of human mind found its way from philosophy into psychology, more precisely psychopathology. Similar to Plato, Freud divided the human mind into three parts: the *id*, the *ego*, and the *superego* (Freud, 1915 [2005]; 1927). The id, as a primitive, habitual and sybaritic system, and the ego, as the rational and reflective component of the mind, very basically compare to modern dual-process theories (Frankish and Evans, 2009).

The subsequent literature[65] applied the conception of a dual-processing mind on various fields, such as learning (Reber, 1993; Dienes and Perner, 1999; Sun, Slusarz and Terry, 2005; Kihlstrom, 2008), decision-making, judgment and reasoning (Tversky and Kahneman, 1974; Kahneman and Tversky, 1982; Evans, 2002; Kahneman and Frederick, 2002; Evans, 2008; 2010; Johnson-Laird, Khemlani and Goodwin, 2015), psychopathology (Klein, Becker and Rinck, 2010; Vrijsen *et al.*, 2012; Wiers *et al.*, 2013; Eberl, 2014; Becker *et al.*, 2015), or social cognition (Epstein, 1994; Chaiken and Trope, 1999; Smith and DeCoster, 2000; Kruglanski and Orehek, 2007; Spunt, 2015). Contemporary dual-process models of mind reflect the idea that interacting systems with different underlying principles determine our behavior.

The term *dual* may be misleading, as it suggests there are exactly two systems. Several dual process models referred to two systems (e.g., Epstein, 1994; Stanovich, 1999, p. 144; Strack and Deutsch, 2004). However, Evans (2009) as well as Evans and Stanovich (2013) noted that there are also models covering more than just *two* systems of mind and thus, do not fit entirely under the umbrella of the term dual process model (e.g., Sloman, 1996; Kahneman, 2011). They brought forward the argument that System 1 should not be mistaken as a single system but as a set of systems, which do not require working memory and thus operate autonomously. That insight recently led scholars to cease using the commonly known distinction between System 1 and System 2 as brought forward by Stanovich (1999) and others (Stanovich, 2004, pp. 34-37; Thompson, 2009; Evans, 2010). As a counterproposal to a generic dual system

64 Plato referred to the today's understanding of the mind as soul.

65 *Here*: Theories originating after the cognitive revolution in psychology beginning in the 1950s (e.g., Miller, 1956; Chomsky, 1959; Bandura, Ross and Ross, 1963a; Neisser, 1967).

model (system 1, system 2), Evans (2009) and Evans and Stanovich (2013) suggested to categorize cognitive processes into type 1 and type 2 processing. In contrast to system 1 and 2, the focus shifts from two distinct systems of mind to two qualitatively distinct forms of processing. This rephrasing seems to be a minor difference. However, it allows describing multiple cognitive or neural systems within one model.

Type 1 processing (intuitive)	**Type 2 processing (reflective)**
Defining features	
Does not require working memory.	Requires working memory.
Autonomous	Cognitive decoupling; mental simulation
Typical correlates	
Fast	Slow
Impulsive	Reflective
Associative	Rule-based
High capacity	Capacity limited
Automatic	Controlled
Parallel	Serial
Nonconscious	Conscious
Biased responses	Normative responses
Contextualized	Abstract
Experience-based decision making	Consequential decision making
Independent of cognitive ability	Correlated with cognitive ability

Table 2: Attributes of type 1 and type 2 processing with reference to Evans and Stanovich (2013, p. 225).

As Evans (2012) and Evans and Stanovich (2013) demonstrated, type 1 and type 2 processing differ in several respects. The so-called *received* view of dual-process theory describes type 1 processing as low-effort, impulsive and automatic. Associative memory networks allow this fast processing of high capacity. However, they are also subject to cognitive biases. On the other hand, type 2 processing is of high-effort, reflective and controlled. Rule-based information processing results in a slow processing speed (see Table 2). Importantly, there is an interaction between both types of processing (e.g., type 1 decisions that led to an impulsive reaction are identified as a maladaptive behavioral response by a post type 2 processing). In the following, the impulsive-reflective distinction by Strack and Deutsch (2004) will be discussed in more detail. This dual process model is the basis for the cognitive bias modification (CBM) conducted in the experiment of this study, but also for numerous other CBM studies (Gladwin *et al.*, 2011; Wiers *et al.*, 2011; Schuck, Keijsers and Rinck, 2012; Amir, Kuckertz and Najmi, 2013; Eberl *et al.*, 2014; Becker *et al.*, 2015; Manning *et al.*, 2016).

The dual process model by Strack and Deutsch (2004) is based on the idea of rule-based and associative processing by Smith and DeCoster (2000) and pursues the objective to offer a model that is not restricted to specific domains but allows to integrate cognitive, behavioral and motivational mechanisms. In developing their model, the authors proposed and theoretically consolidated ten theses that divide into four areas (basic properties and functions [theses 1-3], representation, storage, and processing of information [thesis 4], behavioral control [theses 5-7], and motivation [theses 8-10]). According to their model, behavior is the result of the operation of two distinct but interacting systems that work parallel – the impulsive system and the reflective system (see Figure 3). The two systems can be distinguished by their principles of representation and information processing.

Although the systems work parallel, the authors note an asymmetry, as the impulsive system is always involved in information processing whereas the reflective system may be disengaged. Similar to other dual process models (e.g., Sun, 2002; Kahneman, 2011; Evans and Stanovich, 2013), Strack and Deutsch (2004) described the impulsive system as fast processing while requiring low cognitive effort and having a high capacity. Further, it has a low threshold for incoming information to be processed. On the contrary, the reflective system is slow, consumes a high amount of cognitive capacity to produce a limited output. At the same time, it needs a certain level of arousal for processing information. Whereas semantic relations connect the elements in the reflective system, those in the impulsive system build on associative links that allow faster processing as described before. Those associative links constitutionally build on the principles of similarity and contiguity and can be strengthened by repetitious activation supported by similar contexts. Activating stimuli can trigger different behavioral schemes that include cognitive or affective reactions, as well as motor sequences.

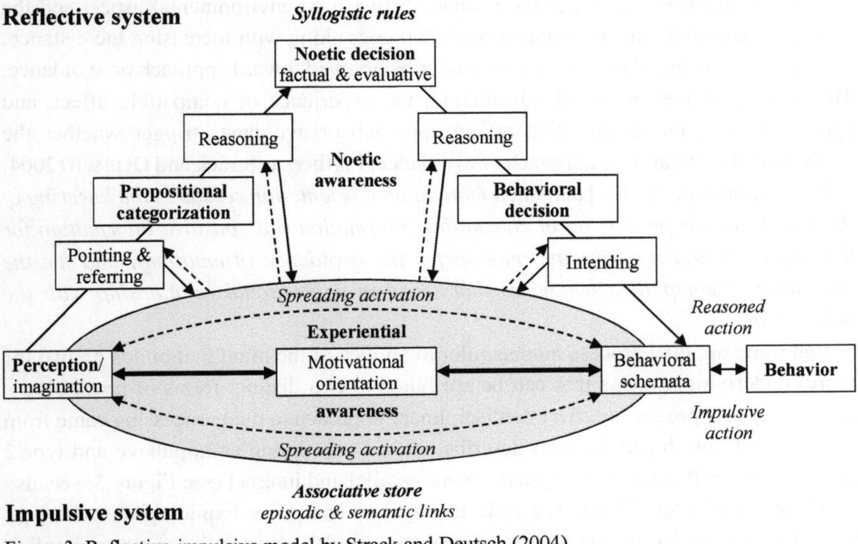

Figure 3: Reflective-impulsive model by Strack and Deutsch (2004).

Note: The solid arrows represent reflective processes, and the dashed arrows represent impulsive processes.

The associations in the impulsive system are not prone to decay, which results in a conception of the impulsive system as long-term memory. However, that also makes these associative links and the resulting behavior hard to manipulate, control or change. In contrast, the reflective system with its semantic relations is determined by truth values for the single relations and follows syllogistic rules. Propositional categorization and reasoning lead to a noetic decision-making process that uses facts to evaluate the informational basis for the subsequent intentional behavioral decision. However, due to the different functioning, the reflective system can be thought of as a temporary storage with a limited amount of information that can be stored and processed relatively flexible. Both systems share a so-called final pathway to behavior, the behavioral schemata. These can be rather abstract, however, for behavior to be executed, it requires a certain threshold of activation.

A characteristic feature of this dual process model is the integration of the motivational orientation and its compatibility with the information processing and the execution of behavior. Motivational orientation refers to the impulsive system that according to the authors can be oriented toward approach or avoidance. Further, the authors brought forward four determinants that may elicit motivational orientation: "[...] *the processing of positive or negative information, the perception of approach or avoidance, the experience of positive or negative affect, and the execution of approach or avoidance behaviors*" (Strack and Deutsch, 2004, p. 231). An approach orientation reflects the readiness to reduce the distance between an environmental aspect and the person. Accordingly, an avoidance orientation goes along with increasing the distance. In a nutshell, the impulsive system can rather be oriented toward approach or avoidance. The valence of the processed information, the experience of compatible affect, and apperception of movements that reflect approach or avoidance trigger whether the motivational orientation is approach or avoidance. Further, as Strack and Deutsch (2004, p. 234) explicated, an "[...] *activated motivational orientation results in the lowering of thresholds for the processing of compatible information (i.e., positive information for the approach and negative information for the avoidance orientation), and for the elicitation of compatible behaviors that stand in a functional relationship with the orientation.*"

Summing up, dual process models refer to an idea of the mind that builds on two (or more) underlying systems that can be attributed to two distinct forms of processing – type 1 or type 2 processing. An interdisciplinary approach to dual processing came from Strack and Deutsch (2004), who described type 1 processing as impulsive and type 2 processing as reflective. Both systems work parallel and interact (see Figure 3; see also Smith and DeCoster, 2000). The reflective system comprises explicit processes (e.g., reasoning, noetic decision-making), whereas the impulsive system incorporates implicit processes (e.g., approach-avoidance, implicit learning). Both systems contribute asymmetrically to the final pathway of behavioral schemata and subsequent behavior. As this model is not limited to a specific domain, it was frequently applied in various research contexts[66] and among those offers a framework for understanding the complex cognitive process, particular processes of learning.

2.2.3 Introduction to the duality of learning

The cognitive process of learning also orchestrates explicit and implicit cognitive processes. Explicit learning as a reflective process can be described as a conscious, effortful and active process that aims to memorize mainly facts (Xie, Gao and King, 2013). On the contrary, implicit learning as an impulsive process occurs effortlessly and mostly without conscious awareness. As explicit learning is generally known, we will focus on implicit learning more in detail. The term *implicit learning* was first mentioned by Reber (1967) in his study on artificial grammar learning (Shanks and St. John, 1994, p. 368). However, there were previous approaches that describe incidental learning activities that have similarities to implicit learning (Thorndike, 1898; Jenkins, 1933; Thorndike and Rock, 1934). Nonetheless, research on implicit learning did not become particularly intense until the 1990s. In the 1980s there were only 15 contributions to research with the term *implicit learning* in the title or abstract, whereas there were 253 articles in the 1990s (Shanks, 2005:204).[67]

The phenomenon of implicit learning is omnipresent and well known in every-day life. We often know more than we can verbalize. This deficient capability of verbalizing the acquired subject is the central characteristic of implicit learning processes (Frensch, 1998; Cleeremans, 2006b). Cleeremans (2006a) named motor skills, such as biking or car driving as examples for this type of learning. These skills are characterized by complex movements, which are hardly or often not at all verbalizable. However, Cleeremans (2006a) did not limit implicit learning to motor skills but broadened it to processes of higher cognitive levels. The grammar rules of one's native language, for example, can often not be verbalized, even though they are applied correctly. Further examples of Cleeremans (2006a) for the implicit learning of higher-order cognitive processes are medical diagnoses, the social ability to judge, or the game of chess. As a first rudimentary understanding of implicit learning, one can refer to it as a process of learning with difficulties of verbalizing the acquired subject (e.g., knowledge, motions, or rules). In the following, further central elements will be discussed to gain a deeper understanding of implicit learning.

Discourse of definitions. Reber (1967) delimited implicit learning from perceptual learning. He defined the latter in dependence on Gibson and Gibson (1955), as a simple process of perception and reaction toward a stimulus, which proceeds without any gain of knowledge. In contrast, (Reber, 1967) described implicit learning as a process, which

[66] According to the Web of Science™ Core Collection, Strack and Deutsch (2004) were cited 1,159 times [accessed on Nov 23, 2016]. According to Google Scholar, 2,364 citations were recorded [accessed on Nov 23, 2016].

[67] According to the *Social Sciences Citation Index*.

sensitizes the learner to certain principles of his environment. Neither does the learner have the intention to learn these principles nor is he aware of the learning process itself. Thus, the learner cannot verbalize the acquired knowledge (Reber, 1967). Many researchers conformed to this understanding of implicit learning. They described implicit learning as an unintentional process of learning, without an awareness of the content being learned (e.g., Reber, 1993; Berry, 1997; Cleeremans, Destrebecqz and Boyer, 1998; Frensch and Rünger, 2003; Jiménez, 2003; Hassin, 2005; Cleeremans and Dienes, 2008; Kaufman *et al.*, 2010). Perrig (1996, p. 212) concisely summed this up: Implicit learning is present "[...] *if a change in an individual's behavior or behavioral potential regarding a situation is identifiable, which results from a singular or repeated experience. This process is to happen without insight, reportable awareness or reportable knowledge being a possible explanation for the change in the individual's behavior.*"[68]

Winkel, Petermann and Petermann (2006, pp. 209-213) also followed this definition. Further, they delineated implicit learning from related terms such as (a) procedural learning, (b) latent learning, and (c) incidental learning. (a) Procedural learning cannot clearly be distinguished from implicit learning. Thus, it is considered to be a possible peculiarity of implicit learning, with a special focus on performance improvement, yet also without access to the acquired knowledge. (b) Latent learning takes place without reinforcement. A change in behavior will only be shown when reinforcement is expected. The acquired knowledge can be verbalized. Creating cognitive maps[69] is a common example of latent learning. (c) Incidental learning is a casual and unintentional process. Implicit learning can also be incidental, yet this is not obligatory. In contrast to the differentiation by Winkel, Petermann and Petermann (2006), Shanks (2010) defined implicit learning synonymously to procedural and incidental learning.

Frensch (1998) subdivided the general process of learning into three subordinated processes: *perception*, *learning*, and *reproduction*. Each of these can but does not have to lapse implicitly. According to his analysis, research concluded on the fact that the sub-process of perception does not happen implicitly, not even within the process of implicit learning. Perception is considered to be a supraliminal process. When it comes to the sub-processes of learning and reproduction, there were dissent opinions in the literature. Some researchers (Lewicki, Czyzewska and Hoffman, 1987; Reber, 1989; Shanks and St. John, 1994; Seger, 1998) only considered implicit learning to be present, when both learning and reproduction occur implicitly, whereas other researchers (Stadler and Frensch, 1994; Buchner and Wippich, 1998; Perruchet and Vinter, 1998)

68 Translated by the author. Original quote: Implizites Lernen liegt vor, „[...] *wenn eine Veränderung im Verhalten oder im Verhaltenspotential eines Menschen hinsichtlich einer Situation feststellbar ist, die auf einmalige oder wiederholte Erfahrung dieser oder ähnlicher Situationen zurückgeht, ohne dass eine Einsicht, berichtbare Erkenntnis oder berichtbares Wissen des betreffenden Menschen die Begründung für die Verhaltensänderung liefern kann*" (Perrig, 1996, p. 212).

69 Laszlo *et al.* (1993) gave an extended overview on the concept of cognitive maps by Tolman (1948).

only required the sub-process of learning to be implicit, but not the sub-process of reproduction. Frensch (1998) further pointed out that the term implicit in itself was interpreted differently. Some definitions used the term implicit synonymously to the term unconscious (Berry and Broadbent, 1988; Shanks and St. John, 1994; Seger, 1998), some in the sense of unaware (Lewicki, Czyzewska and Hoffman, 1987), and some in terms of nonintentional or automatic (Stadler and Frensch, 1994; Perruchet and Vinter, 1998; Cleeremans, 2006b).

2.2.3.1 Research paradigms of implicit learning

Since Reber (1967) performed the first experiments on implicit learning, different experimental paradigms have emerged. Several scholars named *artificial grammar learning* (Reber, 1967), the *control of complex systems*[70] (Berry and Broadbent, 1984) and *sequence learning* (Lewicki, Czyzewska and Hoffman, 1987; Nissen and Bullemer, 1987) as the most common paradigms (e.g., Berry and Dienes, 1993; Cleeremans, Destrebecqz and Boyer, 1998; Cleeremans, 2006b; Kiesel and Koch, 2012, pp. 85-87; Xie, Gao and King, 2013). Further research paradigms are *probability learning* (Reber and Millward, 1968; 1971), *implicit covariation learning*[71] (Lewicki, 1986), *acquisition of invariant characteristics* (Cock, Berry and Gaffan, 1994; Bright and Burton, 2007), *visual search in complex stimulus environments* (Musen and Treisman, 1990), *second language acquisition* (Ellis, 1993; Michas and Berry, 1994), *perceptual learning* (Kolers and Roediger, 1984), and *learning of perceptual categories*[72] (Jacoby and Brooks, 1984). Although various research paradigms have emerged, a matching core in these paradigms is recognizable. In all paradigms, the subjects are exposed to a complexly structured stimulus without being notified of the stimulus or its nature (Reber, Allen and Reber, 1999). Bransford *et al.* (2006) added that implicit learning usually takes place quickly and effortless. In the following, the three first mentioned and most common research paradigms of implicit learning will be discussed in more detail.

Artificial grammar learning. In this research paradigm of implicit learning, a set of different grammatically *correct* strings of letters is presented to the subject in the learning phase. These strings serve as learning stimuli to acquire the proper grammatical rules underlying the letter strings. In this context, grammar refers to a certain structure which forms the basis of the alphabetical strings (see Figure 4). One can obtain a grammatically correct letter strings by following the arrows from the start (IN) to the end (OUT) of this scheme. Here each arrow produces a letter in the chain; circle arrows can repeatedly be followed (Reber, Allen and Reber, 1999; Shanks, 2005).

[70] Also referred to as *dynamic system control* or *control of simulated systems.*
[71] Also referred to as *hidden covariation detection.*
[72] Also referred to as *perceptual categorization.*

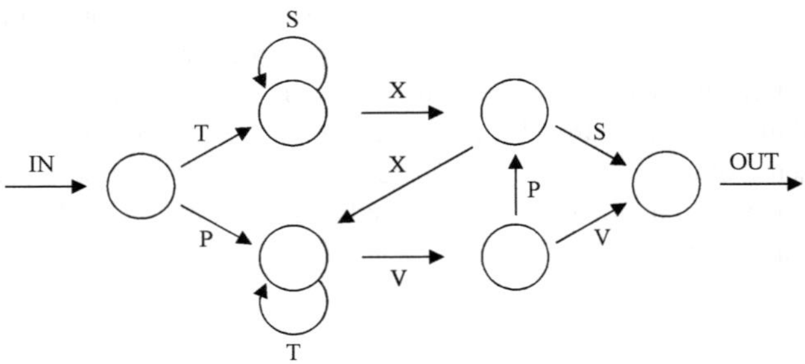

Figure 4: Scheme of an artificial grammar by Reber (1967).

After completing the learning phase, the subjects come to know about the existence of the underlying grammar. There are different configurations of the learning phase. Sometimes subjects only have to view the grammatically correct learning stimuli (see Table 3), in other experiments, they are asked to memorize the letter strings. In the reproduction phase, the subjects receive a set of test stimuli to monitor if and what they learned implicitly. For the subjects, the task in the reproduction phase is to identify all grammatically correct strings (Reber, Allen and Reber, 1999; Shanks, 2005).

Learning stimuli	Test stimuli	
1. PVV	1. PVPV*	9. PVVV*
2. TSXXTVV	2. TSTXS*	10. PVPXVPS
3. PTVPXTVV	3. PVPS	11. SPVPS*
4. TSSSXS	4. TSXTTVPS*	12. PTVPPXVV*
5. PVPS	5. PTTVV	13. TSSSSXS
6. PTTTTTVV	6. TSSXS	14. TTTVPS*
7. TSSXXTVV	7. TVV*	15. VSSXXS*
8. TSXS	8. PVPXVV	16. TXXVVVS

Table 3: Learning and test stimuli in artificial grammar learning.

Note: Grammatically incorrect test stimuli are marked with an asterisk.

Shanks and St. John (1994) critically questioned whether the results of the studies on artificial grammar learning certainly allow concluding that an implicit learning process has taken place. Referring to the *criterion of sensitivity*, they found faults with the fact that the subjects were informed about the existence of grammatical rules at the end of the learning phase. The subjects might be able to construct these rules retrospectively and apply them in the testing phase. They also enunciated the so-called *information criterion* by which they questioned whether the subjects could construct (false) rules through the representation of the test items and thereby biasing the results. Manza, Zizak and Reber (1998) met this criticism with experiments in which the subjects were *not* informed of the existence of the underlying rules, but were told that this was a study on retentiveness. In the learning phase, a set of all letter strings conform to the rules were presented to the subjects. Subjects were instructed to memorize these. After the learning phase, the instructors did not inform the subjects that there was a grammar underlying the letter strings. To check, whether an implicit learning process has taken place or not, another set of grammatically correct *and* incorrect letter strings was shown to the subjects in the reproduction phase. This time, however, the task was to evaluate every single item on an emotion-based scale from one (I do not like this item at all.) to six (I like this item very much.). After the reproduction phase, the instructors asked for the subjects' basis of decision-making. They found that respectively to the mere exposure effect the subjects prevalently preferred the rule-compliant sequences of letters to the non-rule-compliant. Manza, Zizak and Reber (1998) considered this to be a proof for an implicit process of learning.

Control of complex systems. In the first experiment on implicit learning within the control of complex systems, Berry and Broadbent (1984) asked the subjects to regulate the output *P* of a computer simulated sugar factory, thereby imaging a complex and dynamic system. The focus of this study was to analyze the relationship between the performance of the subjects controlling the factory and the ability to verbalize the performance (Cleeremans, 1993, p. 9). The subjects of this experiment took the role of a factory manager. They were asked to bring the output to a predetermined level by varying the number of employees *W*. Further, they were challenged to hold this level of production throughout the following cycles of the experiment. After the subjects had entered the desired number of employees in period t_0, they received feedback in the form of the output in t_1. Then, the number of employees in t_1 could be adjusted to bring the outcome in t_2 to the required value. Again, the subjects received feedback on the production output. This process was repeated according to the predefined number of experiment cycles. The labor productivity remained constant. However, the new production output depended inversely on the production output of the previous period (see equation 1; Berry and Broadbent, 1984).

$$P_t = 2 \times W - P_{t-1} \tag{1}$$

The researchers assumed the principles shown in Equation 1 to be sufficiently complex and unintuitive so that the subjects could not derive the formula from the feedback in the experiment and use it for subsequent calculations (Berry and Broadbent, 1984; Wallach and Lebiere, 2003). Berry and Broadbent (1984) drew the conclusion that with increasing practice and thus with an increasing amount of completed rounds, the subjects showed a better performance without explicitly knowing the principles of the underlying rules. Since the subjects could not verbalize the reasons for their improvement, Taatgen and Anderson (2008) concluded, that an implicit learning process had taken place and that this implicit learning process has an impact on the subjects' performance in solving complex problems. The results obtained by Berry and Broadbent (1984) were replicated in subsequent studies (e.g., Berry and Broadbent, 1987; 1988; Stanley *et al.*, 1989; Dienes and Berry, 1997).

Sequence learning. Cleeremans (2006b) described sequence learning as the dominant form of implicit learning, Abrahamse *et al.* (2010) ascribed a central role to this paradigm, and Kiesel and Koch (2012, p. 86) spoke of the standard paradigm of implicit learning. One of the first studies on this paradigm was carried out by Nissen and Bullemer (1987).[73] Their experiment was designed as a computer-based serial reaction time task. On a computer screen, a star was displayed as a stimulus in one of four possible positions, arranged on a horizontal axis. For each of the four positions, the subjects had a particular key to react to the fade-in of the stimulus. The subjects were asked to do this as quickly as possible. Without the knowledge of the subjects, the stimuli were presented in a fixed sequence in the learning phase. A possible sequence would be D-B-C-A-C-B-D-C-B-A when naming the positions with A, B, C and D from left to right. Each sequence was repeated ten times in a cyclic order and formed a training block. Within a training block, there was no interruption between the sequences. Accordingly, most of the subjects did not become aware of the existence of a sequence. A complete training consisted of eight blocks with 100 presentations each. The test phase also used eight blocks, yet these were not serial sequences but random sequences.

During the training phase, the researchers observed a decrease in reaction times within the particular training blocks. In the test phase, however, no improvement in reaction times was observed. Compared to the training phase, the error rate increased in the test phase. Thus, a negative transfer effect could be noticed which served as an indirect measure of implicit learning. At the end of the tests, the subjects were asked in interviews whether they had perceived a regularity of the presentations. Although some subjects had noticed the serial sequences during the training phase, they showed the same sequence-specific reaction time effects, as the participants who did not notice the regularity. Both groups also showed an increase in the error rate to a similar extent. Hence, the process of implicit learning was verified in this experiment (Abrahamse *et al.*, 2010; Kiesel and Koch, 2012, p. 87). Nissen and Bullemer (1987) further confirmed this by carrying out a modification of their experiment with amnesia patients (Clegg, Digirolamo and Keele, 1998). The effects of implicit learning in sequence learning tasks have been replicated in various studies (Shanks, 2010; Kiesel and Koch, 2012, p. 87). Even though the studies do not always allow a side-by-side comparison due to modifications, the basic results did prove true (Clegg, Digirolamo and Keele, 1998).

The question arises why this research paradigm has the status of being the ***standard paradigm***. Clegg, Digirolamo and Keele (1998) mentioned three reasons to support that conclusion: (1) The processing of sequences is one of the fundamental abilities of the human being, which we use every day. Examples include the sequencing of the sounds while talking or the sequencing of motor movements during writing or driving. (2) Sequencing is easy to explore. Experiments of this paradigm can be implemented relatively simply, and the variables can be manipulated well by researchers. The objectivity of the measured values also contributes to this. Reaction times and error rates

[73] The experiment was carried out in four variants. The basic scheme of the experiment is described here.

allow for high reliability. (3) Sequence learning usually fulfills the requirements that define implicit learning. However, despite the proclamation of many researchers to understand this paradigm as a standard paradigm, there are also critical voices. Goschke (1998), for example, saw the definition of implicit learning as not fulfilled, since the subjects can at least verbalize fragments of the learned. He also criticized the fact that, notwithstanding the positive correlation between the performance provided and the lack of verbalization of the acquired knowledge, it is not possible to clearly differentiate to what extent explicit and to what extent implicit learning and knowledge contributed to the subjects' performance. Concerning the separation of explicit and implicit influences, he saw the need for more research on this paradigm to gain insights on the role of the two forms of knowledge, respectively learning.

Shanks (2010) and Abrahamse *et al.* (2010) critically discussed the role of *consciousness* in sequence learning tasks. In doing so, they differentiated between researchers who believed that in sequence learning tasks, implicit learning is only possible without awareness of the learning process and those who perceived an awareness of the process of learning as non-interfering. Clegg, Digirolamo and Keele (1998) identified open questions within this research paradigm, which can partly be understood as a critique of the research to date, but also as a future direction. For example, they considered the question of the organization of sequentially learned knowledge to be unresolved, while proposing the differentiation between the first sequence and following sequences. From their perspective, it could also be interesting to approach the question, if the results of these simple experimental settings can be applied to more complex or even real situations.

To sum up, this review of the literature on the research paradigms shows that the paradigm of sequential learning is predominant in the research on implicit learning. However, the above discussion on sequential learning can only be understood as a short introduction to gain a basic idea of the conception and some of the fundamental issues, which serves the purpose of this study, though. Despite the brevity of this section, the inherent potential of sequential learning as a paradigm for research is recognizable, and the importance and impact of future research on implicit learning, in general, can be imagined.

2.2.3.2 Impulsive processes and the duality of learning

The introduction to dual process models explained that human behavior arises from an interaction of both, impulsive and reflective processes. While impulsive processing leads to fast and automatic responses that require no attentional resources but have a low flexibility, reflective processing is reasoned, evaluative and slow, and of course requires attentional resources. The first builds on steady associative links that may give rise to cognitive biases, the latter on facts that were explicitly learned (Strack and Deutsch, 2004). The beginning of this chapter also introduced different types learning with its specific characteristics. Importantly, all types of learning share the commonality that both, reflective and impulsive processes are involved. However, the balance between the different types of processes varies.

Kaufman *et al.* (2010) explored the relationship between impulsive processes and implicit learning. They hypothesized that impulsivity and implicit learning are positively correlated. In their experiment, using i.a. a serial reaction time task and the mental rotations test, the hypothesis was confirmed significantly. One of the conclusions that result from this study refers to implicit learning being the most promising approach in modifying impulsive processes. The approach-avoidance task training, that is used in the experiment of this study, belongs to the implicit learning paradigms as it adopts basic principles of other implicit learning paradigms (e.g., serial reaction time task; Brockmeyer *et al.*, 2015; Brockmeyer, Schmidt and Friederich, 2016) – however, it is still a rather young paradigm that has a short but impactful track record in psychopathological research (Rinck and Becker, 2007; Wiers *et al.*, 2009b; 2010; 2011; Becker *et al.*, 2013; Eberl *et al.*, 2013; 2014; Woud *et al.*, 2013b; b; Chambers *et al.*, 2014; Becker *et al.*, 2015; Brockmeyer *et al.*, 2015; Brockmeyer, Schmidt and Friederich, 2016; Kakoschke, Kemps and Tiggemann, 2017).

In laboratory studies, it is possible to separate processes of implicit learning from explicit learning (e.g., Zhuang *et al.*, 2009). However, in practice, the application of one form of learning will frequently be accompanied by the other type of learning. In contrast to the interaction of implicit and explicit processes in dual process models, the interaction between implicit and explicit forms of learning are yet not well understood (Lopes, 2011, p. 27), although there are promising approaches to this topic (e.g., Forkstam and Petersson, 2005; Sun, Slusarz and Terry, 2005). In educational research, for instance, implicit learning is perceived as an approach to counterbalance the predominance of explicit educational models and to develop a learning environment that is more effective and supports individuals with a lower psychometric intelligence, or cognitive impairment (Reber, Walkenfeld and Hernstadt, 1991; Gasparini, 2004; Gebauer and Mackintosh, 2007). Further, the ability to learn implicitly does not decrease in older adults, other than explicit learning. Particularly, that proved true in conditions of learning with time constraints (Verneau *et al.*, 2014).

In a study examining motor skills in sports, Verburgh *et al.* (2016) found implicitly learned motor skills being more durable than explicitly learned ones. The effect was more distinct in early phases of the acquisition of the motor skills as it was over the entire learning period. In consequence, this allows for example athletes using implicit learning techniques to acquire motor skills of a specific level in a shorter amount of time. As the authors noted, the ability to utilize implicit learning for elite athletes may be their key success factor. Further, Sanchez and Reber (2013) studied the role of explicit pre-instruction in implicit motor-sequence learning in an experimental study. They proved that explicit pre-instruction which goes along with building explicit knowledge about the motor sequences does not improve or interfere the performance of the implicit learning process. Similar, Wiers *et al.* (2011, see supplemental material of the article) did not find a significant difference in two experimental settings (with or without explicit instruction) in an approach-avoidance training of alcoholic patients. However, in the more abstract domain of learning atomic bond rules using a variation of artificial grammar learning, Sætrevik, Reber and Sannum (2006) proved true the superiority of explicit learning against implicit learning, even though they found an implicit learning effect. Their results suggested that mere exposure might not be sufficient to learn more complex regular material.

Summing up, the modification of implicit processes as known from dual process models (Strack and Deutsch, 2004) require an implicit approach to learning. However, in practice, implicit and explicit learning are hardly separable. Accordingly, the interaction between both forms of learning is of interest for future research.

2.2.3.3 Methodological challenges

The concept of implicit learning involves the methodological challenge of measuring of the learning process. As mentioned before, learning usually contains both, implicit and explicit learning at the same time. Thus, a particular methodological challenge is the differentiation of implicit and explicit parts of learning (Cleeremans, 2006b). There are approaches using imaging techniques such as positron emission tomography (PET; Rauch *et al.*, 1995; Hazeltine, Grafton and Ivry, 1997) or functional magnetic resonance imaging (fMRI; Schendan *et al.*, 2003; Gureckis, James and Nosofsky, 2011), but a clear distinction between the results of implicit and explicit learning remains difficult. Winkel, Petermann and Petermann (2006, pp. 212-213) saw another challenge in the fact that implicitly learned knowledge cannot be measured directly, but can only be measured by an indirect measure. For example, this indirect measurement can be accomplished by the *mere exposure effect*[74] or by *forced-choice tests*.

Frensch and Rünger (2003) named verbal reports and forced-choice tests as the most common ways of measuring whether implicit learning has taken place. However, they criticized the validity of verbal reports, and therefore they argue for forced-choice tests as a method of measurement. In these forced-choice tests, the participants usually do not choose the answer due to their knowledge, but mostly from intuition and thus unconsciously. As already mentioned in the section about sequence learning, reaction times and error rates are also used as outcome variables. The striking advantage of these measures lies in their reliability. However, they can only be used for certain types of tasks (Clegg, Digirolamo and Keele, 1998), exemplarily for the Approach-Avoidance Task. This brief introduction to the issues on the measurability of implicit learning shows that, in addition to the conceptual challenges for research, there are also methodological problems (Cleeremans, 2006b).

---

74 An application is described in the section *artificial grammar learning*.

2.2.4 Summary

As an introduction to the psychological topic of learning, the history of learning theories was outlined by visiting behaviorism and cognitivism including their main paradigms. To gain a better understanding of the cognitive process of learning, the dual process model was introduced as a framework for all cognitive processes. According to the dual-process model, two systems of cognitive processes interactively control human behavior. The reflective system, which is rather slow and consumes a high amount of cognitive capacity, relies on syllogistic rules, whereas the impulsive system is based on associative links and processes information fast and with rather low cognitive effort. Especially under the condition of automation and in situations with low cognitive capacity the balance between reflective and impulsive cognitive processes shift to the latter. In learning literature, the duality is referred to as the distinction between implicit and explicit learning. In most cases, both of these processes occur parallel whereas explicit learning does not necessarily have to be present. However, in practical learning situations (i.e., outside the laboratory) it is hard to exclude explicit learning completely. It is now almost indisputable in research that implicit learning exists (Berry, 1997; Fletcher, Maybery and Bennett, 2000; Frensch and Rünger, 2003), even though methodological problems come along with the concept of implicit learning.

As shown above, the definitional approaches did not successfully result in a shared comprehensive understanding of implicit learning yet. A clear and scientifically acknowledged differentiation of the concepts of awareness, consciousness, and intention is necessary to overcome the definitional problems. The greatest success in solving this task is to be expected from a cooperation between philosophers, neuroscientists, and cognitive psychologists. This kind of multidisciplinary approach would allow a clearer distinction to related learning concepts as well. Further, it became evident that a side-by-side comparison of the learning mechanisms and research paradigms of implicit learning is difficult as they fundamentally differ in their methodological approaches. Accordingly, also a combination of these mechanisms and paradigms causes problems (Frensch and Rünger, 2003).

In consequence, general statements which are valid throughout the entire field of research on implicit learning are hardly possible, even though the characteristic of the non-verbalizable nature of implicit learning appears to be accepted. Despite the methodological challenges the practical relevance of implicit learning and dual process models is out of question. While in the 1980s and 1990s, researchers mostly focused on proving the existence of implicit learning processes (e.g., Berry and Broadbent, 1984; Nissen and Bullemer, 1987), the 21st century so far showed an increasing number of experiments directly targeting them, attempting to improve learning outcome by integrating insights from research on dual process theories (Wiers *et al.*, 2011; Hayward *et al.*, 2012; Ise *et al.*, 2012; Eberl *et al.*, 2013).

Concluding, within the last 30 years, implicit learning has evolved to become a major field of research in psychology, and it will be of significant future relevance to psychology (e.g., cognitive bias modification) and related disciplines (Cleeremans, 2006b; Shanks, 2010).

2.3 When duality matters in organizations

When it comes to the point where duality matters, there are two main topics: On the one hand, there are cognitive biases that mainly influence the impulsive system and in consequence stress its advantages (e.g., fast processing, high capacity). On the other hand, reflective processes suffer from weaknesses due to the slow process of searching, the need for information for reasoning, and decision-making in general (Nelson and Winter, 1982, p. 18; Evans and Stanovich, 2013). As described above (see Chapter 2.2.2), both systems interact and accordingly back each other. However, also a shift of balance from a more reflective to a more impulsive processing is possible, e.g., by continuous repetition (i.e., organizational routines). However, also the opposite may happen, e.g., when the impulsive processing does not result in behavior that is satisfactory for others like the management. This section views the processing of an organizational routine through lens of the introduced dual-process theory by Strack and Deutsch (2004). This chapter starts with introducing the weakness of cognitive biases, to then show possible consequences for impulsive processing in organizations for approaching the research question.

2.3.1 Cognitive biases

The world we experience is a constructed reality in which no situation occurs twice. Every situation allows finding differences compared to similar situations. Accordingly, in a strict interpretation of constructivism, every situation is new to us (Piaget, 1954). Perceiving a stimulus in one of these situations – possibly the same stimulus across different circumstances – does not necessarily result in the same interpretation, as interpretation hinges on the context. Depending on the input, an individual constructs its subjective reality that is unique to that person (Bless, Fiedler and Strack, 2004, pp. 1-3). In some cases, individuals who experienced the same objective inputs in the same situation may subjectively construct realities that can be so daunting different that one might wonder if these persons were in the same situation. These differences can be a consequence of cognitive biases. As there is a great variety of cognitive biases,[75] it is useful to explain them generally.

The interpretation of a situation (construction) and the subsequent behavioral pattern will regularly follow the criterion of normality across a statistically relevant population.

[75] There are dozens of biases that are subsumed under the generic term cognitive bias (Bazerman and Moore, 2009; Chapter 2). A detailed differentiation would go beyond the scope of this publication.

Those interpretations that significantly deviate from the norm (and rational judgment) are affected by cognitive biases and accordingly result in undesired behavioral responses (Haselton, Nettle and Andrews, 2015). Such an undesired behavioral response is the result of not just one cognitive bias, but often of a co-occurrence of several biases (Wiers *et al.*, 2011; e.g., attentional bias for a specific stimulus, a memory bias for the automatic activation of stimulus-related associations, or a bias toward automatically activated action tendencies). Accordingly, the use of the generic term cognitive bias falls into place as a differentiation and attribution of maladaptive or undesired behavioral patterns to specific biases is often not possible. The research on cognitive biases is extensive[76] and comes from various domains (e.g., clinical and experimental psychology, law, economics, or management). One could imagine the enormous consequences of cognitive biases in distinct settings. Exemplary, in clinical processes of diagnosis or developing treatment plans (Croskerry, 2013); in food-related cues that influence what, when and how much a person eats (Brooks *et al.*, 2011); in substance abuse (Wiers *et al.*, 2009a; Wiers *et al.*, 2015); or for gender and ethnicity stereotypes (Krieger, 1995).

In a highly cited publication on social behavior, Greenwald and Banaji (1995) stressed the idea that human behavior is not always under conscious control. They found that cognitive biases are the driver for the human behavior being implicit and unconscious. By presenting three types of cognitive biases, they highlighted the difficulty in assessing these and postulated the need for indirect measures. There are different examples of cognitive biases in that paper. However, a topic that accompanied both authors also in several other publications are stereotype biases – in particular, gender and ethnic stereotypes (e.g., Banaji and Greenwald, 1995; 2013; Greenwald, McGhee and Schwartz, 1998; Dasgupta *et al.*, 2000; Nosek, Banaji and Greenwald, 2002a; b). These publications showed how implicit those cognitive biases are, and thus how impulsive the subsequent behaviors are. For instance, most people would reflectively confirm that they do not discriminate other races. However, as these studies impressively showed, the majority of people are controlled by their unconscious biases that result in significant discrimination of other races – without being a racist. The same counts true for gender biases. In reflective processing, most people would come to the conclusion that both, female and male, are equally skilled. Assessing their attitudes by using indirect measures (e.g., the Implicit Association Test), reveals on both genders biases for the self and the other gender.

For example, Nosek, Banaji and Greenwald (2002b) showed that female students impulsively perceived themselves negatively toward mathematics and science, and in contrast positively toward arts and language. The opposite applied to male subjects. One might argue that such gender bias depends on the level of education. However, that argument was proven wrong in a recent study by Moss-Racusin *et al.* (2012).

[76] According to the Web of Science™ Core Collection, there are 1,049 publications with the term *cognitive bias* in the title or abstract since 2010 [accessed on Dec 07, 2016].

Conducting a double-blind study in which professors of both genders had to rate applications of equally qualified applicants that were randomly assigned to female or male names, revealed a gender bias regarding the competencies for a laboratory manager position. Male professors, as well as female professors, ascribed male applicants significantly more competencies for the job. Accordingly, the position was offered more often to male applicants than to *identically* qualified female applicants; expectedly for higher wages. The result is notably interesting, as most people of higher education would deny having such a bias when being explicitly asked for it. Thus, boundary points of the duality of mind and economics become evident.

One of the main unsolved and hardly addressed challenges of routine research is the deviation between the ostensive aspect and the performative aspect of a routine. Focusing on the individual level and approaching the problem from a dual mind perspective may be particularly promising in this respect. The performative aspect is located in the individual action, which in turn is interactively determined by the impulsive and the reflective system of each individual. As repetition and limited cognitive resources contribute to shifting the balance between reflective and impulsive processing to the latter, the individual actions become more automatic, at least over time and under stress. This brings especially the impulsive information processing to the focus for understanding the performance, replication und establishment of routines on an individual level and thus may shed light on the problem of misalignment of the ostensive and the performative aspect.

Anticipating the routine that will be examined in the experiment of this study may serve as a suitable example from organization practice. The completion of a flight progress strip (routine) as part of the capability of air traffic control has specific requirements for writing numerals to prevent misreading and accordingly to prevent potential accidents. These requirements are codified as the ostensive aspect in an operations manual (Amt für Flugsicherung der Bundeswehr, 2013) and are trained with explicit methods during the vocational training of becoming an air traffic control officer. As the required writing style deviates from the writing style that students learn in German schools, the air traffic control officers have to undergo a process of relearning to meet the new writing style. In training situations when there is enough cognitive capacity to process the writing style reflectively, the officers are successful in applying the new writing style. However, in practical situations outside the classroom, when the cognitive capacity is required at other domains than writing, the air traffic controllers frequently fall back to the old writing style. That means the balance between reflective and impulsive processing shifts toward the latter. As mentioned earlier, impulsive processing is prone to cognitive biases. It is conjecturable that the cognitive bias involved here is mainly an approach bias toward the old writing style (see also experiment in this study). That means in the performance of the routine of completing the flight progress strip, the approach bias impulsively brings the officers to use the more habitual writing style that does not meet the requirements (i.e., the routine misses its target). At this point, implicit learning as a promising approach in modifying impulsive processes respectively cognitive biases could be a valuable instrument to minimize the deviation between the ostensive aspect of a routine and the performative aspect of a routine. In the subsequent section, the use of implicit learning in organizations will be addressed by approaching the research question.

2.3.2 Approaching the challenge of misalignment

Research in experimental psychopathology offers implicit learning paradigms that directly target maladaptive cognitive biases. A series of studies in psychopathology (Wiers *et al.*, 2009b; b; 2010; 2011; 2015; Gladwin *et al.*, 2011; Eberl *et al.*, 2013; 2014; Sharbanee *et al.*, 2013; Chambers *et al.*, 2014) analyzed the cognitive biases that cause problem drinkers to approach alcohol against the knowledge of the negative consequences. As addictive behaviors are in general "[…] *conceptualized as an imbalance between strong impulsive or associative reactions to drug-related cues and relatively weak reflective or controlled processes* […]" (Wiers *et al.*, 2011, p. 490; see also Chapter 2.2.2), the focus of these studies is the modification of maladaptive action tendencies (cognitive bias) toward the approach of alcohol. Originating in research on anxiety (Rinck and Becker, 2007), the majority of the above studies on alcohol used a training version of the Approach-Avoidance Task for the cognitive bias modification (see Chapter 3.4.2). In several respects, this training compares to implicit learning, in particular to those paradigms using reaction times as measures. Referring to the determinants of implicit learning, the Approach-Avoidance Task training represents a paradigm of implicit learning that allows modifying cognitive biases to converge or meet the norm. This training allows participants to acquire new associations without being able to verbalize these, which is the central characteristic of implicit learning (Frensch, 1998; Cleeremans, 2006b). Further, in a process that is unintentional for the learner, implicit learning sensitizes the learner to react to certain principles of his environment. The retrieved content is outside the learner's awareness (Reber, 1967; Cleeremans and Dienes, 2008; Kaufman *et al.*, 2010). Even the narrow definition of implicit learning that claims this type of learning requires both, the learning and the reproduction to be implicit, cognitive bias modification using the Approach-Avoidance Task training would apply.

A closer exemplary look at cognitive bias modification in alcohol dependence reveals its great potential, which may be applicable to challenges of learning in organizations. Cognitive bias modification succeeded in creating a significant alcohol avoidance bias in alcohol-dependent patients. Thus, alcohol-dependent patients were implicitly trained to increase their implicit avoidance reaction toward alcohol, which resulted in a tremendous long-term effect of a reduction in relapse rates by 15 % (Wiers *et al.*, 2011). That result was replicated and was further strengthened by the finding that the effect of cognitive bias modification on the treatment outcome was mediated by the achieved change in alcohol approach bias, which can be considered to be a proof of the causal effect of the cognitive bias modification to reduce relapse (Eberl *et al.*, 2013). This mediation effect was further supported by Gladwin *et al.* (2011). In line with Strack and Deutsch (2004), the abilities of cognitive control moderated the effect of this very cognitive bias modification for long-term relapse rates in alcohol-dependent patients, showing that training is most effective under conditions of low abilities of cognitive control (Wiers *et al.*, 2013). As to now, these studies are both, comprehensive support for dual process models and a first evidence that cognitive bias modification is of considerable practical relevance. The present study is the first approach to adopt these findings to challenges of learning in the domain of economics, in particular learning of organizational routines as part of organizational research.

When transferring the above results to learning within organizations, the question arises whether implicit learning can change implicit associations toward an organizational routine and whether this would increase the conformity of the performative outcome with the ostensive aspect of a routine. Further, it may suggest that implicit learning in an organizational context may be most useful under certain conditions such as low cognitive capacity or low levels of regulatory control. These research questions will be addressed in the following chapters. The experimental setting is conducted in the style of the cognitive bias modification studies published by Wiers and colleagues cited above approving the transferability of results from psychopathology to organizational routines.

3 Methods

Against the background of the overall research question, whether or not implicit learning can contribute to diminishing the gap between the ostensive and performative aspect of an organizational routine, this chapter introduces the methodological approach in breaking down and answering the overall question. For that purpose, the experimental setting will be presented. The experiment aims to test seven hypotheses assigned to three research questions as well as to answer an exploratory research question. The first research question fundamentally proves if implicit learning allows changing the underlying implicit associations of subjects toward an organizational routine. The second research question then focusses on the ostensive and performative aspect of a routine and asks if implicit learning can increase the conformity between both aspects of a routine. The third question pursues the goal to shed light on the conditions of an effective implementation of implicit learning strategies in organizations. Finally, the exploratory research question looks for possible predictors of the AAT training effect.

3.1 Participants

Fifty-nine candidates for the Bundeswehr air-traffic control (ATC) service were recruited from the German Federal Armed Forces.[77] None of the subjects had started the ATC training before attending the experiment. All subjects accepted the informed consent, which included information about the aim of this study and the core measures. Furthermore, referring to the terms of empirical studies in the German Federal Armed Forces (BMVg, 1990), the consent included information about the option to withdraw from this study, the protection of anonymity and the use of the collected data. For preserving the subjects' anonymity in accordance with the Federal Data Protection Act (BDSG, 1990), each subject generated a specific seven-digit subject code. The code consisted of the first two letters of the subjects' birthplace (two digits), their position in the family birth order (one digit), the first two letters of their mothers' given name (two digits), and their mothers' month of birth (two digits). For instance, a code in accordance with this scheme looks like this: *ma1pe07*.

The five female and 54 male subjects ranged in age from 21 to 30 years ($M = 25.2$, $SD = 2.13$). Except for one male subject who learned German at the age of five, all were native German speakers. Twenty-three point seven percent of the subjects held an intermediate school-leaving certificate (Haupt-/Realschule), 15.3 % held a subject-related entrance qualification (Fachhochschulreife), and 61.0 % a general qualification for university entrance (allgemeine Hochschulreife). At the time of the experiment, 49.2 % had no (completed) vocational training, 38.9 % had a vocational training, and 11.9 % held a university degree. Due to the employment as future ATC officers, all

[77] The German Federal Ministry of Defence approved this study. The assigned registration number is 2/06/14.

M. Eberl, *Organizational Routines Meet Experimental Psychology*, Zukunftsfähige Unternehmensführung in Forschung und Praxis, https://doi.org/10.1007/978-3-658-23562-8_3

subjects have to complete an annual medical checkup (audiometry, eyesight test, color vision, et cetera), which they only pass if they fulfill the basic requirements for ATC officers. Accordingly, hearing disorders, potential or uncorrected amblyopia and color blindness are unlikely to be a confounding factor.

3.2 Materials

In the Federal Republic of Germany, the air traffic control service splits into the military air traffic control service (Bundeswehr) and the civil air traffic control service (DFS Deutsche Flugsicherung GmbH). The military air traffic control service is responsible for all tasks regarding air navigation in the area of authority of the Federal Ministry of Defence (i.e., across all branches). In modern times the sovereignty over the airspace is important, and thus the military air traffic control service is directly responsible to the Inspector of the German Air Force.[78] This chain of command highlights the role of air traffic control service in the Bundeswehr as a core competence. During peace times, both organizations, civil and military, work in large parts according to the same (European) standards (Mensen, 2014, pp. 74-76). Nonetheless, the organizations maintain their individual operations manuals. For the Bundeswehr, it is the *Besondere Anweisung für die Militärische Flugsicherung 2-100*, which governs all procedures for military air traffic control units of the Bundeswehr, but also for remote units (e.g., during missions; Amt für Flugsicherung der Bundeswehr, 2013, pp. 00-01).

Categorizing air traffic control and its associated services (e.g., aeronautical information services) according to the hierarchical organizational structure suggested by Salvato and Rerup (2010), it would fall into the category of organizational capabilities (see Chapter 2.1.2). As routines are the building blocks of capabilities (Parmigiani and Howard-Grenville, 2011), air traffic control comprises multiple routines (e.g., handling aircraft flying on crossing tracks, or issuing traffic information based on radar information). One of these routines and the one that is central to the experiment of this study is maintaining a flight progress strip. This task can be identified as an organizational routine as it fulfills the characteristics of routines introduced before (see Chapter 2.1.1.1). The performance occurs for each aircraft that moves in the controlled sector or at ground. In civil aviation, these movements can be several hundred per day (e.g., at Frankfurt Airport there were up to 1.467 airplanes starting or landing on a peak day in 2014; Fraport AG Frankfurt Airport Services Worldwide, 2015, p. 12). Finally, the routine of maintaining a flight progress strip involves several actors (e.g., the colleagues on the working position next by, but also the pilots, ground staff, or air traffic controllers from other sectors or aerodromes) and thus meets the characteristic of the collective nature of routines.

[78] The structure of the Bundeswehr and its branches is subject to continuous change. The structure explained here, refers to the time the experiment was planned (i.e., 2013).

Flight progress strips document several sets of data about the aircraft in the controlled sector or aerodrome (see Figure 5): (a) times (e.g., estimated time of departure or arrival, or estimated time over significant point); (b) levels (e.g., requested, cleared, assigned, or coordinated level); (c) aircraft information (e.g., aerodrome of destination, aircraft identification, number and type of aircraft, or wake turbulence category); (d) procedure information (e.g., departure and approach procedure, coordinating procedure); en-route and additional information (e.g., departure route, slot, or transponder frequency). Much of this information is codified in numerals (e.g., the flight level, or the heading), but also in symbols, abbreviations and phrase contractions (Amt für Flugsicherung der Bundeswehr, 2013, pp. 27–21 - 27–12).

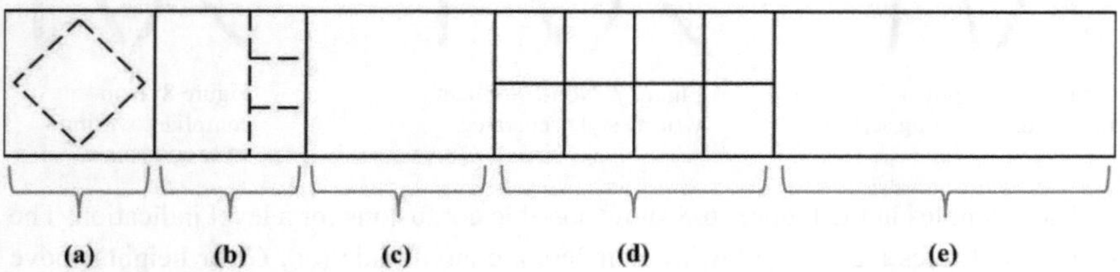

Figure 5: Schematic patterned layout of a flight progress strip according to Amt für Flugsicherung der Bundeswehr (2013, pp. 27–23).

Note: The flight progress strip structures as follows: (a) time box; (b) level box; (c) call sign box; (d) procedure box; (e) en-route and additional information.

Common German writing style non-compliant	Approved in air traffic control compliant
0	0
1	1
7	7
9	9

Table 4: Writing styles of numerals (Amt für Flugsicherung der Bundeswehr, 2013, pp. 27–13).

The *Besondere Anweisung für die Militärische Flugsicherung 2-100* provides the air traffic controller with the approved abbreviations and symbols, but also with the approved writing styles for specific numerals (see Table 4). The manual has to govern in detail how the entries on the flight progress strip need to be carried out, as confusions could entail enormous consequences. These instructions meet the level of individual action.

Numerals on a flight progress strip can be marked in different ways with different meanings. For example, a check mark indicates the coordination of a concerned entry on the flight progress strip; an arrow on the right side of the corresponding entry indicates a climb/descent; or a horizontal line through the corresponding entry indicates that the cleared level was reached by aircraft (Amt für Flugsicherung der Bundeswehr, 2013, pp. 27–11).

Figure 6: Compliant standardized writing style.

Figure 7: Non-compliant writing style separated.

Figure 8: Non-compliant writing style condensed.

The examples in the Figures 6-8 show possible confusions for a level indication. The letter *A* indicates that the following numbers are an altitude (cf., *G* for heights above ground). The numbers signal the altitude in hundreds of feet (i.e., A71 for an altitude of 7.100 ft.). Figure 6 indicates an altitude of 7.100 ft. using the approved writing style that is compliant to the *Besondere Anweisung für die Militärische Flugsicherung 2-100*. It differs to the common German writing style as taught in elementary school (see Table 4). Exemplarily, the approved writing of the seven does not have a horizontal line in the middle, or the one does not have a diagonal line at the top. Figure 7 shows the writing according to the common German writing style with a decent separation between the characters. However, even with this separation, the non-compliant writing style may cause confusion. One might interpret the last character, the one, as an arrow indicating that the aircraft is climbing to 700 ft., instead of having a coordinated altitude of 7.100 ft. In Figure 8 the confusions can be even worse, as there are two possible misinterpretations due to the condensed spacing: (1) It could be misinterpreted as the fact that the airplane left the altitude of 7.100 ft., which would be indicated by a horizontal line through the characters A71. (2) It could also be interpreted as the sequence of actions of an airplane that climbed to 700 ft. (upwards pointing arrow), reached 700 ft. (horizontal line through the arrow) and finally left 700 ft. (horizontal line through the characters A7. Both interpretations would be wrong and could have fatal consequences, as the airplane would still maintain the altitude of 7.100 ft.

Air traffic controllers that learned and use the writing style as it is common in Germany (in the following referred to as Old Writing Style; OWS), need to relearn the approved writing style (in the following referred to as New Writing Style; NWS) during their vocational training as ATC officer. Handwriting, or more precisely the production of handwritten characters by the combination of strokes is a process that is highly automatized (Berninger, Mizokawa and Bragg, 1991; Medwell and Wray, 2007). Over many years this motor skill became habituated by the subjects of this experiment. Accordingly, it is difficult to explicitly relearn this motor skill as tried in the air traffic control training. During practical training sessions or in their day-to-day job, the ATC officers fall back into the OWS in stressful situations (e.g., practical exams in the simulator or high intensity of traffic). That observation is in line with the dual-process model as introduced before (see Chapter 2.2.2). In stressful situations, the cognitive capacity may not be sufficient to process the writing of specific numerals reflectively, so that automated processes prevail in such circumstances. The result is a conflict between the impulsive action tendency and the result of a reflective processing. The latter would lead to a decision that meets the requirements of air traffic control (i.e., the *Besondere Anweisung für die Militärische Flugsicherung 2-100*). However, the first is driven by the implicit motivational orientation of the actor that is characterized by a period of learning and application of the OWS. This discrepancy between the reflective and impulsive processing can be viewed as an approach bias toward the OWS (Wiers *et al.*, 2011; Watson *et al.*, 2013; Cousijn, Luijten and Wiers, 2014).

To modify this cognitive bias (i.e., the approach bias) and to retrain the subjects' automatic action tendency to approach the NWS is the goal of the experiment in this study. By using the Approach-Avoidance Task training paradigm, the subjects should implicitly learn to approach the NWS for the numbers 0, 1, 7, and 9. Besides indirect measures (e.g., Implicit Association Test), also direct measures (e.g., a behavioral task with different cognitive loads) are used to monitor the success of relearning. The behavioral task transfers the implicitly relearned writing style from the computer screen to the actual production of handwritten numerals on a sheet of paper. Before describing the experimental tasks in more detail, the research questions and hypotheses in the next section reflect the aggregation of the line of thoughts in the previous chapters.

3.3 Research questions and hypotheses

Research question I: Does implicit learning change implicit associations toward an organizational routine?

- H1: The AAT training will increase the approach tendency toward the NWS and generalize to untrained pictures.
- H2: The training effect will generalize to another implicit measure (IAT).

Research question II: Does implicit learning increase the conformity of the performative outcome with the ostensive aspect of a routine?

- H3: The training group will make fewer faults in the behavioral task (writing numerals in NWS) than the control groups.
- H4: The training effect will be more distinct in a situation of high cognitive load.

- H5: The size of the training effect mediates the error count in the behavioral task (HCL).

Research question III: Under which conditions is the implementation of implicit learning strategies most effective?

- H6: Low levels of regulatory control will predict an increased training effect on an implicit level (AAT).
- H7: Low levels of regulatory control will predict a decreased error rate on a behavioral level (behavioral task).

Exploratory research question: Which factors predict the AAT training effect?

3.4 Experimental tasks

3.4.1 Approach-Avoidance Task: Assessment version

Rinck and Becker (2007) introduced an indirect measure to assess behavioral tendencies toward stimuli in a computerized joystick classification task, the Approach-Avoidance Task (AAT). The fundamental idea behind the AAT is that human beings have an automatic behavioral tendency to avoid stimuli that are valenced negatively and to approach stimuli that are valenced positively. While avoidance tendencies are related to arm extension (pushing the joystick), approach tendencies are related to arm flexion (pulling the joystick; Cacioppo, Priester and Berntson, 1993; Rinck and Becker, 2007). The assumption is that it is easier for subjects (i.e., they have a faster reaction time) to push away stimuli that are associated with avoidance and to pull stimuli that are associated to approach (compatible assignment) than the other way around (incompatible assignment). In a comparative study on fear of spiders, Reinecke, Becker and Rinck (2010) found a sufficient[79] test-retest reliability ($r = .35$, $p < .01$) and a good internal consistency (ranged between $r = .66$ and $r = .70$) for the AAT. In the same study, validity correlations between the AAT effect and a validated self-report questionnaire on fear of spiders ranged from $r = -.45$ ($p < .001$) to $r = -.59$ ($p < .001$). The adaptability of the results by Reinecke, Becker and Rinck (2010) to this study is limited, as they conducted their study in a different field of research. However, it is a reference point.

The stimuli that are used in this study are pictures of three categories counterbalanced in landscape and portrait format (see Table 5), presented singly centered on the computer screen in a quasi-random order (no more than three consecutive pictures with the same format or contents). The order was the same for all subjects within the particular stage of testing (pretest, posttest). By using standardized instructions in written form, the participants were asked to ignore the contents of pictures but to react to their format by pushing or pulling the joystick as fast and accurate as possible until

[79] Compared to other RT-based measures on group level, knowing that the reliability is insufficient on an individual level.

the detent of the joystick (angle of approx. 30°). Pushing the joystick, smoothly decreased the size of pictures, whereas pulling it increased the size of pictures, respectively. When reaching the detent of the joystick pictures disappeared, and the reaction times were taken as the final reaction time. This zooming effect induces the sensation of approach and avoidance (Neumann and Strack, 2000; Wentura, Rothermund and Bak, 2000; Kawakami *et al.*, 2007; Wiers *et al.*, 2010). The joysticks were tightly attached to the tables to prevent a delay of the zooming feature and to absorb a potential slip of the device, which would cause a bias in the reaction times (Woud *et al.*, 2013a).

Category	Writing Style	Picture format	Picture contents	Condition 1 (trials)	Condition 2 (trials)
1	NWS	Portrait	0, 1, 7, 9	Pull (80)	Push (80)
		Landscape		Push (80)	Pull (80)
2	OWS	Portrait	0, 1, 7, 9	Pull (80)	Push (80)
		Landscape		Push (80)	Pull (80)
3	No change	Portrait	2, 3, 4, 5, 6, 8	Pull (24)	Push (24)
		Landscape		Push (24)	Pull (24)

Table 5: Schematic description of the assessment Approach-Avoidance Task.

Note: Each numeral in category one and two was used in two different handwriting styles, i.e., there was a set of eight stimuli for NWS in portrait format, a set of eight stimuli for NWS in landscape format, et cetera.

The AAT at pre- and posttest consisted of 20 practice trials with gray rectangles to learn to respond to the format of pictures and 368 test trials with numerals as stimuli (see Appendix A). However, of these 368 trials, there were just 320 relevant for analysis (category one and two). The interval between the trials was 300 milliseconds.

$$Approach\ Bias_{Category\ x} = \frac{M_{RT\ Category\ x\ (incompatible\ trials)} - M_{RT\ Category\ x\ (compatible\ trials)}}{SD_{RT\ Category\ x}} \quad (2)$$

For calculating the approach bias, a procedure analog to the improved scoring algorithm of the Implicit Association Test was used (IAT; see Chapter 3.4.3). Trials with reaction times above 10 seconds were deleted before calculating the approach bias and participants having at more than 10 % of the trials an RT below 300 milliseconds were excluded completely. The approach biases were calculated for category one and two separately, i.e., there is one approach bias for NWS and one for OWS. Formula 2 shows the schematic calculation of an approach bias.

3.4.2 Approach-Avoidance Task: Training version

The approach bias retraining paradigm was coined by Wiers *et al.* (2010) in the domain of substance abuse. Using the experimental logic of the attentional bias retraining

(MacLeod *et al.*, 2002), the recently developed alcohol Approach-Avoidance Task (Wiers *et al.*, 2009b) was modified to a training version. In this modified version, subjects' automatic action tendencies toward alcohol were retrained with the aim either to avoid or to approach alcohol. Wiers *et al.* (2010) changed the contingencies of the percentage of congruent and incongruent pictures that were pushed (*avoidance*) or pulled (*approach*). More precisely, for those subjects who were in the avoid-alcohol condition, 90 % of the alcohol-related pictures were displayed in push-format, and 10 % of alcohol-related pictures were presented in pull-format. In the same group, pictures of soft-drinks came with reversed contingencies, i.e., 10 % of soft-drink-related pictures appeared in push-format and 90 % in pull-format. In contrast, for the subjects from the approach-alcohol condition, all contingencies were reversed, i.e., of the alcohol-related pictures 10 % came in push-format and 90 % in pull-format, and of the soft-drink-related pictures, 90 % were shown in push-format and 10% in pull-format. The contingencies were set to 90 % (and not to 100 %) to reduce the probability that subjects become aware of the manipulated contingencies; this is consistent with the studies by MacLeod *et al.* (2002) and Schoenmakers *et al.* (2007). However, later studies used contingencies of 100 % without subjects gaining awareness of the manipulated contingencies (Wiers *et al.*, 2011; Eberl *et al.*, 2014). Compared to the assessment AAT the total number of trials in push-format (184) and pull-format (184) remained constant (see Table 6).

Category	Writing Style	Picture format	Picture contents	Condition 1 (trials)	Condition 2 (trials)
1	NWS	Portrait	0, 1, 7, 9	Pull (144)	Push (16)
		Landscape		Push (16)	Pull (144)
2	OWS	Portrait	0, 1, 7, 9	Pull (16)	Push (144)
		Landscape		Push (144)	Pull (16)
3	No change	Portrait	2, 3, 4, 5, 6, 8	Pull (24)	Push (24)
		Landscape		Push (24)	Pull (24)

Table 6: Schematic description of the Approach-Avoidance Task training.

The AAT training used here was similar to the assessment AAT described above, in Chapter 3.4.1. However, the contingencies for the relevant categories were changed from 50 % to 90 %, i.e., 90 % of the pictures containing the NWS were presented in pull-format (*approach*), and 90 % of the pictures containing the OWS appeared in push-format (*avoidance*). Deviant from the assessment AAT, only four pictures per category and format were used to allow a close generalization to untrained pictures in the posttest. The training consisted of 368 trials, 320 of them were in the relevant categories one and two. As in the assessment AAT, the post-trial pause was 300 milliseconds.

3.4.3 Implicit Association Test

The Implicit Association Test (IAT; Greenwald, McGhee and Schwartz, 1998) allows assessing the strengths of implicit associations between concepts indirectly in a computerized categorization task (Greenwald, Nosek and Banaji, 2003). It can be used to measure impulsive behavioral tendencies (Strack and Deutsch, 2004; De Houwer, 2006). In a review across different domains, Nosek, Greenwald and Banaji (2006) found a stable and satisfactory test-retest reliability (*median* $r = .56$) compared to other reaction time-based measures. Others (Banse, Seise and Zerbes, 2001; Greenwald and Nosek, 2001), reported internal consistencies for IAT scores that are quite satisfactory (*average* $\alpha > .80$). In a meta-analysis of 122 reports (184 independent samples, 14,900 subjects) across different domains, Greenwald *et al.* (2009) calculated a moderate predictive validity of $\overline{r} = .274$. Breaking their results down to comparable domains that are preference related, they found higher predictive validities for consumers ($\overline{r} = .323$) and political preferences ($\overline{r} = .483$).

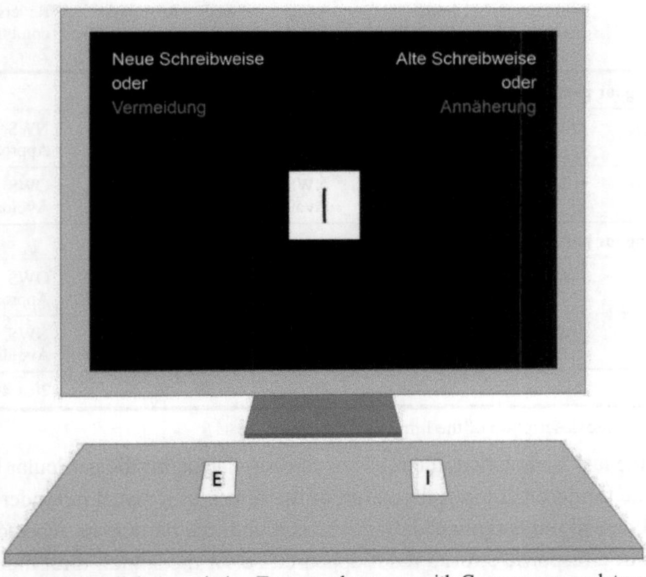

Figure 9: Implicit Association Test sample screen with German nomenclature.

This study used a variation of the standard IAT with seven blocks and the improved scoring algorithm as described by Greenwald, Nosek and Banaji (2003). The subjects sorted stimulus items into four concepts by pressing the left (*e*) or right response key (*i*) on the keyboard of the computer. Two concepts are target categories (*OWS: 'Alte Schreibweise'; NWS: 'Neue Schreibweise'*) and two concepts are attribute categories (*approach: 'Annäherung', avoidance: 'Vermeidung'*). These concepts merge into a compatible combination (*OWS* and *approach*; *NWS* and *avoidance*) and an incompatible combination (*OWS* and *avoidance*; *NWS* and *approach*), which are tested in separate blocks (see Table 7). Block one, two and five are practicing blocks (20 trials each) to get used to the task and the assignment of the keys to the categories. The third (20 trials) and the fourth block (40 trials) represent the initial combined task, and the sixth (20 trials) and seventh block (40 trials) represent the reversed combined task. In the practicing blocks, target and attribute categories appear separately, whereas in the combined blocks both appear simultaneously, i.e., one target and one attribute category appear together on each side of the screen (see Figure 9). The assignment of the target categories to the left or right key differed between subjects of condition one and two, i.e., subjects of condition one started with the compatible combination and subjects of condition two started with the incompatible combination (Greenwald, McGhee and Schwartz, 1998; Wiers *et al.*, 2002; Nosek, Greenwald and Banaji, 2006).

Block	**1**	**2**	**3 + 4**	**5**	**6 + 7**
Description	Initial target practice	Initial attribute practice	Initial combined task 1 + 2	Reversed target practice	Reversed combined task 1 + 2
Key Mapping for participants of condition 1					
Left Key (*E*)	OWS	Approach	OWS Approach	NWS	NWS Approach
Right Key (*I*)	NWS	Avoidance	NWS Avoidance	OWS	OWS Avoidance
Key Mapping for participants of condition 2					
Left Key	NWS	Approach	NWS Approach	OWS	OWS Approach
Right Key	OWS	Avoidance	OWS Avoidance	NWS	NWS Avoidance
Trials	20	20	20 + 40	20	20 + 40

Table 7: Schematic description of the Implicit Association Test.

During the task completion, the relevant category labels for the particular block were visible at the top-left and top-right corner of the screen as a visual reminder of the key mapping. Each stimulus remained on the screen until the participant reacted correctly. In the case of a response error, a red *X* appeared below the stimuli until the participant pressed the correct response key. Each trial had a post-trial pause of 250 milliseconds (Nosek, Greenwald and Banaji, 2006, pp. 271-272). The background color of the computer screen was black, and the font color for the target category labels was white whereas it was green for the attribute category labels. The font size of the on-screen text was five percent of the display height, displayed in *Arial* font. Stimuli presented for target categories were squared pictures (300 x 300 pixels; see Appendix A) of the numbers zero, one, seven, and nine in OWS and NWS. For attribute categories, words reflecting *approach* and *avoidance* were used as stimuli (see Appendix B). Each category (both target and both attribute categories) had eight stimuli, i.e., altogether there were 24 stimuli used in pretest and 32 stimuli in the posttest.

$$D - score_{condition\ 1} = \frac{\left(\frac{M_{RT\ Block\ 6} - M_{RT\ Block\ 3}}{SD_{RT\ Block\ 3\ and\ 6}}\right) + \left(\frac{M_{RT\ Block\ 7} - M_{RT\ Block\ 4}}{SD_{RT\ Block\ 4\ and\ 7}}\right)}{2} \quad (3)$$

Greenwald, Nosek and Banaji (2003) suggested an improved scoring algorithm to calculate the IAT effect (D-score). Before calculating the D-score, all trials with RTs greater than 10,000 milliseconds were deleted and all subjects that reacted to more than 10 % of the trials faster than 300 milliseconds were excluded. Finally, the D-score (exemplarily for condition one) calculates as shown in Formula 3. The calculation of the D-scores in this study followed the improved scoring algorithm of Greenwald, Nosek and Banaji (2003).

3.4.4 Rating of test materials

According to dual-process theories implicit and explicit processes are interrelated (Strack and Deutsch, 2004), this proposition is supported by several studies across different domains (e.g., Nosek, 2005; Woud *et al.*, 2013b). Wiers *et al.* (2010; 2011) as well as Woud and colleagues (2008; 2011; 2013a; b) assessed explicit evaluations of stimulus items using a direct rating task. Participants had to rate the stimuli that were

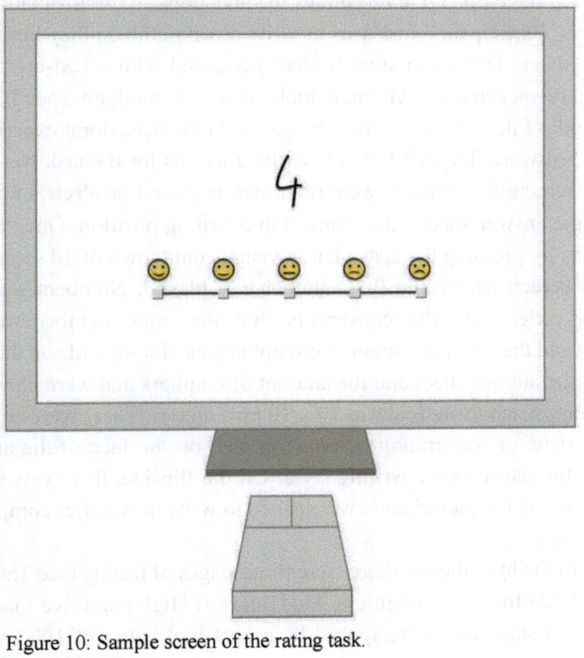

Figure 10: Sample screen of the rating task.

presented during the AAT or IAT on a Likert scale (see Appendix A). Different scales were used across those studies, but essentially participants had to rate if they have a positive or negative attitude toward the presented stimulus. Some studies found a relationship between implicit and explicit evaluations (Wiers *et al.*, 2011), while others did not (Woud, Becker and Rinck, 2008).

In the rating task applied here, participants had to rate the pictures used during the AAT and IAT on a 5-point bipolar smiley scale. This non-numeric and non-verbal Likert scale showed cartoon-like pictures as anchors, as they polarize more than pictures with detailed facial expressions (Reynolds-Keefer and Johnson, 2011). Participants were instructed about the task in an on-screen briefing. They were asked to rate the presented stimulus either neutral or positive respectively negative according to the strength of their attitude. The 28 stimulus pictures (numerals in NWS and OWS) were presented singly centered on the computer screen in random order. Below the stimulus item, the rating scale was displayed (see Figure 10). Participants answered by clicking one of the anchors using the mouse. Once the participant clicked on an anchor point, the computer screen turned blank for 1000 milliseconds until the next item appeared.

3.4.5 Behavioral task

For testing, if a potential implicit training effect transfers to the behavioral level, an applied task was developed that resembles the vocational writing situation of air traffic control officers. Participants' task was to write down numbers they heard on a headset to an answer sheet. The audio stimuli were generated with a text-to-speech software (www.fromtexttospeech.com; German male voice in medium speed) and saved as Waveform Audio File Format for the application in the behavioral experiment software (Millisecond Software, Inquisit Lab 4.0.4). Instructions for the task were displayed on the computer screen: Participants were requested to put on headsets, to pick up the pen and to place the answer sheets in a comfortable writing position. Once they confirmed the instructions by pressing the space bar, a visual countdown of 10 seconds elapsed on the computer screen before the first number was played. Numbers were played in a quasi-random order with the constraints that the same number was not played consecutively and that the same number did not appear side-by-side on the answer sheet. The fields on the answer sheet and the amount of numbers that were played equaled for the specific stage; each form field was 10 x 10 millimeters. There were no numbers (e.g., subject code, date, or registration number) printed on the face of the answer sheet to avoid biasing the participants' writing style. On the flipside, there was a field to enter the subject code, which participants were asked to write down after completing the task (see Appendix C).

According to the hypotheses, there were three stages of testing (see Table 8): (1) Low cognitive load, (2) Increased cognitive load, and (3) High cognitive load. (1) The 160 stimuli played in stage one were spaced by a post-trial pause of 1000 milliseconds to ensure that participants could complete the task without missing any numbers. (2) In stage two, the same amount of stimuli was played, but the post-trial pause was reduced to 500 milliseconds, which leads to an increased cognitive load and a higher degree of impulsive processing (Strack and Deutsch, 2004). (3) Similar to stage two, in stage three the 160 stimuli were spaced by 500 milliseconds. However, to increase the cognitive load to a higher level, participants had to take an additional task. They had to memorize and not to write down 40 terms (not being numbers), that were played randomly among the stimuli being numbers. These terms derive from Projekt Deutscher Wortschatz (2014), which offers a database of the most frequently used German nouns. In principle, starting from the top of the list the most frequently used nouns were chosen for this task.

Stage	**Trials**		**Post-trial pause (milliseconds)**	**Application**
	Numbers	**Terms**		
Low cognitive load	160	-	1000	Pretest, Posttest
Increased cognitive load	160	-	500	Posttest
High cognitive load	160	40	500	Posttest

Table 8: Basic characteristics of the behavioral task.

However, several terms were omitted as they may lead to confusion during testing (e.g., the German term for success, problem or example) or were not articulated well by the text-to-speech software (e.g., the German terms church, percent, or path). Also, due to their frequency of occurrence some names of months and weekdays were not used for testing. When participants finished stage three, a list of 40 nouns was displayed, in which they had to flag the words they memorized in stage three. All three stages had a different order of stimuli. However, the order was the same for all subjects within the specific stage. Numbers that have a defined writing style in the air traffic control operations manual (0, 1, 7, 9) were played 25 times each. All other numbers (2, 3, 4, 5, 6, 8) were just played 10 times each (see Appendix D for a complete list of stimuli used in this task).

In the pretest, the behavioral task was conducted to assess the writing style of the relevant numbers (0, 1, 7, 9) before taking the implicit training. Respectively, participants were instructed just to write down the played numbers to the answer sheet. Whereas in posttest, participants were explicitly instructed to stick to the NWS required in ATC during all three stages. Four raters independently evaluated the answer sheets based on predefined rules. The raters tracked errors that either indicated the wrong writing style (OWS) and the approach to writing a number in the wrong writing style.

3.4.6 Stroop color-word task

Recent studies showed strong evidence that impulsive processing depends on regulatory control (RC) functions. A person with a high RC is assumed to be able to regulate an impulsive into a reflective behavior while a person with a low RC is not able to do so (Grenard *et al.*, 2008; Houben and Wiers, 2009; Wiers *et al.*, 2009a; etc.). In this study the well-known Stroop color-word interference task (Stroop, 1935) was used to assess RC, as it "[…] *appears to have reasonable reliability and validity* […]" (MacLeod, 1991, p. 166).[80] The Stroop task allows comparing the time required for naming congruent and incongruent stimuli, i.e., it belongs to the reaction time-based measures. It allows assessing "[…]*the ease with which a person can maintain a goal in mind and suppress a habitual response in favor of a less familiar one*" (Strauss, Sherman and Spreen, 2006, p. 477). In the completely computerized version used here (Houben and Wiers, 2009), subjects were asked to name the ink color (red, green, blue, black) of stimuli presented singly centered on the computer screen by pressing one of four response keys (*d, f, j, k*) on the keyboard of the computer. Each key was assigned to one ink color; the assignment did not change during testing. As a reminder for participants, the key mapping was displayed on the screen throughout the task (see Figure 11).

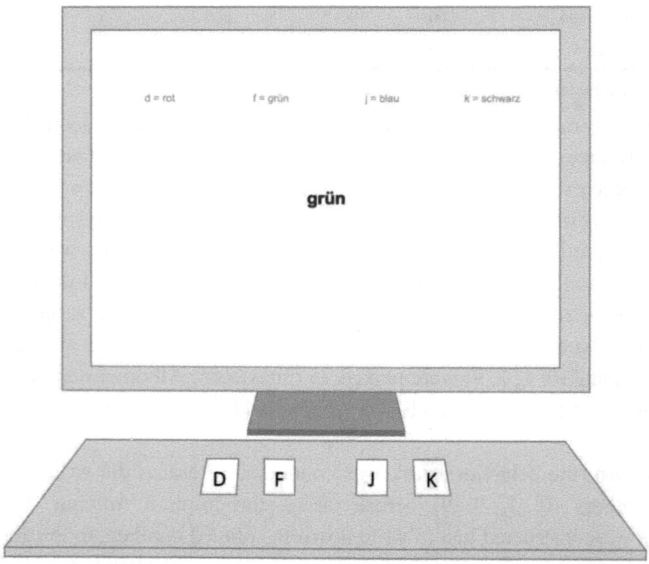

Figure 11: Sample screen of the color-word interference task; showing an incongruent trial.

The stimuli can be either (1) congruent or (2) incongruent. (1) Stimuli of the congruent category are the words *red* (*German*: rot), *green* (*German*: grün), *blue* (*German*: blau) or *black* (*German*: schwarz) displayed in the ink color of their meaning, e.g., the word *green* is displayed in green ink. (2) Stimuli of the incongruent category

[80] For a comprehensive review on the reliability and validity, see Strauss, Sherman and Spreen (2006, pp. 490-495).

were also the words *red*, *green*, *blue*, and *black*; however, they are not displayed in the ink color of their meaning, but in an incongruent ink color. Exemplarily, the word *red* is displayed in the ink color green, blue, or black. The basic concept behind the Stroop task is that reading is more automatized and practiced than naming ink colors, which results in conflicting (slower or wrong) responses for incongruent trials. Whereas this is not the case for congruent trial, the automatized response matches the reflectively processed response of naming the ink color, which leads to a faster RT (MacLeod and MacDonald, 2000).

Before the test block began, all participants took a practice block to get used to the task and the key mapping. This block consisted of 48 trials which showed meaningless symbols (*&&&&,= = = =, % % % %, # # # #*) in red, green, blue and black ink color as stimuli. The test block consisted of 64 trials: 32 congruent trials and 32 incongruent trials. When the subjects' response was correct, after a post-trial pause of 200 milliseconds the next stimuli appeared. In the case of a wrong response, the stimuli disappeared, a gray X displayed for 400 milliseconds, and then the next stimuli appeared (i.e., subjects had no option to correct errors). In both blocks, the practice and the test block, the stimuli were displayed in a quasi-random order with the constraint that no more than two consecutive stimuli of the same color appeared.

$$Stroop\ score = \frac{M_{RT\ incongruent\ trials} - M_{RT\ congruent\ trials}}{SD_{RT\ all\ trials}} \quad (4)$$

For the calculation of the Stroop score, the standardized mean reaction times of the congruent trials were subtracted from the standardized mean reaction times of the incongruent trials (see Formula 4). The higher the difference score is, the more difficulties do the subject have to suppress the predominant response, i.e., the higher the interference.

3.4.7 Demographic questionnaire

The pretest survey assessed basic demographic and potential interfering variables to gain a composite picture of the sample. First, participants generated their individual seven-digit subject code as their anonymous identifier during the experiment. Then their sex, age (month and year of birth), native language, and education level (general and vocational education) was surveyed based on the recommendations of the Federal Statistical Office for demographic surveys in Germany (Statistisches Bundesamt *et al.*, 2010, pp. 29-49). As most of the tasks in this experiment are computer-based tasks, participants' computer usage pattern might interfere the results of the tests. Accordingly, participants were asked how many hours they played computer or video games during the last week and if this was a typical week. In the case, that the last week was not a typical week, participants had the chance to adapt their answer to a typical week by choosing from a 4-point Likert scale (*considerably less*; *less*; *more*; *considerably more*). Additionally, the participants were asked to check those input devices in a list, which they use for playing computer games and which of them they use most. Similar to the questions about playing computer games participants were asked about their further computer usage (e.g., for working or surfing the internet).

3.4.8 Funneled debriefing

At the end of the posttest, the subjects answered a five-item funneled debriefing questionnaire (Chartrand and Bargh, 1996; Wiers *et al.*, 2010), in which they were probed for awareness of the implicit training situation and the experimental manipulation. All questions were in an open-answer format to minimize interference.

The funneled debriefing questionnaire started with general questions to then getting more and more specific with each question: (1) "What do you think is the purpose of this study?" (*German*: „Was denken Sie, ist das Ziel dieser Studie?"), (2) "Do you think the tasks in this study are linked? If so, in which way?" (*German*: „Denken Sie, zwischen den einzelnen Aufgaben dieser Studie besteht eine Verbindung? Wenn ja, welche?"), (3) "Do you think your performance in a particular task influenced your performance in another task? If so, please explain in more detail." (*German*: „Denken Sie, Ihre Leistung in einzelnen Aufgaben hat die Leistung in anderen Aufgaben beeinflusst? Wenn ja, beschreiben Sie dies näher."), (4) "Did anything attract your attention notably during participation?" (*German*: „Ist Ihnen während der Teilnahme an dieser Studie etwas in besonderem Maße aufgefallen?"), and (5) "Do you think the joystick task influenced you in any way? If so, how?" (*German*: „Denken Sie, die Joystickaufgabe hat Sie beeinflusst? Wenn ja, wie?").

In this computerized questionnaire, each question appeared separately on the screen. Once subjects answered a question and navigated to the next question, they had no option to return to the previous question. Each question had to be answered with a minimum of four characters (the German word for *no* has four characters) and was limited to 700 characters.

3.5 Study design, conditions and experimental manipulation

This study was conceptualized as an independent group[81] pretest-posttest design (e.g., Greenhoot, 2003, pp. 92-96; Shaughnessy, Zechmeister and Zechmeister, 2011, pp. 187-188). Unbeknownst to participants, they were randomly assigned to one of three groups: experimental group (EG), placebo group (PG), or non-training group (NTG). The EG was trained using the Approach-Avoidance Task training, the control group one (PG) received a sham training, and the control group two (NTG) did not receive any training. Compared to repeated measures designs[82], using an independent group design has the advantages that there are no order or practice effects. However, for independent group

[81] Also referred to as between-subjects design.
[82] Also referred to as within-subjects design.

designs, a larger population is needed, and there is a risk that the randomized groups are too heterogeneous (Kantowitz, Roediger and Elmes, 2009, pp. 64-71). Potential experimenter effects could not be ruled out completely in this study, as the limited availability of personnel did not allow realizing a double-blind experiment (Shaughnessy, Zechmeister and Zechmeister, 2011, pp. 200-201). The experimenters were one research assistant and one student assistant, both from the Bundeswehr University Munich.

Besides the assignment to one of three groups, participants were assigned counterbalanced to one of two conditions, i.e., there were six possible combinations (EG1, EG2, PG1, PG2, NTG1, and NTG2). These conditions were relevant for the Approach-Avoidance Task and the Implicit Association Task. In the Approach-Avoidance Task, participants in condition one were instructed to pull pictures in portrait format and to push pictures in landscape format, whereas participants in condition two were instructed to pull pictures in landscape format and to push pictures in portrait format (see Table 6). In the Implicit Association Task, participants in condition one began with the compatible combination (OWS and words for approach; NWS and words for avoidance) in the initial combined task and completed the Implicit Association Task with the incompatible combination (OWS and words for avoidance; NWS and words for approach) in the final combined task. For participants in condition two, this assignment was reversed, i.e., they began with the incompatible combination in the initial combined task and completed the Implicit Association Task with the compatible combination (see Table 7).

3.6 Apparatus

The laboratory was located in an air-conditioned and automatically vented room without windows. The lighting was artificial and uniformly bright across all workstations. The noise level was very low, as the computers reside inside cabinets and most surfaces are composed of sound absorbing materials. In the laboratory, there were 20 workstations (e.sigma Systems GmbH, model: KOFA™ classroom console) that can be controlled from the administrator console. All workstations were equipped identically: Chairs (König + Neurath AG, model: LAMIGA), computers (operating system: Microsoft® Windows® 7 Professional SP1[83]; hardware: Intel® Core™[84] i5 3GHz processor, 8GB RAM), monitors (AG Neovo Technology, model: X-22, resolution: 1920 x 1080 pixel) on adjustable rigs, keyboards (ZF Electronics GmbH, model: G83-6104), mice (Logitech, model: Mouse M100™[85]), joysticks (Logitech, model: Extreme 3D Pro

[83] Microsoft and Windows are either registered trademarks or trademarks of Microsoft Corporation in the United States and/or other countries.

[84] Intel and Intel Core are trademarks of Intel Corporation in the U.S. and/or other countries.

[85] Mouse M100 and Extreme 3D Pro Joystick are either registered trademarks or trademarks of Logitech in the United States and/or other countries. All other trademarks are the property of their respective owners.

Joystick™, J-UK17), and headsets. Further, all instructions, tasks, and questionnaires were realized and conducted in the psychological experimentation software Inquisit Lab (version: 4.0.4) by Millisecond Software.

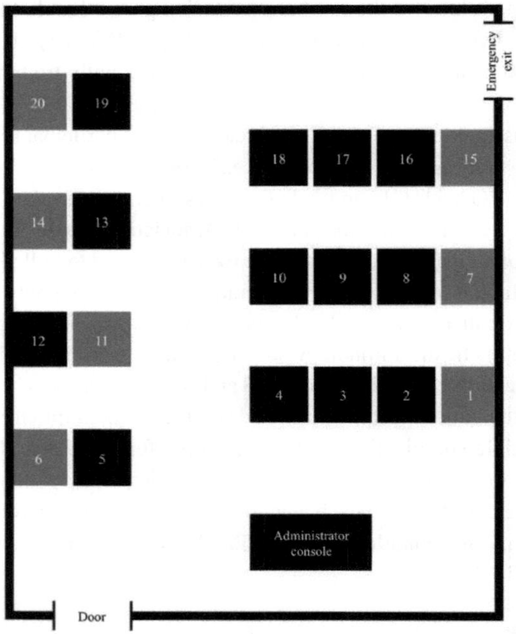

Figure 12: Laboratory seating arrangement during the experiment.

Note: Only the greyed-out workstations (1, 6, 7, 11, 14, 15, 20) were used during the experiment.

To prevent visual distraction related to movements of other participants or the tasks displayed on other computer screens, participants were seated well-spaced out so they would not disturb each other (see Figure 12). Due to technical problems that could not be solved by the IT technicians before the start of the experiment, it was not possible to use workstation 12. The participants who were planned to use this workstation were placed at workstation 11 instead. All monitors were adjusted at the same position relatively to the console desk. The keyboards and joysticks were positioned centered in front of the computer monitor. The distance of keyboards respectively joysticks and the computer monitors was the same across all workstations. The joysticks were tightly attached to the console desks so they could not slip or be moved during the experiment. Across all workstations, the headphones were adjusted to the same volume level. However, the participants were informed that they could adjust the volume according to their personal preference.

3.7 Procedure

The participants arrived at the casern in which the laboratory was located on Sunday 10 p.m. latest. The experiment started the next day and was conducted on five consecutive days, from Monday to Friday. All participants had on-site accommodation and the opportunity to take all meals in the mess. The participants could choose between two different weeks to take part in the experiment. In the first event (June 30 – July 4, 2014), there were 21 participants, and in the second event (July 28 – August 01, 2014), there were 38 participants. This disequilibrium originates from the vacation season in Germany. On Monday morning, the participants were informed about the study and the option to withdraw at any time. All groups completed the pretest on Monday, after a short break the EG and PG had the first of four training sessions (Eberl *et al.*, 2014). From Tuesday to Thursday, the EG and PG received a daily training. On Thursday, after the last training session, participants of the EG and PG took a short break. Afterward, all participants (EG, PG, NTG) completed the first part of the posttest. The second part of the posttest was conducted on Friday.

The pretest measures were operated in a fixed order after the participants accepted the informed consent and answered the demographic questionnaire they completed the behavioral task, the rating of test materials, the Implicit Association Test, the Stroop task, and the assessment version of the Approach-Avoidance Task. The posttest also had a fixed order. However, it was split into two parts to ensure that all participants finish the experiment by Friday noon. On Thursday, the participants completed the first part, including the rating of test materials, the Implicit Association Test, and the assessment version of the Approach-Avoidance Task. The second part on Friday comprised the behavioral task and the funneled debriefing.

	Event 1			Event 2		
	n (EG)	n (PG)	n (NTG)	n (EG)	n (PG)	n (NTG)
Run 1	3	2	2	3	2	2
Run 2	2	3	2	2	2	1
Run 3	2	2	3	1	2	3
Run 4	-	-	-	3	2	1
Run 5	-	-	-	2	3	2
Run 6	-	-	-	2	2	3
Overall	7	7	7	13	13	12

Table 9: Assignment of participants to groups and runs.

The subjects were tested collectively with a maximum of seven at once (see Table 9). Each run consisted of participants from all groups (EG, PG, NTG) to avoid a bias due to the time of day or uncontrollable extraneous variables (e.g., noise). The experimenters arranged the seats so that each participant used the same workstation during all stages of the experiment. The laboratory has 20 similar workstations, of which seven were used during the experiment. The participants of alternating groups were assigned counterbalanced to each workstation from run to run to prevent biases due to workstation-specific factors (e.g., different pressure point of keyboards or joysticks). Exemplarily, in the first run, workstation one was assigned to a participant from the EG; in the second run, it was assigned to a participant from the PG, and in run three, it was assigned to a participant from the NTG, et cetera.

The experiment was embedded into a general program hosted by the *Bundeswehr Air Traffic Service Office*. Presentations and activities during this program aimed to inform the candidates about topics regarding their future vocational training as air traffic controllers. The schedule of the general program and the experiment were coordinated. Accordingly, idle times for the participants were reduced as far as possible.

4 Results

4.1 Research question I: Does implicit learning change implicit associations toward an organizational routine?

4.1.1 H1: The AAT training will increase the approach tendency toward the NWS and generalize to untrained pictures.

The AAT training effect was tested with a 2 (Time: pretest, posttest) x 2 (Writing Style: NWS, OWS) x 2 (Trained Stimuli: yes, no) x 3 (Group: EG, PG, NTG) mixed ANOVA. There was no statistically significant main effect. However, there were significant interaction effects for Writing Style x Group $F(1, 56) = 3.209$, $p = .048$, $\eta_p^2 = .103$; Time x Writing Style, $F(1, 56) = 16.677$, $p < .001$, $\eta_p^2 = .229$, which both became redundant by a significant three-way interaction of Time x Writing Style x Group, $F(2, 57) = 5.860$, $p = .005$, $\eta_p^2 = .173$. The four-way interaction and the main effect Trained Stimuli were not significant (close generalization).

For both Writing Styles, a 2 (Time: pretest, posttest) x 2 (Trained Stimuli: yes, no) x 3 (Group: EG, PG, NTG) mixed ANOVA was conducted separately in the follow-up analysis. In the case of NWS, there was a significant effect of Time, $F(1, 56) = 11.342$, $p = .001$, $\eta_p^2 = .168$ superseded by a significant interaction between Time x Group, $F(2, 56) = 6.035$, $p = .004$, $\eta_p^2 = .177$. Both, the three-way interaction and the main effect Trained Stimuli were not significant (close generalization). For OWS there was only a significant effect of Time, $F(1, 56) = 4.710$, $p = .034$, $\eta_p^2 = .078$.

Figure 13 visualizes the results above and shows that the D-score depends on the interaction of group assignment with writing style and time of measurement. As indicated by the Time x Group interaction for NWS there were significant differences between the three groups in their change of approach bias from the pretest to the posttest. Accordingly, paired-sample t-tests were conducted to compare the mean D-scores of the pretest and the posttest within the particular group. The participants of the EG had a significant change from avoidance of NWS in the pretest ($M = -.074$, $SD = .237$) to approach of NWS in the posttest ($M = .304$, $SD = .284$), $t(19) = -5.180$, $p < .001$, which represents a large effect, $d = 1.356$. Neither for the PG nor for the NTG a significant change of the approach bias was found.

M. Eberl, *Organizational Routines Meet Experimental Psychology*,
Zukunftsfähige Unternehmensführung in Forschung und Praxis,
https://doi.org/10.1007/978-3-658-23562-8_4

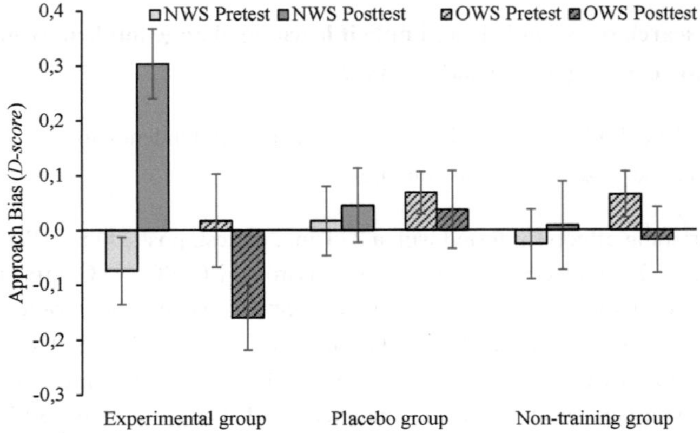

Figure 13: D-scores of the Approach-Avoidance Task for the experimental and the two control conditions separately for NWS and OWS. D-scores calculate as the difference between the standardized mean reaction times for approach movements to pictures and avoidance movements to pictures. A positive D-score value indicates an approach tendency and a negative value an avoidance tendency. Error bars indicate ±1 SEM.

4.1.2 H2: The training effect will generalize to another implicit measure (IAT).

The generalization of the AAT training effect to the IAT was tested with a 2 (Time: pretest, posttest) x 3 (Group: EG, PG, NTG) mixed ANOVA. There was a significant main effect of Time, $F(1, 56) = 9.701, p = .003, \eta_p^2 = .148$, and a statistically significant interaction effect of Time x Group, $F(2, 56) = 20.145, p < .001, \eta_p^2 = .418$. As can be seen in Figure 14, the participants in the EG significantly changed from a slight approach bias toward OWS in the pretest ($M = .066$, $SD = .490$) to a considerable approach bias toward NWS in the posttest ($M = -.474$, $SD = .495$), $t(19) = 8.736$, $p < .001$, which represents a large effect, $d = 1.096$. Both, PG and NTG had no significant change in their approach bias.

Obviously, the groups differed in their D-score levels in the pretest and the posttest (see Figure 14). In the pretest, the difference between EG and PG was not statistically significant. However, the pretest approach bias of EG ($M = .066$, $SD = .490$) and NTG ($M = -.792$, $SD = .475$) differed significantly, $t(37) = 5.550$, $p < .001$, and also the approach bias of PG ($M = -.244$, $SD = .641$) and NTG ($M = -.792$, $SD = .475$) differed statistically significant, $t(37) = 3.019$, $p = .005$. The posttest values of EG and PG, and of EG and NTG had no significant difference. However, the difference between the control groups, i.e., PG ($M = -.200$, $SD = .600$) and NTG ($M = -.715$, $SD = .491$) was significant, $t(37) = 2.925$, $p = .006$. Compared to the EG and the PG, the NTG has a conspicuously strong approach bias for NWS in both, the pretest and the posttest. There were no outliers found that might cause this bias.

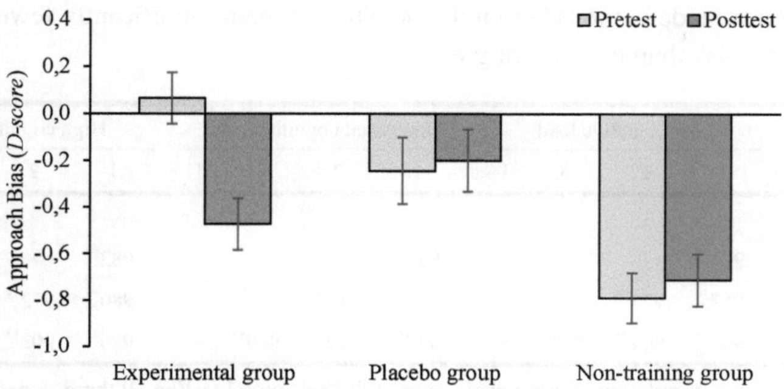

Figure 14: D-scores of the Implicit Association Test for the experimental and the two control conditions separately. D-scores calculate as within-subjects standardized difference scores, in which the latency of categorizing approach words and OWS pictures together and categorizing avoidance words and NWS pictures together was subtracted from the latency of categorizing avoidance words and OWS pictures together and categorizing approach words and NWS pictures together. A positive *D-score* value indicates an approach bias toward OWS, a negative value an approach bias toward NWS. Error bars indicate ±1 SEM.

4.2 Research question II: Does implicit learning increase the conformity of the performative outcome with the ostensive aspect of a routine?

4.2.1 H3: The training group will make fewer faults in the behavioral task (writing numerals in NWS) than the control groups.

The participants' handwritten answer sheets were evaluated by four raters separately. The evaluations of the four raters were tested for inter-rater reliability for each stage (LCL, ICL, HCL). Table 10 shows the Pearson product-moment correlation coefficients between the raters' evaluations. The inter-rater reliability was strong and highly significant, $r > .900$, $p < .001$. Due to the high inter-rater reliability, the follow-up analysis was conducted with the evaluation values of the rater A.

The ANOVA showed a significant difference between the groups in the number of errors in the behavioral task (including all three stages: LCL, ICL, HCL), $F(2, 56) = 3.738$, $p = 0.030$, $\omega^2 = .085$. Omega squared represents the effect size and is medium to high (Kirk, 1996). The subsequent independent sample t-tests allowed for comparing the groups. The average error rate of the EG ($M = 9.100$, $SD = 6.512$) and the PG ($M = 17.350$, $SD = 16.978$) differed slightly significant, $t(38) = -2.029$, $p = .050$, and also the average error rate of EG and NTG ($M = 19.000$, $SD = 10.630$) differed significantly, $t(37) = -3.527$, $p = .001$. The difference between the control groups (PG, NTG) was not statistically significant. These results indicate that the groups differ in the number of error made in the behavioral task. The EG made significantly fewer errors in the behavioral task than the control groups.

Measure	Low cognitive load				Increased cognitive load				High cognitive load			
	1	2	3	4	1	2	3	4	1	2	3	4
Rater A	–				–				–			
Rater B	.922**	–			.979**	–			.982**	–		
Rater C	.957**	.973**	–		.983**	.985**	–		.980**	.972**	–	
Rater D	.909**	.904**	.914**	–	.947**	.947**	.949**	–	.926**	.903**	.932**	–

Table 10: Inter-rater correlations for the evaluation of the behavioral task in all three stages.
Note: $N = 59$; ** $p < .001$.

4.2.2 H4: The training effect will be more distinct in a situation of high cognitive load.

The groups did not differ in the first two stages (LCL, ICL), however, in stage three (HCL) the groups showed a significant difference, $F(2, 56) = 8.328, p = .001, \omega^2 = .199$, which represents a large effect size (Kirk, 1996). The average error rate of the EG ($M = 3.250$, $SD = 3.654$) and the PG ($M = 8.350$, $SD = 6.459$) differed significantly, $t(38) = -3.074$, $p = .004$, and also the average error rate of EG and NTG ($M = 8.737$, $SD = 3.347$) differed significantly, $t(37) = -4.882$, $p < .001$. The difference between the control groups (PG, NTG) was not statistically significant. These results indicate that the groups only differed in the HCL condition significantly. The EG made significantly fewer errors in the HCL stage than the control groups.

4.2.3 H5: The size of the training effect mediates the error count in the behavioral task (HCL).

This hypothesis assumes that the change in approach bias as it is an objective of the AAT (training effect), would mediate the error count of the HCL stage in the behavioral task. It is assumed that a lager value for the change in approach bias predicts a reduced error count of the behavioral task. The change in approach bias was calculated as shown in Formula 5 from the *D-scores* of the AAT. Positive values indicate a change from approaching OWS to NWS and negative values vice versa. The more the value differs from zero, the stronger was the change in approach.

(5)
$$Change\ in\ approach\ bias = (\text{NWS}\ D\ Score_{post} - \text{OWS}\ D\ Score_{post}) - (\text{NWS}\ D\ Score_{pre} - \text{OWS}\ D\ Score_{pre})$$

Based on the mediation model for multicategorical independent predictor variables of Hayes and Preacher (2014) a mediation path analysis was conducted with a general linear model approach (Figure 15). In this model, the group that received no intervention (NTG) is the reference group and was compared to the other groups. Accordingly, there were five pathways analyzed: Path (a_1) $b_{a1} = 0.087$, $p_{a1} = .613$; Path (c'_1) $b_{c'1} = -1.147$, $p_{c'1} = .068$; Path (a_2) $b_{a2} = 0.376$, $p_{a2} = .030$; Path (c'_2) $b_{c'2} = -5.222$, $p_{c'2} < .001$; and Path (b) $b_b = -0.191$, $p_b = .718$ (Table 11).

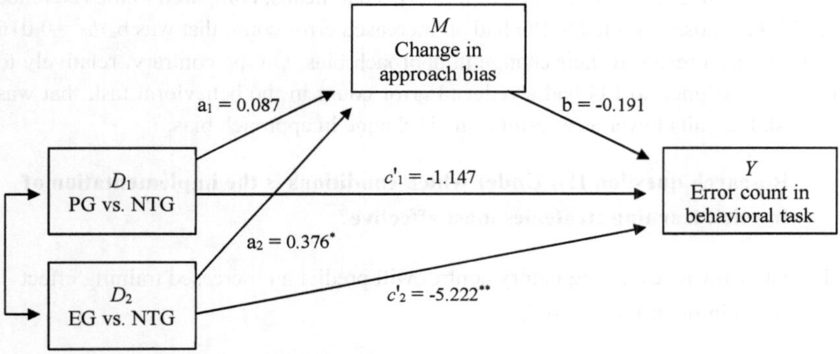

Figure 15: Mediation of error count in behavioral task.

Outcome:		***M* (Change in approach bias)**		**_Y_ (Error count in behavioral task, HCL)**		
		Coefficient (*SE*)		Coefficient (*SE*)		Coefficient (*SE*)
Constant	i_1	0.157 (0.123)	i_3	7.530** (0.453)	i_2	7.500** (0.441)
D_1	a_1	0.087 (0.171)	c_1	-1.164 (0.622)	c'_1	-1.147 (0.615)
D_2	a_2	0.376* (0.168)	c_2	-5.151** (0.643)	c'_2	-5.222** (0.606)
		$R^2 = 0.156$ $F(2,48) = 4.422$, $p = .017$		$R^2 = 0.637$ $F(3,48) = 27.438$, $p < .001$		$R^2 = 0.636$ $F(2,48) = 41.848$, $p < .001$
M					b	-0.191 (0.525)

Table 11: Mediation model coefficients and standard errors for the presumed influence of the change in approach bias on the error count in the behavioral task.

Note: Outliers in the behavioral task error count were removed from the sample, $N = 51$. * Statistically significant at no more than the .05 level, ** Statistically significant at no more than the .01 level.

The results indicate that PG changed their approach bias 0.087 units more than NTG and that EG significantly changed their approach bias 0.376 units more than the NTG. Besides, holding the training condition constant, those who achieved a higher change in approach bias also achieved a lower error count in the behavioral task ($b_b = -0.191$). However, neither for D_1 nor for D_2 there was a statistically significant relative indirect effect of Group (training condition) on the error count in the behavioral task through the change in the approach bias: (D_1) $b_{a1}b_b = 0.016$, 95% BCa CI [–.185, .450], and (D_2) $b_{a2}b_b = -0.072$, 95% BCa CI [–.778, .643]. That means, compared to the reference group (NTG), those assigned to PG had an increased error count that was $b_{a1}b_b = 0.016$ units higher as a result of their change in approach bias. On the contrary, relatively to NTG, those assigned to EG had a reduced error count in the behavioral task that was $b_{a2}b_b = -0.072$ units lower as a result of their change in approach bias.

4.3 Research question III: Under which conditions is the implementation of implicit learning strategies most effective?

4.3.1 H6: Low levels of regulatory control will predict an increased training effect on an implicit level (AAT).

It is assumed that the training effect that is represented by the change in approach bias as shown in Formula 5 will be predicted by a measure of regulatory control (RC). More precisely, lower levels of RC will predict an increased training effect on an implicit level (AAT) compared to higher levels of RC. Participants completed a Stroop Test to measure their RC respectively their lack of RC. The data was analyzed in three major steps: Firstly, the complete sample was analyzed for a Stroop effect and then probed for significant differences in the Stroop score. Secondly, the Stroop effect was calculated for each group separately and tested for significant differences to ensure there is no interference between the groups. Finally, the relationship between RC and the training effect was analyzed in a mixed model ANCOVA.

	EG (n = 20)		PG (n = 20)		NTG (n = 18)	
	M_{congr} (*SD*)	$M_{incongr.}$ (*SD*)	$M_{congr.}$ (*SD*)	$M_{incongr.}$ (*SD*)	$M_{congr.}$ (*SD*)	$M_{incongr.}$ (*SD*)
RT raw	806.231 (168.413)	962.155 (194.970)	780.219 (132.982)	904.805 (212.102)	814.233 (129.412)	959.977 (192.203)
RT standardized	2.454 (0.827)	2.896 (0.875)	2.618 (0.668)	3.000 (0.742)	2.411 (0.653)	2.795 (0.630)

Table 12: Raw and standardized mean reaction times from Stroop test reported separately for groups.

Note: Raw RTs reported in milliseconds.

Analyzing the complete sample using a paired-sample t-test showed a significant Stroop effect for both, standardized, $t(58) = 10.576$, $p < .001$, and not standardized RTs, $t(58) = 9.288$, $p < .001$. On average, participants were faster naming congruent trials, $M = 801.371$, $SD = 142.689$ ($M = 2.486$, $SD = 0.714$ for standardized RTs), compared to incongruent trials, $M = 939.247$, $SD = 197.714$ ($M = 2.879$, $SD = 0.762$ for standardized RTs). The Stroop score as a measure for RC was calculated as the difference between the standardized mean RTs for incongruent and congruent trials (see Formula 4, p. 113). The more positive the value is, the weaker is the participants' RC, i.e., the participant has a higher interference for incongruent compared to congruent trials. Across all groups, the average Stroop score was $M = 0.393$, $SD = 0.285$. One case (NTG) was excluded from the sample for the follow-up analysis, as it was an outlier (± 2 *SD* Stroop score). Analyzing the groups separately using a one-way repeated-measures 2 (Condition: congruent, incongruent) x 3 (Group: EG, PG, NTG) ANOVA yielded no significantly different Stroop effects between the groups,[86] $F(2, 55) = 0.408$, $p = .667$, $\eta_p^2 = .015$. Running the same ANOVA with standardized RTs showed similar results, $F(2, 55) = 0.176$, $p = .839$, $\eta_p^2 = .006$. Mean RTs are shown separately for the groups in Table 12.

To examine the influence of RC on the strength of the AAT training effect, a 2 (Time: pretest vs. posttest approach bias) x 3 (Group: EG, PG, NTG) mixed model ANCOVA with RC as a covariate was performed. The results indicate a significant main effect of Time, $F(1, 52) = 21.650$, $p < .001$, $\eta_p^2 = .294$ and significant interaction effects for Time x Group, $F(2, 52) = 14.282$, $p < .001$, $\eta_p^2 = .355$, for Time x RC, $F(1, 52) = 11.094$, $p = .002$, $\eta_p^2 = .176$, and most importantly a significant three-way interaction of Time x Group x RC, $F(2, 52) = 3.727$, $p = .031$, $\eta_p^2 = .125$. Separate analyses were performed for the trained (EG) and the untrained groups (PG, NTG) to break down the three-way interaction effect. For the trained group the interaction Time x RC remained significant, $F(1, 18) = 12.867$, $p = .002$, $\eta_p^2 = .417$. Neither the PG, $F(1, 18) = 0.002$, $p = .965$, $\eta_p^2 = .000$, nor the NTG, $F(1, 16) = 3.993$, $p = .063$, $\eta_p^2 = .200$, showed a statistically significant interaction of Time x RC.

These results indicate a moderating role of RC on the prediction of the AAT training effect. On average, participants with lower levels of RC have a higher benefit of the AAT training than participants with higher levels of RC have.

4.3.2 H7: Low levels of regulatory control will predict a decreased error rate on a behavioral level (behavioral task).

In this hypothesis, it is supposed that participants with lower levels of RC will perform the behavioral task of writing down numbers with a reduced error rate compared to those

[86] *Here*: Interaction of Group x RT.

with higher levels of RC. As shown in the analysis of hypothesis six, a Stroop effect as a measure for RC was found and did not differ significantly between the groups.

The relationship between RC and the error rate in the behavioral task was analyzed using a univariate ANCOVA. The covariate, RC, was not significantly related to the participant's error rate in the behavioral task, $F(1, 52) = .048$, $p = .828$, $\eta_p^2 = .001$. Running the ANCOVA separately for each group did not yield any significant relationship of RC and the error rate. This result denotes that RC could not predict the error rate in the behavioral task in this experiment.

4.4 Exploratory research question: Which factors predict the AAT training effect?

Three forced entry regressions were performed, to examine the relationship between the training effect and the RC for the EG. The first model examines the relation between the training effect (DV) and Stroop score (IV). The second model includes the Stroop score and the pretest measures from the IAT and the AAT[87] as predictors. In the third model, the Stroop score and two demographic variables (typical duration of computer utilization and the typical duration of computer gaming) were used as predictors of the training effect.[88] Before conducting the regressions, zero-order correlations for the predictors were calculated.[89] There were no statistically significant correlations between the predictors found (see Table 13).

The first regression model (see Table 14), a simple linear regression, revealed RC being a predictor of the training effect, $\beta = -0.646$, $t(18) = -3.587$, $p = .002$. RC also explained a significant proportion of variance in the training effect, $R^2 = .417$, $F(1, 18) = 12.867$, $p = .002$. RC remained a significant predictor of the training effect in regression model 2 and 3. In model 2, RC ($\beta = -0.221$, $t(16) = -3.426$, $p = .003$) and the AAT pretest D-score ($\beta = -0.672$, $t(18) = -5.118$, $p < .001$) were found to predict the training effect significantly. Testing RC in one model with the demographic variables duration of computer utilization and duration of computer gaming yielded similar results. RC remained a significant predictor ($\beta = -0.681$, $t(16) = -3.640$, $p = .002$) of the training effect. However, the demographic variables had no predictive value.

---

[87] The AAT pretest measure calculates as the difference between the AAT approach bias for NWS and OWS.

[88] The sample size of n = 20 for the EG necessitated to split the regression, as a regression with five predictors would require a sample of approximately n = 43 even when there is a large effect size to expect (Field, 2013, p. 314).

[89] Typical duration of computer utilization and computer gaming were treated as continuous variables in the correlation and regression to keep down the number of predictors in the model and accordingly to prevent a decrease of power as the sample size is relatively small.

	1	2	3	4	5
1. Regulatory control (Stroop score)	–				
2. IAT *D-score* (pretest)	.029 [-0.377, 0.522]	–			
3. AAT *D-score* (pretest)	.333 [-0.226, .693]	.322 [-0.098, 0.725]	–		
4. Computer utilization	-.279 [-0.588, 0.067]	.010 [-0.530, 0.637]	-.117 [-0.552, 0.280]	–	
5. Computer gaming	.026 [-0.441, 0.561]	-.209 [-0.630, 0.209]	-.239 [-0.568, 0.103]	.430 [-0.104, 0.814]	–

Table 13: Correlations between regulatory control, IAT *D-score*, AAT *D-score*, Computer utilization, and Computer gaming utilization as product moment correlation coefficients.

Note: BCa bootstrap 95% CIs reported in brackets. * Statistically significant at no more than the .05 level, ** Statistically significant at no more than the .01 level. All data was standardized (z-scores).

	b	***SE B***	***ß***	***p***
Model 1				
Constant	0.612	0.099		< .001
Stroop score (RC)	-0.336	0.094	-0.646	.002
		R^2 = .417, *F*(1, 18) = 12.867, *p* = .002		
Model 2				
Constant	0.538	0.084		< .001
AAT *D-score* (pretest)	-0.249	0.049	-0.672	< .001
Stroop score (RC)	-0.221	0.064	-0.425	.003
IAT *D-score* (pretest)	0.078	0.090	0.108	.398
		R^2 = .783, *F*(3, 16) = 19.286, *p* < .001		
Model 3				
Constant	0.615	0.097		< .001
Stroop score (RC)	-0.354	0.097	-0.681	.002
Computer utilization	0.166	0.105	0.317	.131
Computer gaming	-0.055	0.118	-0.096	.651
		R^2 = .499, *F*(3, 16) = 5.312, *p* = .010		

Table 14: Linear regression models of predictors of the training effect.

5 Discussion

This study brings together two fields of research: Organizational routines and experimental psychology. Addressing the overall research question, whether implicit learning can diminish the gap between the ostensive and performative aspect of an organizational routine, this study showed the synergetic value of consolidating insights from research on routines and experimental psychology. In this final chapter, some of the main theoretical and experimental insights will be recapped and will be integrated into the results of the experimental study. The structure of the contributions of this study corresponds to the conceptual themes that were introduced in the theoretical background of organizational routines and divide into a vertical, a horizontal and a time perspective.

- The ***vertical perspective*** highlights the varying impact dual processes respectively impulsive processes across the hierarchy of (collective) entities in organizations. This perspective contributes to routine research by bridging the micro-macro gap through aligning inappropriate routine performances to the ostensive aspect respectively the above entities.
- The ***horizontal perspective*** discusses the role of implicit learning strategies in the context of replication as a mechanism to spread a routine in an organization. The Approach Avoidance Task training proved to be an efficient instrument to replicate a part of a routine across several individuals in a way that the result of the replication corresponds to the organizational ostensive aspect.
- The ***time perspective*** addresses change in and of organizational routines and contributes to routine research by integrating cognitive bias modification as a seminal approach for controlling the change of organizational routines and for escaping situations of path-dependence.

5.1 Summary

Following the basic approach of this thesis, to offer a comprehensive understanding of the theoretical background, this section gives a recap of the main theoretical ideas introduced in Chapter 2 on organizational routines, learning as a fundamental topic for routines, and the duality of learning. Subsequently, the results of the behavioral experiment on cognitive bias modification will be summarized and interpreted.

5.1.1 Organizational routines – the manifold and blurry concept

Organizational routines suffer from conceptual blurriness and while processing routine literature one will quickly realize that the "[…] *term is used by many people in many different contexts, and, it seems, to describe many different 'things'*" (Becker, 2004, p. 664). The authors on routines built on diverse sets of data and theoretical foundations. There are those that are mainly interested in the output of routines (capabilities

M. Eberl, *Organizational Routines Meet Experimental Psychology*, Zukunftsfähige Unternehmensführung in Forschung und Praxis, https://doi.org/10.1007/978-3-658-23562-8_5

perspective), or in contrast those that seek to open up the black box to explain the functioning of routines (practice perspective). In other words, there are those who use a bottom-up approach and construct their understanding of routines from the individual level (e.g., habits), as against those who strictly put forward the organizational level and redline the individual actor from their models. At some points in literature, it appears as if an organizational routine allows to explain all and nothing: An organization's output and its utilization of resources; its internal dynamics of change, social conflict, learning and even the dynamics of decay; its mindful but also mindless actions; and so on and so forth.

The approach taken here offers a more holistic view and tries to integrate the various schools of thought at best possible – knowingly that an entirely holistic picture is unobtainable. However, the reader learned about the origin of routine research at the level of habits and the subsequent development of the concept including the influential writings of Simon, March, and Cyert, as well as Nelson and Winter (Simon, 1947; March and Simon, 1958; Cyert and March, 1963; Nelson and Winter, 1982). Based on those publications and the subsequent literature, four widespread characteristics of organizational routines were introduced: *recurrence*, as well as the *patterned*, the *processual* and the *collective nature*.

As discussed in Chapter 2.1 in more detail, organizational routines constitute by their *recurrence*, which allows them to become automatic in their processing. The characteristic of the *patterned nature* of routines is essential in many definitions. However, it is also a point of ambiguousness, as literature describes patterns of behavior, action, activities, or interaction. Even if there is a taxonomy within these kinds of patterns, they at least allow choosing a level for establishing a routine within the organization. The *processual nature* of routines describes the link between an organization as a structured object and its function of organizing as a process, much in the sense of the ostensive-performative distinction by Feldman and Pentland (2003) and its link to structure and agency. Becker's (2004) approach of exemplifying the processual nature of routines by using three dimensions made the magnitude of automaticity involved in routines quickly comprehensible. The three dimensions include the frequency of repetition, the regularity of the frequency, and the time pressure the routine actors face while performing a routine. Finally, the *collective aspects* of a routine are obvious throughout literature. They underline the immanent heterogeneity of routines and accordingly of organizations. This collective nature also involves the idea of distributed heterogeneous knowledge that may impede organizations in achieving a constant performance level.

Building on the essence of routines' characteristics, four influencing analogies were introduced as they show the thinking of the protagonists of routine research: Routines interpreted as *rules* compare to computer programs in the way of repetitious, explicit and conditional if-this-then-that sequences. The *routines as genes* analogy has a strong evolutionary biological background and integrates the thoughts of Darwin's evolutionary theory into routine research. Accordingly, only those organizations which exercise routines that are well adapted to environmental needs and challenges will survive. Routines viewed as *grammatical models* draw the parallel to linguistic models of grammar and describe routines as a set of possible actions that the actor can combine to various grammatically correct forms of the routine. Finally, the analogy of routines as *procedural memory* aligns with the idea of declarative and procedural knowledge as known from psychology. Routines encapsulate the procedural knowledge (i.e., know-how), which is relatively automatic and inarticulate (cf., declarative knowledge).

Summing up, the analogies cover a broad variety of influences from other fields of research but do not necessarily allow for orientation. Whether routines are seen as rules, genes, grammatical models or procedural memory, it may appear that all of these analogies center around keywords borrowed from other domains, such as mathematics, biology, linguistics, or psychology. The introduced analogies do certainly not have the explanatory power for routines as they have in their original context, for example, the role of genes in biological evolutionary theory.

Research typically advances by falsification and incremental gain of (new) knowledge. In this regard, one might interpret the path that routine research followed as indispensable in approximating a clear understanding of the concept. However, the combination of the explanatory approaches so far – even if some of them proved as weak – helped us to develop a rich, but a still blurry understanding of how organizations accomplish their work by using routines and what can be achieved by smooth functioning routines. Six effects demonstrate the potential output of organizational routines:

(1) *Coordination and control* results from the patterned and repetitious nature of routines that makes subsequent actions predictable and thus allows for controlling current and future performances.

(2) *Building truces* refers to the ability of routines to spread a shared understanding of repetitious processes in organizations; at least to a level that enables the actors to overcome or at best to resolve conflicts that arise from different individual motivations.

(3) *Regularity and reduction of uncertainty* arise from the inherent patterns of routines that provide the actors with stability and courses of action in uncertain situations.

(4) *Path-dependence* or in an extreme form lock-ins stem from the recursive relationship of action and history in organizational routines that conserves past decisions at the abstract level of the routine, which in consequence shapes the performance.

(5) *Preservation of knowledge* is one of the core effects of routines that involves artifacts for keeping the declarative knowledge and the actual performance of the routine for sustaining the procedural or tacit knowledge.

(6) *Economizing cognitive resources* is one of the desired effects organizations wish for by applying routines, as they have bound cognitive resources and an efficient use of these resources in standard situations enables them to handle non-routine situations successfully.

5.1.2 Learning at the heart of routines: Toward an integrated approach to variation in organizational routines

Routines, as described in this publication, are an organizational concept that builds on individuals as the foundation. Characterized by recurrence, patterns, the processual nature and the collective embedment, routines allow the organization members to perform the organization's tasks more efficiently. Routines are a form of organizational memory and preserve knowledge of both kinds, tacit and declarative (Miner, Ciuchta and Gong, 2008; Miller, Pentland and Choi, 2012). Before the knowledge about the characteristics and in particular the contents of a routine become part of the organizational memory and can be performed, it first has to be acquired – in organizations usually by experiential learning (backward-looking logic; Gavetti and Levinthal, 2000; Eggers and Kaplan, 2013). As described earlier, the role of individuals is bold regarding routines. Due to the collective nature of routines and the embeddedness into the organizational structure, the role individuals take in organizational routines is not necessarily apparent. However, using the approach of methodological individualism allows to break down collective entities, such as routines, into individual actions and the knowledge fractions held by individuals. The acquisition of this knowledge and actions occurs on the individual level; as Herbert Simon (1991, p. 125) sustentative noted, "[a]*ll learning takes place inside individual human heads*." In consequence, that means that "[o]*rganizations learn only through individuals who learn*" (Senge, 1990, p. 124).

Alongside with perception, interpretation, and the moderation of personal interests, *learning* of routine knowledge belongs to the individual psychological processes that precede the performance of a routine. These individual psychological processes take place with each repetition of a routine and may even go along with the execution of actions in a routine. However, the individual's learning curve for routines is on a diminishing scale. Accordingly, with each repetition of a routine, the individual actor will learn less. This idea is in line with the routines' effect of economizing cognitive resources. Nevertheless, individual cognition can also be the impeding factor for the accumulation of routine knowledge in organizations and the homogenous functioning of routines (Rice and Cooper, 2010, pp. 131-133). Exemplarily, the personal interests of the organization members may oppose the organizational goals and thus prevent the advancement and innovation of a routine. Bringing together the points above leads to one of the unsolved challenges in routine research, the deviation between the ostensive and performative aspect of routines or in other words, the variance between the performances of the same ostensive aspect by different actors. In particular, this issue becomes relevant if an organization aims for the deliberate change of a routine.

Change, in general, is a central topic in the field of routines. It *requires* (re)learning of parts of the routine or in some cases even the complete routine to evolve from the current state to the next state of the routine (Feldman and Pentland, 2003; Farjoun, 2010). Basically, two forms of change can be distinguished: deliberate change (e.g., modeling of grammatical rules) and non-deliberate change (e.g., mutation, or drift). Each of these forms can be approached from an individual or an organizational perspective, which can be conflictive (e.g., agency dilemma). Not only today's dynamic technological progress, but also the decreasing life-cycles of products, services, and organizations per se require the change of routines and importantly an organization that is open to change.

The management's and leader's chance to entirely control change in organizations, whether it concerns routines or other areas, is very limited. On average only one of three change initiatives is successful (Kotter, 1996; Aiken and Keller, 2009). One of the frequently named reasons why change initiatives in organizations fail is the missing anchorage in the organizational culture, which is a key element to shape individuals into a collectively acting organization (see Chapter 2.1.2.2). The shared assumptions, values, and beliefs that are the basis for an organizational culture are also the basis for the reflective interpretation of routines and rules underlying routines in the sense of Wittgenstein (1956, I.113; see also Reynaud, 2005). To create or change an organizational culture is a time-consuming and slow "[…] *process that is exceptionally difficult*" (Schein, 1985 [2004], p. 243; see also p. 36). The leader and/or management thus will regularly fail in adapting the culture so as to the actors interpret the changed routine as it was intended. Such misinterpretation of the deliberately changed routine – frequently reflected in a changed ostensive aspect – results in performances that do not meet the expectation formulated by ostensive aspect. That means the ostensive and the performative aspect are decoupled and in a variety of cases also the different performative aspects among each other.

In consequence, both, the cognitive constraints for learning but also the challenges in regard to organizational change and culture result in routines that are missing the target. Organizations often successfully accomplish the task to create or change the codified or in artifacts expressed part of their routine's ostensive aspect (i.e., the ideal schematic form of a routine) that should give the actor reference, guidance, and explanation while performing a routine (Feldman and Pentland, 2003). However, as outlined in Chapter 2.1, this structural element does not necessarily result in the desired performance. On the contrary, the implementation of such a structural element may result in resistance (e.g., the NIH syndrome). In those cases, the organization is not able to keep the balance between stability and change as needed for survival. In fact, often the contrary occurs: Organizations create a misbalance between change and stability that has two extremes. On the one hand, it may lead to an endless circle of change initiatives.

Each circle conceived to *optimize* or also to outweigh the recent change initiative, which presumably did not lead to the routine that was targeted. However, an endless journey like this can be stressful for the individuals in terms of emotion, motivation, and orientation. In contrast, the other extreme would be an organization or management that does not dare to initiate change and accordingly results in a rigid organization with rigid routines. Both of these extremes make organizations increasingly incapable of sustainably developing, taking action, and participating in the market.

By breaking these thoughts down to the individual level, it becomes apparent that the learning mechanisms used by organizations are not as fruitful as one might expect. Most learning in organizations has an explicit character (e.g., reading manuals, or ex-cathedra teaching). However, as highlighted in the introductive section about learning theory (Chapter 2.2.1), psychology has to offer a variety of other forms of learning. Since psychology is a natural science[90] and accordingly in most cases uses experimental and quantitative approaches to its research topics, all of the introduced forms of learning are well probed and documented. That becomes evident when viewing the learning paradigms that were introduced in Chapter 2.2.1. All of the original studies for these paradigms were replicated manifold. Research on organizational routines is often the opposite, a collection of cases based on qualitative data, which usually is not replicable and has limited generalizability. At this point, routine researchers may learn from psychological research, especially from experimental psychology that offers a wide body of in-depth knowledge about the methodological foundations that are regularly overlooked in case studies or qualitative approaches in general (Narduzzo and Warglien, 2008).

Integrating those fundamental ideas into routine research could advance routine research substantially on both, the individual and the collective level. For example, in Geiger's and Schröder's (2014) conceptual paper on the rule-based nature of routines, they integrated reinforcement as part of operant conditioning (behavioral psychology) into their conceptual approach. However, they did not use the existing body of knowledge on this type of learning in-depth (or did not demonstrate it). They neither distinguish between positive or negative reinforcement in their model nor do they prove the model experimentally in a subsequent study. In other fields of research, it looks different. So, in the research on work-related compensation models, there are experiments using the profound knowledge of the behavioral concept of operant conditioning (e.g., Cadsby, Song and Tapon, 2007). Or, giving another example, the influence of organizational culture on the drift and dynamics of routines is, as highlighted earlier, crucial for understanding the failure of routines and the replication of routines. Bertels, Howard-Grenville and Pek (2016) picked exactly that topic for their qualitative case study. Without going into the theory of social learning. They basically described the socially learned organizational culture as a driver for the interpretation

[90] Knowingly that others would put emphasis for psychology on humanities or social sciences.

and specific performance of routines. Again, other areas of research on organizations do use the methodology and existing psychological knowledge about social learning systematically (e.g., Celen, Kariv and Schotter, 2010).

These two examples point directly to the fundamental problem in research on organizational routines: Scholars from this domain seem to be reinventing the wheel again and again. The approach taken here tries to avoid that shortcoming by building a rich foundation for both, the theory of organizational routines as well as the psychology of learning. As learning is at the heart of routines, we should address the numerous and obvious theoretical holes by integrating the well-proven knowledge from other domains to achieve a symbiosis of routine research and related fields of research.

5.1.3 What experimental psychology can contribute to research on routines

The duality of learning. Experimental psychology has, as mentioned, a large treasure chest of models, methods, and paradigms that could be fruitful for various domains. That counts true for the research on organizational routines too. One of these models is the duality of learning that builds on the duality of mind with the impulsive-reflective distinction of information processing (Strack and Deutsch, 2004). There is explicit learning on the one hand and implicit learning on the contrary. Explicit learning is a process that occurs consciously in which the individual is willingly engaged and accordingly explicit learning enables the learner to select the contents that should be learned. Implicit learning as introduced earlier (see Chapter 2.2.3) differs in several respects. The central characteristic of implicit learning is the individual's missing ability for verbalizing what has been acquired. In other words, the individual knows more than she or he can express (Frensch, 1998; Cleeremans, 2006b). Hence, the process of implicit learning often occurs without the insight or awareness of the learning situation and the contents to be acquired (Reber, 1967; Perrig, 1996, p. 212). Also, the intention to learn does not have to be present. This every-day phenomenon is not limited to the common examples like riding a bicycle or dribbling a basketball. It can also be found in complex tasks of higher-order cognitive processes like medical diagnosis or playing chess (Cleeremans, 2006a).

To date, there is little known about the interaction of implicit and explicit learning (Lopes, 2011, p. 27). In practical learning situations that usually do not come along with the chance of controlling the situation as it is possible in laboratories, it is to expect that both forms of learning cannot be clearly separated from each and thus occur simultaneously. As proven by Sanchez and Reber (2013; see also Wiers *et al.*, 2011), explicit pre-instruction does not influence the result of the implicit learning situation, although it leads to explicit learning. As implicit and explicit learning interact, it is surprising that implicit learning finds little attention in organizational research and especially in research on organizational routines. Disregarding implicit learning (and also impulsive processes in general) in organizational change processes such as the advancement or replication of organizational routines results in the issues illustrated in Chapter 5.1.2. Including implicit learning paradigms as standard tools to the methodological portfolio of routine researchers could advance and accelerate the purposeful gain of insights on organizational routines. Using a paradigm like the Approach-Avoidance Task training facilitates to focus on the process of implicit learning. The Approach-Avoidance Task training used in the experiment of this study fulfills the above-mentioned characteristics of implicit learning and builds on the fundamental principles of other implicit learning paradigms, such as Serial Reaction Time Tasks (Brockmeyer *et al.*, 2015; Brockmeyer, Schmidt and Friederich, 2016).

The duality of mind. The distinction between explicit and implicit learning, made in the duality of learning, is crucial in understanding how the different types of processing in the dual process theory (see Chapter 2.2.2) can be modified. Reflective processing (type 2) is conscious and builds on rules and explicit knowledge, which leads to noetic decision-making about the behavioral schemata to apply in a given situation. Changing the rules or the explicit knowledge can be achieved by explicit learning rather easily and consequently, results in changing the behavioral schemata that arise from the reflective processing. On the contrary, impulsive processes are nonconscious and base on associative knowledge. Thus, type 1 processing is fast, highly automatic, of low effort and high capacity. However, as this type of processing is rather inaccessible for the modification by explicit learning, it requires a different approach. Implicit learning allows accessing those impulsive processes that are at the bottom of the individual's automatically retrieved behavioral schemata and skills (e.g., writing numbers in a specific way). Kaufman *et al.* (2010) provided evidence that implicit learning is the most promising approach to change impulsive processes. As high cognitive loads, e.g., in air traffic control, reduce the individual's ability to process information reflectively and derive behavioral schemata by this conscious processing, it is substantial to be able to modify such impulsive processes to not result in an organization that does not learn and suffers from rigid processes.

Summing up, in this study, challenges of organizational research meet methodological approaches and insights from experimental psychology, in particular from the psychology of learning. Thus, the experiment conducted in this study allowed for successfully modifying impulsive processes in organizational routines by applying a paradigm of implicit learning, the Approach-Avoidance Task training. More specifically, the organizational routine of completing a flight progress strip, which is part of the capability of air-traffic control, was modified. The subjects implicitly relearned the writing style of specific numerals to meet the requirements of air-traffic control, as formulated in the ostensive aspect (i.e., operations manual).

5.1.4 Experimental study: Implicit learning in organizational routines

The experiment conducted in this study is the first experiment that transfers cognitive bias modification using the Approach-Avoidance Task training as a paradigm of implicit learning from experimental psychology to economics. Against the background of conceptual and methodological issues in research on organizational routines, a small piece of a routine should be implicitly relearned by the subjects. Based on the military capability of operating air traffic control, the routine of completing a flight progress strip offered a skill of manageable scope to conduct this experiment as a fundament for further research. This skill is writing specific numerals (0, 1, 7, and 9) in specific styles that are subject to the requirements of air traffic control. The subjects, fifty-nine candidates for the Bundeswehr air-traffic control service, were split into one training and two control groups. In an independent group pretest-posttest design, the training group was tested against the control groups and received four Approach-Avoidance Task training sessions. The training effect and its generalization were quantified with two implicit measures (AAT, IAT) and a behavioral task. Additional tasks (e.g., Stroop color-word task) were conducted to complement the main data.

Four research questions were addressed with this experiment. Three of these questions build on hypothesis testing, the fourth is an exploratory research question and thus omnidirectional. As shown in the results section, five of the seven hypotheses proved true, and two did not. This section discusses the results as a basis for the implications in the subsequent section.

Research question 1. The first research question asks if implicit learning does change implicit associations toward an organizational routine. Two hypotheses were proved to answer this question. Hypothesis one (H1) assumes that the AAT training will increase the approach tendency toward the new writing style and generalizes to untrained pictures. The results of the ANOVA indicated a training effect (AAT D-score) that depends on the interactions of the group assignment (experimental group, placebo group, and non-training group) with the writing style (new writing style, old writing style) and with the time of measurement (pretest, posttest). The subsequent paired-sample t-tests proved the first part of this hypothesis true and revealed a highly significant change in the approach tendency toward the new writing style for the experimental group. Importantly, for both control groups, there was no significant change in the approach tendency toward the new writing style. Also, the close generalization of the training effect, which is the second part of this hypothesis, proved true. The posttest used additional pictures that were not employed in the pretest and also not in the training sessions. There was no statistically significant difference between trained and untrained pictures in the posttest, which means that the subjects did not develop an approach tendency toward the training material by the mere exposure effect, but developed an approach tendency toward the new style of writing.

After the close generalization with the same measure proved true, the second hypothesis (H2) assumes that the training effect will generalize to another implicit measure, the Implicit Association Test (IAT). As the IAT is also an indirect measure, this generalization occurs within the same type of reaction time-based measures. The D-score of the IAT is a within-subject difference score that combines the latency in approaching/avoiding the new and the old writing style. An ANOVA provided evidence of a highly significant interaction effect of time (pretest, posttest) and group (experimental group, placebo group, and non-training group). Based on the assignment to the groups, the subsequent paired sample t-tests revealed that there was a highly significant change from an approach tendency toward the old writing style in the pretest to an approach tendency toward the new writing style in the posttest for the experimental group which received training. For the control groups, there was no significant change in the approach bias. Accordingly, the hypothesis proved true as the training effect could be verified with another implicit measure than the AAT.

Regarding the first research question, the two hypotheses clearly indicated that it succeeded to change implicit associations by implicit learning. Both measures used here indicated this change on a highly significant level. Substantially, this was proven within the same implicit measure (AAT) with a close generalization onto new materials, but also with a different implicit measure (IAT) as a further generalization. The outcome of this research question is fundamental for this experimental study and also for the application of the AAT training outside the field of clinical psychology. There was no study found, that used the AAT training as a paradigm of implicit learning in other than psychological applications yet. So, the experiment conducted here can be viewed as the seminal work to bring such type of implicit training into economics and importantly in a setting that allows for practical day-to-day use in organizations.

Research question 2. The second research question approaches more specifically the issues of routines in practice and asks if implicit learning increases the conformity of the performative outcome of a routine with its ostensive aspect. Routine research repeatedly highlighted the deviation of routines when processing from the ostensive to the performative aspect. In other words, the tangible outcome of a routine (i.e., the performance) does not meet the ideal schematic form of the routine (i.e., the ostensive aspect). That omnipresent issue was addressed here with a transfer task. It was tested if the training effect that proved true by using an implicit measure transfers to the behavioral level. As introduced in the section on dual process models (Chapter 2.2.2), implicit and reflective processing occur parallel – at which the impulsive system is always involved but the reflective system not necessarily. This is due to the high amount of cognitive capacity the reflective system requires, and low amount of cognitive capacity impulsive system requires. Furthermore, reflective processes can be changed rather easily, whereas impulsive processes are hard to change. The behavioral task conducted in this experiment consisted of three different stages with varying cognitive loads (i.e., under low, increased, and high cognitive load). The higher the cognitive load, the lower the free cognitive capacity for reflective processing of how to write the numbers according to the task requirement (i.e., writing down the audio stimuli in the new writing style). Three hypotheses were prepared to answer the research question.

The first hypothesis to answer this research question states that the training group will make fewer faults in the behavioral task than the control groups (H3). This hypothesis views the complete behavioral task with the three different levels of cognitive load (i.e., low, increased, and high cognitive load) and allows for proving if the training effect that was verified for the training group (EG) with an implicit measure transferred to the behavioral level. Expectedly, the training group differed significantly from the control groups, whereas the control groups amongst each other did not show a significant difference. Accordingly, the training took effect on the behavioral level in a task that compares to a realistic setting in air traffic control. That insight is of value as it puts the path for applying the training outside the laboratory. Measuring the training effect on the implicit level shows that it succeeded to modify the impulsive processes (research question 1). However, it does not reflect a change in the behavioral schemata and the actual behavior. Demonstrating the training effect with the behavioral task is accordingly a purposeful step toward the practical advantage of implicit learning in modifying organizational routines.

As the generalization on the behavioral level succeeded and prior research suggested that the impulsive system shows to advantage more in situations of reduced cognitive capacity, the next hypothesis picks up that insight. The second hypothesis (H4) to support answering this research question assumes that the training effect will be more distinct in a situation of high cognitive load. In other words, in a situation of less cognitive capacity for reflective processing. For reference, the training effect needs to be viewed in comparison to the control groups, as they did not show a significant training effect. The training group did not differ significantly from the control groups in the conditions of low and increased cognitive load, which denotes that all groups had a similar point of balance between impulsive and reflective processing in those conditions. It may also show that all groups had enough free cognitive capacity to process the task of writing the numerals in the new style reflectively and thus the implicitly manipulated impulsive processes did not take effect significantly. However, in the condition of high cognitive load, the groups showed significant differences. The trained group significantly outperformed the placebo and the non-training group and made fewer faults. Because the condition of high cognitive load requires more cognitive capacity than the other conditions, it involves more impulsive and less reflective processing for the writing of the numerals.

Accordingly, the implicit training effect shows to advantage more distinct in situations of a high cognitive load than in situations of a lower cognitive load. For the specific task of writing numerals in air traffic control, this insight is useful. It enables organizations, such as the Bundeswehr, to assure a low level of faults (or even no faults at all) in situations of high cognitive load (e.g., high volume of inbound traffic, or in an emergency procedure). So far, these were the typical situations for air traffic controllers to revert to their old writing style. In consequence, the positive result of proving this hypothesis has a profound meaning for air traffic control in practice: In situations of low and medium cognitive load (e.g., normal operation), the air traffic controllers have the cognitive resources to follow the requirements of writing at least by processing the skill of writing reflectively. However, in situations of a high cognitive load with less capacity for reflective processing, they now fall back on the modified impulsive process – the new writing style.

The last hypothesis (H5) attributed to this research question assumes that the size of the training effect mediates the error count in the high cognitive load condition of the behavioral task. Accordingly, the subjects that realized a larger training effect are expected to make fewer faults in the high cognitive load condition of the behavioral task, and in contrast, subjects with a lower training effect are supposed to have a higher error count in that situation. Applying a mediation model for multicategorical independent predictor variables that uses the change in the approach bias as the predictor variable, the mediation effect of this predictor on the error count of the behavioral task was analyzed (see Chapter 4.2.3). The non-training group served as reference. The results verify the prior results and show both, a significant training effect (change in approach bias) for the training group and a highly significant lower error count for the training group in the high cognitive load condition of the behavioral task. In contrast, for the placebo group, there were no significant effects. However, besides confirming the prior results, the current hypothesis (H5) could not be proved true. The path that describes the effect of the training groups' significantly higher change in the approach bias did not result in a significantly lower error count in the behavioral task.

For two reasons the result is not entirely surprising: (1) The population size is rather small. For the mediation analysis, the group size in this experiment is at the lower bound and thus may be more likely biased than in a larger population with correspondently larger groups. However, the population in this experiment was the complete sample of students that have not started their air traffic control class at that time. One might argue, that it would be possible to include following students in the subsequent years to achieve a larger sample. Due to restrictions of time, costs and other resources, that was not possible. (2) The mediation model applied here to test the mediation of the training effect on the error count in the high cognitive load condition of the behavioral task is, like most models, a simplification of systems that are too complex to view them to the full extent. As the human mind is probably the most complex system that we know, it would be surprising if the simplification that the mediation model reflects meets the processes occurring in the black box called human mind. That challenge accompanies many studies in psychopathology that try to shed light on the cognitive processes of the human mind. So, the mediation model taken here should be seen as nothing more than an attempt to illustrate something we do not understand entirely (i.e., the human mind) with the limited methods and knowledge that we have available today. There might be other cognitive processes that we do not even know today but which influence both, the training effect as well as the error count in the behavioral task. Accordingly, the result of the mediation analysis is not clearly allegeable from a today's point of view.

Research question 3. The third research question views the aspect of a successful implementation of an implicit training as conducted in this experiment. It asks under which conditions the implementation of implicit learning strategies is most effective. As prior research identified a potential role of regulatory control for implicit learning, the focus for this research question is on this factor as a predictor of the success of an implicit training. The regulatory control was measured with the well-known Stroop color-word interference task. Two hypothesis were tested to answer this research question.

First, it was hypothesized that low levels of regulatory control will predict an increased training effect on an implicit level (H6); measured with the Approach-Avoidance Task D-score. In more detail, the lower the level of regulatory control, the higher the training effect that will be realized with the Approach-Avoidance Task training. The analysis of covariance yielded a significant predictive influence of the individual's regulatory control on the size of the training effect for the training group. In contrast, for both control groups, there was no significant covariation of the regulatory control on the extent of the approach bias. Accordingly, the size of an individual's regulatory control serves as a predictor for the training effect. As hypothesized, the individuals with a low level of regulatory control will more likely realize a strong training effect than those with a high level of regulatory control.

On the basis of this insight, it can be assumed that subjects of a higher regulatory control also have a higher cognitive capacity. A higher regulatory control consequently qualifies those subjects for a more reflective processing than those with a lower cognitive capacity. Here, it is crucial to highlight that higher/lower cognitive capacity is irrespective of intelligence. As mentioned earlier, implicit learning is to the greatest extent irrespective of intelligence, age, and other cognitive factors. Here, regulatory control refers to the individual's ability to suppress an impulsive process that would result in an automatic behavior. Those individuals that do not have that ability are not able to bypass the impulsive action tendency into a reflective process to deliberately make their decision about an action based on balancing the consequences, information, and other influencing factors. A limitation for the relevance for practice in an applied setting, such as an organization, is that the training effect is an implicit measure that not necessarily reflects a behavioral change in the performance of a routine or similar. However, to countervail this weakness, the next hypothesis complements to the current hypothesis and transfers the idea of regulatory control being a predictor of the success of the implementation of an implicit training to the behavioral level.

Accordingly, the next hypothesis (H7) assumes that a low level of regulatory control will predict a decreased error rate on the behavioral level. This assumption was tested in an ANCOVA using the error count of the high cognitive load stage of the behavioral task and as a covariate the Stroop effect as a measure for the regulatory control. As the results indicate, the hypothesis did not prove true. There was no significant predictive effect of the regulatory control for the error count in the behavioral task verifiable. Besides the population size, there might be another explanation for this result. All subjects were recruited from the career path of military air traffic control service and are rather homogenous regarding age and education. However, most importantly the subjects were preselected for this career path by accomplishing a selection procedure that focusses on cognitive factors (e.g., multi-tasking, decision-making, perception, attention, and logical reasoning). Only subjects that perform above a predefined threshold will be accepted for the training as air traffic controller. Accordingly, in all probability, the subjects of this experiment outperform an average population regarding their cognitive abilities such as regulatory control. Against this background, the results realized in this experimental study become even more valuable as it is to expect that a normally distributed population would go along with lower levels of cognitive abilities (in particular executive functions) and accordingly with higher training effects, or in general with more distinct results proving the applicability of cognitive bias modification in organizational settings.

Nevertheless, regulatory control did not prove true being a predictor for the error rate in the behavioral task; it appears as a promising predictor for the effectiveness of the implementation of an implicit learning strategy based on the Approach-Avoidance Task. As highlighted, on an implicit level this is the case. However, on the behavioral level and with the population of this experiment, regulatory control did not allow any prediction of the prospective result in the behavioral task. Although this research question cannot generally be answered for both levels, the implicit and the behavioral level, it at least allows for predicting the implicit training effect. Thus, a short (< 5 minutes), inexpensively scalable and reasonably reliable, as well as valid test, enables organizations to predict whether the organization members will realize a training effect or not. This prediction can be a first indicator of the effectiveness of the implementation of an implicit learning strategy. As the behavioral level is the level where the outcome of such strategy becomes a tangible performance, the role of regulatory control as predictor should be addressed in future studies to clarify its power in projecting behavioral changes.

Exploratory research question. In this research question, possible factors were explored that might predict the AAT training effect for the trained subjects (i.e., exclusively for the EG). Three regression analyses tested the predictive potential of five variables. The first model tested the Stroop score as a predictor for the training effect and found a significant predictive value of it. Additionally, the Stroop score as the measure of regulatory control also allowed explaining a proportion of the variance of the training effect within the training group, which further supports the results of hypothesis H6. The Stroop score also remained a significant predictor in the following regression models.

Besides the Stroop score, the second model tested the pretest D-scores of the Approach-Avoidance Task and the Implicit Association Test as predictors for the training effect. The pretest D-score from the Approach-Avoidance Task turned out to be a highly significant predictor for the training effect. Accordingly, the AAT pretest allows identifying those subjects that most likely will achieve a certain training effect and thus allows to sort out those who will not reach a specific threshold (e.g., determined by a cost-value analysis). In contrast, the pretest D-score of the Implicit Association Test could not be verified as a significant predictor, which is interesting as it is also an implicit measure. However, it does not link the compatibility of the stimulus to an approach/avoidance-reaction in the form of a body movement, but to a category that the subject assigns to the stimulus by the press of a key. This may be less intuitive than the joystick movement of the AAT.

Finally, the third regression model additionally tested for the predictive value of computer utilization and computer gaming (both determined as continuous time variables). These computer-usage-related variables were of interest, as the Approach-Avoidance Task training is computer based and one might expect a bias for those subjects that regularly use a computer or a joystick. As the analysis showed, there was no significant predictive value of the computer utilization and also not of the typical computer gaming experience of the subjects. These results are not surprising, as the population was rather homogeneous regarding age and educational background. Thus, it was expectable that basic requirements needed to perform the joystick-based Approach-Avoidance Task training compliantly were existent in all subjects of that age, especially as the movements are very limited and intuitive.

Summing up, the results of the exploratory research question allow for formulating an entry criterion for the Approach-Avoidance Task training that might reflect a cost-benefit equation. Those subjects that realize a predefined result in the pretest version of the Approach-Avoidance Task and the Stroop color-word interference task might benefit to a larger extent than the costs of the training charge the organization. Such entry criterion would further be supported by a mediation analysis (see hypothesis 5) that proved true and showed the impact of the training effect on the behavioral level. A replication of this experiment using a larger population is highly suggested in this respect.

Recapitulating the overall results of the experiment, it can be put on the records that it is possible to modify behavior in organizations using implicit training methods. In particular, the experiment contributed to the unanswered and hardly addressed issue of diminishing the variation between the ostensive and performative aspect of an organizational routine. This study should be seen as a first step toward closing this gap and offers a replicable experimental approach for conducting further research using implicit training methods. As this study addressed and answered the question whether or not the Approach-Avoidance Task training works in an organizational setting, further research might focus on the questions *by what* and *for whom* the implicit training works.

The contributions this study made to these questions are rather limited and should be seen as a first impression of the equifinality that could be achieved by implicit training methods in organizations.

5.2 Implicit learning in organizations and its role from different perspectives

Interpreting organizations in the thought of the dual process theory by Strack and Deutsch (2004), allows focusing on the qualities of processes that result in the actual behavior of an organization. One might wonder if there are systems in organizations that compare to the reflective system and the impulsive system as known from the above introduced dual process model (see Chapter 2.2.2). Expectedly, there is no overall answer to this question as organizations do not have a brain in the sense of human or animal biology. However, analyzing the organizational constructs that lead from perception and imagination to behavior from the perspective of dual process theories may be fruitful in understanding how organizations function in general, what the roles of routines are, and where to locate the individual within the firm. In the following, three perspectives discuss the contributions of this study. First, a vertical perspective views the role of dual processing in organizations on its different hierarchical levels and discusses the impact of implicit learning within the hierarchy. Second, the horizontal perspective focusses on implicit learning as a mechanism of replication of routines, and thus to distribute routines in an organization. Finally, the time perspective examines implicit learning against the background of the time-dependent dimensions of change and path-dependence.

5.2.1 A vertical perspective: Duality in organizations and its role for different dimensions

This perspective locates organizational routines in the intra-organizational hierarchy of collective entities. Further, the following line of thought combines the insights from the dual process model introduced earlier with this hierarchical multi-level perspective. In doing so, the role of automatic processes for organizations becomes clearer, and the idea of organizational impulsive processing will be developed. Based on these thoughts the impact of implicit learning strategies for modifying such impulsive processes will be discussed. Finally, the implications and limitations of the implicit modification of impulsive processes will be portrayed for the vertical perspective.

If there is something like a typical organization, its hierarchy of structuring and (collective) entities could be described from top to bottom by vision, strategy, dynamic capabilities, capabilities, organizational routines, individual competencies, skills, and actions (Salvato and Rerup, 2010). Each of these entities involves approaches to problem-solving, decision-making or behavior that can be more or less reflective (e.g., accounting) or respectively impulsive (e.g., hand writing). Alongside this hierarchy, from top to bottom, the entities and the related processes move from an abstract level to a tangible and concrete action-oriented level. Importantly, the lower a process resides in this hierarchy, the more frequently it is applied, developed and/or changed.[91] The following examples illustrate these thoughts on three different levels of the hierarchy: Vision and strategy, organizational routine, and the individual levels.

Vision and strategy. For example, *Amazon.com, Inc.* altered its vision statement only a couple of times since it was founded in 1994, mainly adapting it to the wider range of goods and services offered. The result, a statement comprising the organization's principles and future direction, should guide organization members through decision-making processes on a profound basis without requiring a reevaluation of the route in each iteration (Lipton, 1996; Kantabutra and Avery, 2010). Accordingly, the reflective application of this vision as nucleus of the strategies that direct the particular fields of organizational activities toward the environmental needs processes at rare intervals. In contrast, there are billions of fulfilled orders since the founding year; e.g., in 2015, *Amazon.com, Inc.* processed hundreds of orders per minute around the globe (Amazon.com Inc., 2016).

Developing a strategy out of a vision – a vision that pursues the goal to last a couple of years or in many cases even the whole life-cycle of an organization – is a process that involves several dimensions (analysis of the current situation, environmental assessment, identification of desired future strategy, connecting the present and desired state, and testing the strategy; Lipton, 1996; O'Brien and Meadows, 2001). These dimensions make applying a vision and its transfer it into a strategy a complex process of thought and reasoning. Accordingly, the balance between reflective and impulsive processing shifts strongly in the direction of the first (i.e., reflective processing). Along the path of reflective processing in the dual process model (perception, imagination, referring, reasoning, decision-making and intending) of Strack and Deutsch (2004), there are parallels to the above-mentioned dimensions in aligning a strategy to the vision and the environmental needs. By the noetic decision-making process in strategy formulation, an organization abstractly prepares to recall specific behavioral schemas that are compatible to the vision and that finally result in actual and perceivable behavior on the subordinated levels.

Organizational routines. Hierarchically below the levels of the vision and the organization's strategies, routines take a less abstract role and orient more in the direction of tangible behavioral outcome. As introduced in the previous chapters (e.g., Chapter 2.1.1), there are various conceptions of what an organizational routine is. These conceptions allow locating routines on the continuum between reflective and impulsive processing at different points, depending on the conceptual approach. So, viewing routines from the perspective of grammars of action makes them highly deliberate

[91] It is recognized that the vision and strategy should be ubiquitous on all levels below. However, here it is referred to the processing of these entities in actively shaping the levels below.

decision-making processes in which actors need to choose reflectively from a predefined set of possible actions (Pentland and Rueter, 1994; see also Chapter 2.1.1.2, section: Routines as grammatical models). In contrast, viewing routines as part of an organization's procedural memory (i.e., on the basis of associations) assigns them attributes like automatic, path-dependent, tacit, inarticulate, unconscious, or dependent on the actor's orientation (Cohen and Bacdayan, 1994; Egidi, 1996; Egidi and Narduzzo, 1997; see also Chapter 2.1.1.2, section: Routines as procedural memory). Even though Pentland and Rueter (1994, p. 492) describe routines in their analogy more as reflective processes, they highlight that routines "[…] *can be more or less repetitive, more or less automatic, embody more or less variety, search, and so on.*"

In the sense of Becker's (2004; see also Chapter 2.1.1.1, section: Processual nature) dimensions of the processual nature of routines (frequency of repetition, regularity of the frequency, time pressure) and their value, one could assume that routines can be processed both, reflectively and impulsively. However, when viewing the effects of organizational routines (see Chapter 2.1.4), the majority of these effects reflect the objectives that organizations pursue by applying routines. One of the more significant effects respectively objectives of routines is to economize cognitive resources within the organization. Furthermore, organizations also seek the regularity and reduction of uncertainty by applying routines, alongside with the preservation of knowledge. More specifically, as organizational routines often have regular and short frequencies of repetition, and mostly occur with the intention to make processes more efficient in respect of time, human capital, as well as resource allocation in general, the balance of reflective and impulsive processing shifts to the latter – at least over time. Accordingly, organizational routines could be conceived as an instrument to strengthen the impulsivity of a firm in accomplishing their tasks. In other words, routines often produce responses that compare more to impulsive processed responses than to reflective processed ones – on an organizational level.

As an example of such organizational routine, it can be referred to the routine of a recurrently executed service encounter in a fast food restaurant that follows a recognizable pattern, involves interaction and is processual in its nature (see Figure 16). The frequency of repetition and its regularity is high. In many cases, that routine processes under time pressure to keep the speed of service on the desired level. Without considering the emergence of this routine (deliberate search vs. evolutionary process), the repeatedly execution of this routine becomes fast and automatic, and the connections between the single steps become increasingly associative in their nature, which is the basis for impulsive processes.

Steps such as the reception of a customer or the compilation of the order process highly automatic and thus can be compared to impulsive processing as known from the dual process model but on an organizational level. These steps are executed without any or at least with a minimal reflective effort of the organization (e.g., the perception of a customer spreads the activation for the behavioral schema of smiling, greeting, and order initiation). However, this routine also has reflective processing steps in it. For example, cashing up the customer will involve reasoning, as well as factual and evaluative decision-making (e.g., how to make up the change). Importantly, the introduced dual process model involves interaction between the reflective system and impulsive system (e.g., to make use of experiential shortcuts). Transferring this idea to the example of the service encounter routine and the step of making the change in cashing up a customer, the employee may first impulsively make the change from the experiential background but will parallel reevaluate this impulsively started process reflectively. That denotes that there is also interaction between the reflective and impulsive level possible, similar to the model described by Strack and Deutsch (2004).

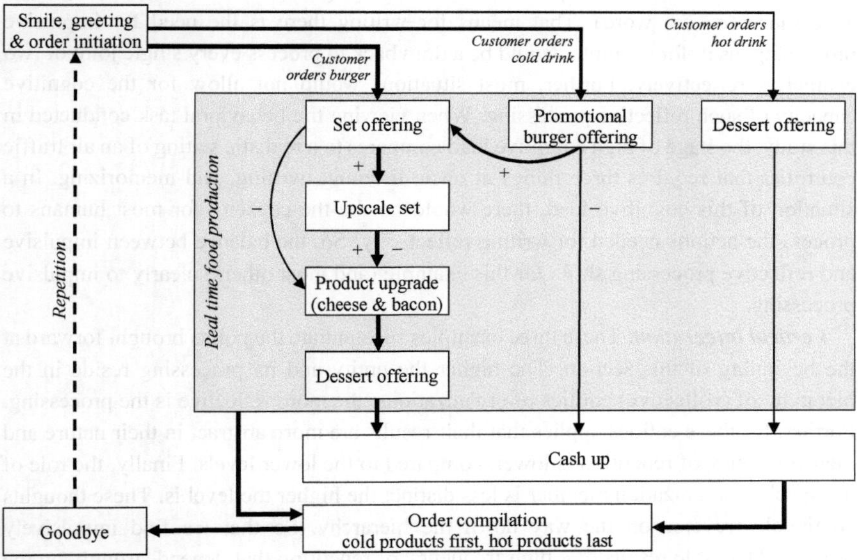

Figure 16: Simplified service encounter routine in a fast food restaurant.

Note: The higher the weight of an arrow, the more preferred is that process. The lighter the weight of an arrow, the faster the process needs to be liquidated as it ties resources inefficiently.

Individual levels. Individual skills and actions are the levels below routines and obviously assign to individuals. However, in the sense of methodological individualism, these are the levels that allow explaining the superordinate levels. So, here these individual levels are conceptualized as the building blocks of the collective entities. Both, individual skills and actions are usually applied without adjustment across the different collective entities that superordinate them (e.g., routines, or capabilities). In contrast, processing a vision, capability or routine is in most cases unique to the setting within the organization. Individual skills can be broken down into their single actions, which reflect the smallest piece of behavior in organizations.

For example, handwriting numbers or letters belongs to the category of psychomotor skills. These skills combine sets of coordinated cognitive and motor processes (van Galen, 1991; VandenBos, 2015, p. 861). Breaking down the skill handwriting into its smallest parts results in the actions for drawing the single strokes that compose a character. Due to frequent repetition, in most humans on a daily basis, the strokes of handwriting become highly automatic. The movements that are applied to make the strokes for characters or numbers base on an associative network. Especially in writing cursive this becomes clear, as the processing speed needs to be relatively high to guarantee a smooth motor sequence that joins the single characters into a homogenous appearance (e.g., a word). That means for writing there is the need for impulsive processing, as it, for example, would be a drawback to process every single joint of two characters reflectively. Further, most situations would not allow for the cognitive capacity of such reflective processing. When viewing the behavioral task conducted in this study, the stage of high cognitive load compares to a realistic setting of an air traffic controller that requires three things at once: listening, writing, and memorizing. In a situation of this cognitive load, there would not be the capacity for most humans to process the actions needed for writing reflectively. So, the balance between impulsive and reflective processing shifts for this example (and most others) clearly to impulsive processing.

Vertical integration. These three examples substantiate the points brought forward at the beginning of this section. The higher the entity and its processing reside in the hierarchy of (collective) entities of organizations, the more reflective is the processing. Further, for these entities applies that their results are more abstract in their nature and their frequency of repetition is lower, compared to the lower levels. Finally, the role of the specific organization member is less distinct the higher the level is. These thoughts continually reverse on the way down the hierarchy. So that we find impulsively processed tangible results of a high frequency of repetition that depend strongly on the performance of an individual on the level of action.

However, viewing the organizations in the sense of methodological individualism and as a conglomerate of individuals that process for example routines, puts the individual (and interpretative) differences in processing center-stage. Regarding the reflective processes, there can be differences in the declarative knowledge but also in the logics for reasoning or the normative basis for evaluation that lead to a behavioral decision. For the impulsive processes, there can be differences in the experiential awareness or the associative store. Individuals may lack significant portions of these aspects to carry out a routine and its required actions. In other situations, these aspects might be weak or maladapted to the normative requirements of the routine and thus result in a cognitive bias.

These differences adjust the balance between reflective and impulsive processing from individual to individual differently, as there are no duplicates in humankind. However, with a frequent repetition and habituation that balance inevitably shifts in the direction of impulsive processing (Ouellette and Wood, 1998; Aarts and Dijksterhuis, 2000; Strack and Deutsch, 2004). Then, the execution is driven by the associative stores of the individuals and their motivational orientation. Both have the potential to cause cognitive biases, which can lead to misfiring of routines from time to time, or even permanently (Cohen and Bacdayan, 1994). For collective entities in general, that implicates an increasing impact of an individual cognitive bias or maladaptive processing on the organization that goes along with the increasing role of the individual in the collective entity.

Within the vertical perspective and its hierarchical framework of behavioral entities in organizations, routines are the level that combines the individual competencies, skills, and actions into a collective performance. Accordingly, this is the level where the individual level with its heterogeneous performances needs to be orchestrated for the first time into a homogenous organizational performance that is determined by the ostensive aspect of a routine (i.e., the ideal schematic form of a routine, which describes the organization's targeted performance). However, one might argue that a single routine does not have the ability to determine the outcome or overall performance of an organization. This point becomes obvious when viewing routines of different complexity, for example, a service encounter in a fast-food restaurant versus the preparation of an enterprise's annual report. The examples show the different scope of a routine's effect on the outcome an organization. More specifically, a single service encounter in a fast-food restaurant might not harm the overall outcome of that organization. However, an annual report that misses its goal could result in a misinterpretation of the balance sheet and the profit and loss statement by the shareholders. Accordingly, the shareholder value might drop dramatically and thus jeopardize the organization's future and outcome. That means an organizational routine of appropriate scope may utterly be determined for the outcome of an organization.

These points are essential to assess the results of the experiment in this study from the standpoint of an organization. Viewing the relevant topics covered here (i.e., organizational routines, dual processes, and implicit learning) from the vertical perspective allows for identifying routines as the appropriate hierarchical level for integrating implicit learning strategies into the organization. At this level, the balance of impulsive and reflective processing (at least over time) has a strong weight on impulsive processing. Further, the role of individuals in organizational routines is distinct and more recognizable than in the above collective entities. It is also the lowest level at which cognitive biases and maladaptive processes may spread through the interaction between the individuals across the organization. By the implementation of an implicit learning strategy at this level it is possible to homogenize the impulsive processes that lead to a significant portion of the routine's outcome and to modify these to the specificity that produces the intended performance.

These insights contribute to the micro-foundational discussion in the field of routines. Pentland and Hærem (2015) broached the issue of whether a (mindful) organizational routine can include impulsive processing (they refer to it as System 1 - intuitive processing), what role the individual and the differences between them play in this view. This study clearly addressed that topic and thus contributes to the micro-foundational discussion in clarifying the role of individuals and their impulsive processing in the organizational context. Homogenization between the ostensive and performative aspect can be considered as a substantial effect of the modification of impulsive processes by implicit learning. The modification can be conceived an adjustment of individual differences to meet an organization-wide standard that allows for stability and continuity in the outcome. As Pentland and Hærem (2015) claim that organizations need meta-routines to control their current organizational routines actively, the implicit training conducted here can be understood as a meta-routine. It allows to willingly change a routine by reconfiguring the individual contributions to the routine (see also Winter, 2003; Lewin, Massini and Peeters, 2011). To close this section and to highlight the importance of the contribution made by this study, it is referred to Nelson and Winter (1982, p. 125). They state that an "[...] *individual lacking skills appropriate to the situation may respond awkwardly, but an organization lacking appropriate routines may not respond at all*." With the implementation of an implicit learning strategy, both of these issues can be addressed. Based on the implicit training approach on the level of individual psychological processes taken here, this study brought up evidence that it is possible to close a potential gap of inappropriate routines in organizations.

5.2.2 A horizontal perspective: Implicit learning as replication mechanism

The horizontal perspective discusses the role of implicit learning strategies in the replication of organizational routines. In other words, how implicit learning strategies can support the horizontal distribution of routine knowledge throughout the organization and possibly also from one to another organization. Implicit learning strategies may contribute to some of the challenges that accompany the replication of organizational routines ever since. In this section, the challenges of replication will be highlighted, and the potential contributions of an implicit learning strategy as used in this study will be discussed. Further the limitations of the utilization of such learning strategy will be shown for the horizontal perspective (i.e., replication).

Replication is a challenging process that does not work efficiently or at reasonable costs for the most cases. Different mechanisms of routine replication could be found in literature and organizational practice. Most commonly organizations approach replication by sending internal (e.g., senior employees) or external experts (e.g., consultants) to the new business unit to transport and integrate the existing routine knowledge. However, these mechanisms often fail and bring about substantial challenges and consequences for the organization: high costs, not-invented-here syndrome, a low speed of replication, missing local adaptation, and the difficulty of transferring tacit knowledge.

In more detail, sending internal experts from the source to the receiving part of the organization is a cost intensive process. These costs do not only include financial aspects, such as moving and traveling costs or expatriate compensation but also costs that result from the loss of workforce and knowledge in the sending business unit. Also, the consultancy of external experts that can be used as agents for collecting, transferring and implementing the routine knowledge is cost-intensive. Similar for both of these mechanisms is the frequently observed resistance against external knowledge in the receiving unit, which is known as the not-invented-here syndrome. Depending on the organizational culture, employees in the part of the organization that should receive the routine knowledge are incredulous about the external knowledge. In the extreme cases, the receiving unit does not adopt any of the knowledge that did not originate from their own unit. Further, the speed of replication is crucial to organizations as it is a determining factor for the rate of growth that can be realized. Particularly in industries with short business and product life cycles, slow rates of replication can result in a competitive disadvantage (Kogut and Zander, 1992).

However, replication involves another field of conflict: By applying routines, organizations seek to achieve a performance that is homogeneous and in many cases standardized throughout the organization. At the same time, there is the need for contextual adaptation when replicating a routine. Hodgson (2009) highlighted that organizations cannot be successful in replicating routines and maintaining the routines' value if they do not adapt the routine and the inherent knowledge to the receiving business units cultural and economic context. So, there is the need to replicate routines and be able to finely adapt routines to the receiving unit's context to allow a smooth and purposeful functioning. Finally, one of the challenges of routine replication is the successful transfer of tacit knowledge components of routines. As this knowledge is barely expressible or even completely non-verbalizable, organizations use the mechanisms of experiential or social learning as the approach of choice (e.g., by expatriation). However, in those cases, the results are hardly controllable and there is no guarantee that such learning imparts the intended knowledge to transfer. The conglomeration of these challenges of replication shows the theoretical lack but also the practical need for a learning mechanism that supports a reliable and successful replication.

The Approach-Avoidance Task training, respectively Cognitive Bias Modification contributes to successfully face these challenges. The Approach-Avoidance Task training conducted in this experiment consists of two assessment and four training sessions. That means the total expenditure of time is relatively small (overall approx. 70 minutes), which reflects rather little costs compared to the mechanisms mentioned above. This study focused on a detail of a routine and did not pursue the objective to replicate an entire organizational routine. Replicating a complete organizational routine would require multiple training sequences that cover the various actions involved in a routine. If such design would work in practice is in question and needs to be tested in a follow-up study. However, an Approach-Avoidance Task training could be a promising complementary to other forms of learning and mechanisms of replication. In non-critical areas of replication that proved to quickly transfer the required knowledge at reasonable costs without resistance, conventional learning and replication strategies may still be the first choice. On the contrary, in critical areas (e.g., writing style of numerals in the air traffic control service), the use of the implicit learning paradigm as shown in this study might be helpful to reduce the costs for replication and to lessen the impact of resistance against external knowledge or even to avoid the perception of the incoming knowledge as external. As there is less or no resistance to expect and the time required for conducting the implicit training in such critical areas is lower than with other forms of learning, the overall speed of replication is supposed to increase.

The Approach-Avoidance Task training can also contribute to the challenge of transferring tacit knowledge. There are several cases conceivable in which tacit knowledge can be expressed on a computer screen by using well prepared visual stimuli. Exemplarily, for the writing style transferred in this experiment, it is hard to exactly explain the required movements for the action of creating a numeral in the targeted style. However, approaching the transfer not by the attempting to teach the movements but by raising an impulsive approach tendency to write in the new style, shifts the focus to motivational orientation. The subject got manipulated to implicitly develop a motivation to accomplish a result: Writing the numerals in the new style. Even though literature does not allow for explaining the subliminal psychological processes underlying this kind of learning entirely, the studies do allow for proving the change in the approach tendency and the subsequent behavior (e.g., Brockmeyer *et al.*, 2015; Kakoschke, Kemps and Tiggemann, 2017).

Finally, the possibly necessary adaptation of parts of the routine to the local context of the receiving units can be achieved by the Approach-Avoidance Task training (see also Chapter 5.2.3). As the computerized training uses picture materials for training, the organization can use different sets of pictures depending on the context without changing the basic learning strategy (e.g., replacing Arabic numerals with simplified Chinese numerals). The basic psychological processes are the same in humans of different (cultural) contexts so that the implicit learning strategy can remain the same across various locations and cultural contexts. In contrast, traditional forms of learning strongly depend on, for example, the cultural background and thus have the need for adaptation to succeed (Hofstede, 1986; Liu and Vince, 1999).

In addition to the discussion about the mechanisms of replication, literature offers a limited but interesting discussion about the preferable replication strategy (Konlechner and Güttel, 2010). The two strategies that literature portrays are the template-based and the principle-based replication. The template-based replication strives for replication the source routine without any modification or variation into the target context. Differently, the principle-based approach seeks to transfer a set of rules, norms and processual principles of a routine instead of a one-to-one copy (Baden-Fuller and Winter, 2007). So, the question whether choosing a template-based or the principle-based approach accompanies the planning phase of routine replication. Depending on the requirements and the context of a replication there are arguments for both approaches. However, the advantages of the principle-based approach are compelling. The constellations under which an organizational routine arises are determined by the specificity of the context and the involved actors' mindsets (Reynaud, 1996). Becker (2004, p. 651) emphasizes, "[…] *the probability that routines can be replicated exactly is low* […]" as the above-mentioned constellations are too complex.

In contrast to the template-based approach, the principle-based approach allows for innovation while replicating a routine. Also, the self-adjusting ability to adapt a routine to a new context is a strength of this method; even though the adjustments occur within the boundaries of the replicated principles. To give an example: So far, most military air navigation service units use flight progress strips made of paper, others already use paperless strips that are operated on a touch-sensitive display. Besides the historical roots, the paper strips still have its reason. A mission in a crisis region may require working without constant power supply or with an improvised tower. At this point, there would be the need for at least two routine templates, one for the paperless flight progress strips and one for the traditional paper strips. However, there would only be the need for one set of principles. Irrespectively of the assessment which of the replication strategies is predominant, an approach using implicit learning strategies can contribute to both of these replication strategies. It is possible to train the underlying principles of a routine implicitly (e.g., using the paradigm of Artificial Grammar Learning) but also to train specific templates (e.g., using the sequence learning paradigm). The AAT training, in particular, can contribute to both strategies and thus allows organizations to be flexible in choosing a replication strategy from case to case.

Nelson and Winter (1982, p.112) noted that is a difficult process to create a "[…] *new routine where none existed before*". Frequently, that is the case for the replication of organizational routines (e.g., transfer of a production routine to a newly build factory). The AAT training and implicit learning strategies in general, are a promising approach to face this difficult process. For the replication of organizational routines, this study emphasizes the potential of the Approach-Avoidance Task training for practical applications. Even though in this experiment the transfer covered just a piece of a routine – small but crucial – the importance of a follow-up study on a larger scale becomes evident. For example, it needs to be proved in more detail how the simultaneous transfer of several parts of a routine affects the results of the implicit training. Further, a study using the Approach-Avoidance Task training for the replication of a routine (or its parts) between different cultural contexts may bring forward valuable insights. Besides showing the potential benefit of the application of implicit learning strategies for the industry, one of the substantial contributions of this study to the field of replication is that the results were generalized and allow for replication due to the experimental laboratory approach. Thereby, this study opposes the repeated critique that most studies on routines and especially on the replication of routines are only collections of case studies with limited value in making general insights (e.g., Hodgson, 2003; 2008).

5.2.3 A time perspective: Implicit modification of routines

This section takes a time perspective on organizational routines that focusses on the aspect of routine change and the role of cognitive bias modification in inducing and controlling this change. One of the most recurrent themes in routine research is the discussion about change, stability, and the rigidity of routines (see Chapter 2.1.3.2). Regarding this topic, there are things that organizations seek and others that may represent a threat to the operations or even the existence of an organization. For example, the mutation (i.e., the non-deliberative change) of the writing style of numerals on a flight progress strip represents a threat to the operating capability of air navigation service due to an accordingly malfunctioning high-reliability routine (i.e., maintaining a flight progress strip). In consequence, such obviously minimal evolutionary mutation may have fatal consequences as the actual altitude could be misinterpreted. In particular, this proves true when the mutation spreads across multiple but not all actors. However, in other cases than high-reliability organizations, mutations might be acceptable or "[…] *not always deleterious*" (Nelson and Winter, 1982, p. 116). Besides change, this section also discusses the impact of the cognitive bias modification for the organizational phenomenon of path-dependence, which is one of the effects that can result from the use of routines in organizations (see Chapter 2.1.4). In particular, it will be discussed how cognitive bias modification can support organizations to build routines on the future requirements instead of the previous experience. Further, the role of cognitive bias modification as to instrument to revert a routine to a previous point in time will be highlighted.

Change. One might ask, what is it in regard of routines that organizations are looking for? Literature and the case studies available draw the picture that many organizations are looking for flexibility within stable patterns that allows for intended change propelled and controlled by the management. The objective lies in transforming the (visionary) thinking of the management into an evolvement of the innovative potential of the organization to become or remain competitive. Thus, as "[m]*odeling the firm means modeling the routines and how they change over time*" (Nelson and Winter, 1982, p. 128), one of the management's major tasks is balancing stability and change within an organization in the course of time (Feldman, 2003). More organizations succeed in maintaining stability than in modeling their routines intentionally to innovate their thinking, services, and products. The deliberate change of routines is difficult as

Pentland and Hærem (2015) made the note and the management is missing the instruments to bring their intentions into action, i.e., into the performative aspect of a routine.

The AAT training, as shown in this study, contributes at this decisive point. During the experiment a part of an organizational routine was intentionally modified, in particular, the action of writing specific numerals in a new and in air traffic control required writing style. Subjects retrained their current and in Germany common writing style of the numbers 1, 7, and 9. As a result of the training, the subjects adopted the new writing style and deployed it in favor over the old style. That means a couple of actions within the routine changed while the rest remained the same. For example, the positions for noting the specific information on the flight progress strip or the symbols that are used as shortcuts remained the same for this routine. Only the writing of three distinct numerals was modified. On a more abstract level, the experiment showed that cognitive bias modification using the AAT training changed certain actions of a routine within an unchanged and stable (grammatical) pattern. As yet, in the ostensive-performative model of Feldman and Pentland (2003), a management-induced deliberate change was only possible by approaching the ostensive aspect and thus changing the abstract and schematic form of an organizational routine.

Applying the training method shown in this study allows for the first time to directly access the level of action. This is the performative aspect, respectively the part of a routine that produces the tangible output. Against the opinion of other researchers, it is well possible to tackle deliberate change in organizational routines – experimentally and replicable proven. Accordingly, the implicit learning mechanism represented by the Approach-Avoidance Task training contributes to the research gap identified by Pentland and Feldman (2008) with an alternative approach to modifying the ostensive aspect. They found that a deliberate change at the ostensive level does not necessarily result in the expected change of the performative aspect that the organization primarily seeks. Now, alternatively and in a variety of cases, it is possible to inject the desired and intended change directly into the level of action. Such directly injected alteration supersedes a lengthy and iterative process of designing an ostensive aspect which will be interpreted by the actors in the desired way and results in the intended tangible outcome.

Further, the Approach-Avoidance Task training allows organizations to overcome some of the impeding factors for deliberate change, such as the actor's limited intelligence and processing capacity, as well as inertia and cultural or organizational biases (Rice and Cooper, 2010, pp. 131-133). Another advantage of the computerized Approach-Avoidance Task training is the rather low cognitive effort that the actor needs to relearn parts of an organizational routine. The effort is reduced to the handling of the computer program with the joystick, that means, for example, pushing away landscape pictures and pulling portrait pictures.

Having the ability to change an organizational routine willingly and precisely without undergoing an iterative process of approximating to the desired state allows for tackling the argument that suboptimal routines will survive in organizations and prevent innovation. This argument bases on the thought that organizations stick with suboptimal routines as long as they result in satisfactory outcomes, although there would be a superior alternative routine. This line of thinking is mainly driven by perceiving change as cost driver (March and Simon, 1958; Becker, 2004, pp. 140-141, 173-174). Of course, such short-term thinking is a barrier for innovation. Change, respectively innovation then becomes a consideration of the losses by applying a suboptimal routine versus the costs for changing the routine. As mentioned earlier, the Approach-Avoidance Task training is a relatively inexpensive strategy to transfer the knowledge of a routine but also to change it. Coming from a cost-driven thinking, an implicit training like the Approach-Avoidance Task training may reduce the costs of change and thus contribute to realizing the innovative potential of an organization (i.e., to forward-looking thinking that at least pays off in the long-term). In today's digitalized world, a teenager with a computer that is connected to the internet can disruptively renew an entire industry – that means the change needed for the innovation in and of organizations is not just a trend but the basis for economic survival. Cognitive bias modification can be the facilitator for organizations to maintain or increase their speed of change to remain competitive.

Path-dependence. As yet, organizational *"[r]outines build on the past"* (Becker, 2004, p. 653) and the decisions of yesterday determine the actions of the organization's tomorrow. Once chosen a routine or letting it emerge, it is hard for organizations to escape the taken path. In those cases, it is not possible to adapt a routine to new circumstances before the current state of the routine begins to malfunction. Organizations are missing the instruments to align their routines on the future requirements proactively and irrespectively of the previous path. Instead, they become reactive in adapting their routines as they can only choose from those options that the previous path allows at the current intersection. Further, path-dependence hinders or even prevents organizations of retracing the current state of their routines in cases of a decay of the historical path (e.g., due to employee turnover). Accordingly, re-setting a routine to a prior point in time becomes impossible as, for example, the current employees do not hold the knowledge developed along the path but only know the current state of the routine (Levitt and March, 1988; Becker, 2004).

Cognitive bias modification might contribute to both of the challenges originating from path-dependence, the challenge to proactively determine the path of a routine irrespectively of the previous path, and also to the challenge of resetting a routine to a prior point in time. Regarding the first issue, this study has experimentally proven that it is possible to advance a routine actively. The subjects were candidates for the air traffic control service and hence a future part of the routine of maintaining a flight progress strip. However, against the background of their school education, they learned to write differently than required in air traffic control. So far, the candidates frequently had problems with adapting their writing style to the requirements of air traffic control. It was an iterative process using explicit forms of learning to develop their writing style as required in air traffic control. In some cases, they could not adapt and accordingly failed in the final practical exam. Those candidates involved, the routine of maintaining the flight progress strip was malfunctioning. Similar, air traffic controllers that are already on duty and had learned the new style reflectively, fall back to the old writing style in situations of high cognitive load (see also Weick, 1990).

The training conducted here allows for dissociating the prior from the future path. Even though the old writing style does not belong to the path of the routine in a strict sense, it nevertheless has a strong influence on the individual level to the performance of the routine.[92] On the one hand, the result contests the conclusion that Weick (1990) made in his analysis of the Tenerife air disaster, which illustrates that humans fall back to first learned responses in situations high cognitive load. On the other hand, this study succeeded in proactively shaping the performance of a routine without reference to the previous path. Especially for fast moving industries that experience disruptive changes, this path-independence could be of enormous value to remain competitive.

Addressing the question of Schulz (2008), who asked what keeps a routine on track, this study offers an experimentally proven instrument to adjust and shape the track a routine follows. When conceiving the ostensive aspect as track (i.e., the ideal schematic form of the routine), the Approach-Avoidance Task training enables the organization to keep the routine on this track and minimize or even extinguish a variation between the ostensive and the performative aspect. However, crucial at this point is that this implicit training assesses the motivational orientation of the individual actor to keep the routine on track intrinsically. Metaphorically speaking, the ostensive aspect is the road, the performative aspect is the car, and the Approach-Avoidance Task training (i.e., cognitive bias modification) is the steering wheel to keep the vehicle on the road to reach the destination. Additionally, the Approach-Avoidance Task training can contribute to the challenge of reverting the routine to a previous point in time. Whether an employee knows the historical path or not is not crucial. As long as it is possible to express the former state in an implicit training (e.g., on a computer screen for the Approach-Avoidance Task training), it is possible for the organization to radically escape out of the gridlocked situation of path-dependence.

5.3 Conclusion

This study brought together organizational routines and experimental psychology to examine the role of implicit learning in the context of routines. Framing both concepts,

---

92 Conducting the same experiment with air traffic controllers that already accomplished the vocational training and are on duty would expectedly result in a similar outcome for those who fall back to the old writing style from time to time.

organizational routines, and implicit learning, in the relevant theory allowed for developing a broad and well-founded understanding of the concepts and their delineation from cognate concepts. The understanding of organizational routines was built by following the historical path of routine development and depicts them a concept which allows for explaining how organizations accomplish their work. Based on the commonly associated characteristics of routines (i.e., recurrence, patterns, the processual nature, and collective social nature) and the frequently used analogies, some of the relevant topics in routine research were highlighted (e.g., change and stability, replication, or the effects of routines). Also, the importance of individual actors for the functioning of routines, and, in consequence, for the operation of organizations was elaborated.

The conceptual and methodological issues of routine research lead to one of the major issues of organizational routines: Building on the ideal schematic form of a routine (ostensive aspect), organizations try to achieve a specific, homogenous and controllable outcome (performative aspect). In many cases, the alignment between the ostensive and the performative aspect is not successful, and routines deviate from intended outcome – they miss the target. This experimental study clearly addresses this issue. As yet, organizations have limited mechanisms to align the actual performance of a routine to the intended outcome. This experimental study introduced cognitive bias modification as a mechanism to approach the challenge of aligning the ostensive and performative aspect. Using the Approach-Avoidance Task training as implicit learning paradigm, the subjects writing style of numerals was re-learned implicitly to match the style required for air traffic control.

Contributions. The results of the study were approached from three perspectives (vertical, horizontal, and time perspective) to allow for differentiating the contributions. Taking a ***vertical perspective*** on the (collective) entities in organizations shows an increasing role of impulsive processes the lower the level gets. Accordingly, it is most promising to implement an implicit learning strategy at the level of transition between individual and organizational level, which is the organizational routine. Modifying the individual skills that shape the routines allows for orchestrating the overall performance of a routine to a homogenous level that accords with the ostensive aspect. Further, routines have the potential to escalate vertically and take influence on the levels above. That enables organizations to modify not only the individual associative store but also the organizational associative store.

There are various prospective use cases in organizations: Exemplarily, an organization that aims for equal opportunities for women and men may suffer from a biased human resource management routine, which preferably promotes men in the executive positions. That organization could modify the potentially underlying cognitive bias toward men by using an implicit training and thus adapt it to gain equal opportunities for both genders. That would allow the organization to adapt its routine and realize the human resource strategy of equal opportunities (i.e., vertical escalation).

A comparable case could be drawn for the objective of ethnic diversity in a recruitment routine. Both examples could have a tremendous impact on organizations and should be put on the research agenda.

The ***horizontal perspective*** on the role of implicit learning for organizational routines focusses on the replication of routines between different parts of the organization. Integrating the results of this study into the horizontal view and interpreting the Approach-Avoidance Task training as a mechanism for replication allows depicting the contributions of implicit learning to the crucial challenges of replication. The compact Approach-Avoidance Task training can reduce costs for the process of replication while increasing the speed at the same time. Further, it allows for homogenization of the outcome as well as localization to the local circumstances and requirements. Finally, the training also allows for overcoming organizational resistance against external knowledge (not-invented-here syndrome) as well as it allows for transferring tacit knowledge if it can be expressed by pictorial stimuli.

Besides the general value of developing the ability to replicate tacit knowledge and overcoming the not-invented-here syndrome, these contributions might have substantial value for the use of implicit learning strategies in the field for two reasons: First, today's globalized economy requires organizations to be able to participate in any relevant market across the globe. That requires the organizations to replicate and adapt their business models and the adherent processes to the new market very quickly at minimized costs. Second, the increasing number of franchise chains and organizations that produce across the globe aim for consistent standards. For example, the perception of quality depends on factors like the cultural background. Implicit training strategies can support organizations to bring the perceived level of quality to the required level. Replication could be one of the most promising fields for the application of implicit learning strategies in practice. Future studies should cover the replication of larger parts of a routine as well as cross-cultural replication.

The ***time perspective*** highlighted the contributions of implicit learning strategies for change in and of routines, as well as the contributions of implicit learning to deal with the path-dependence of routines. Routines change is particularly crucial for the innovation of routines over time. Being able to control change initiatives precisely allows organizations to prevent unnecessary iterative loops and to recall the innovative potential of an organization that otherwise would not be realized. For the second aspect, path-dependence, implicit learning enables organizations to escape out of the trap of being limited in the choice of the next developmental step of a routine. Further, the training as conducted here, allows organizations to erase disadvantageous steps and to revert to a previous stage of the routine. These two time-related aspects facilitate organizations in realizing the objective they look for in applying routines: flexibility within stable patterns. Additionally, one of the effects that organizations want to achieve with routines is control, which is in tension with innovation though. Being able to control change makes it possible to loosen this tension, and to stimulate innovation in a controlled environment. Within the time perspective, future research can contribute to clarifying the potential of implicit learning as a mechanism to control the change of routines to direct the innovative path the routine goes.

Limitations. Alongside with these contributions, there are several limitations. Regarding this experimental study specifically, there are two main limitations: First, the rather small population needs to be kept in mind when interpreting the results. As mentioned earlier, due to the limited resources it was not possible to test a larger population. From a statistical perspective, the groups had a sufficient size and the essential power. However, larger groups would have realized a larger power. Second, this experiment can only be seen as groundwork for the implementation of implicit learning into organizations, as the part of the routine that was relearned by the subjects was rather small. This limitation is one that should be addressed in future research with a strong focus. On a general level, there is an ethic concern that goes along with cognitive bias modification in organizations. Exposing organization members to a situation that does not allow them to realize that they are learning and especially what they are learning is ethically difficult justifiable. In specific countries, this type of learning could also have legal aspects that would prevent organizations from applying implicit learning without the agreement of the participants. However, as other studies showed that explicit pre-instruction is not disadvantageous for the success of implicit learning, ethical concerns could be overcome. Another general challenge for the Approach-Avoidance Task training that might limit the practical application could be the challenge to express knowledge in pictorial stimuli. Accordingly, it might be of value to examine other forms of implicit learning to overcome this limitation (e.g., Artificial Grammar Learning).

Future versions of the Approach-Avoidance Task training could benefit from advances in the areas of virtual reality or force-feedback devices that might allow for more realistic training environments with a stronger reference to the behavioral level. Concluding on the research on organizational routines as "[…] *deceptively complex phenomenon* […]" (Pentland and Hærem, 2015, p. 481), it is to assert that routines are an entity that involves both, individual as well as group behaviors (i.e., social and group dynamics). Unfortunately, most of the scholars that contribute to the field of routine research do not integrate the store of knowledge that experimental and social psychology already reliably proved – a point that Michael D. Cohen (1991) already brought forward in *Organization Science* in the 1990s (see also Narduzzo and Warglien, 2008). So, instead of reinventing the wheel, routine researchers are called to intensify collaborations with other domains to stop collecting single cases and create replicable and in best case experimentally proven results.

Appendix

A Numeral stimuli

Numerals used as stimuli for the new writing style:

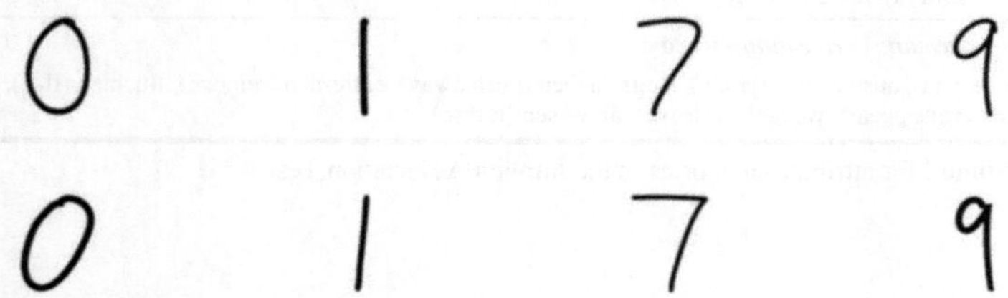

Numerals used as stimuli for the old writing style:

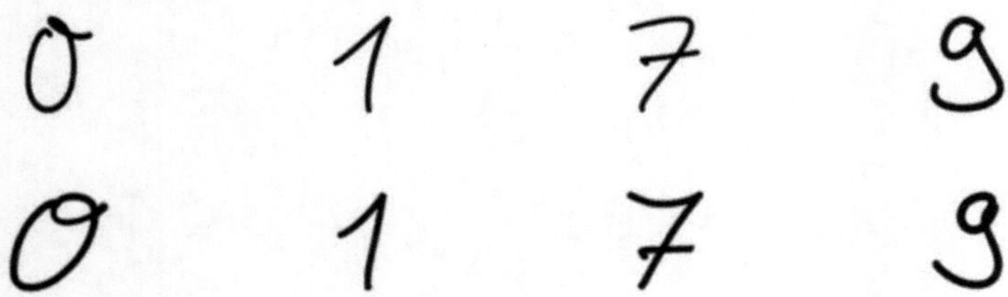

Numerals used as stimuli irrespectively of the writing style:

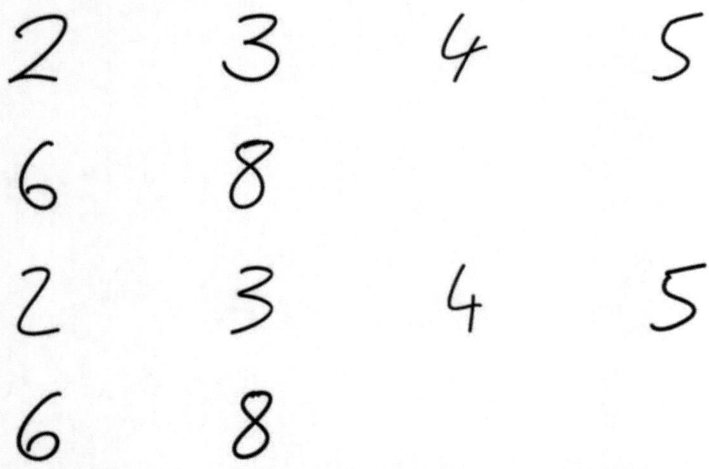

Table 15: Numeral stimuli.

M. Eberl, *Organizational Routines Meet Experimental Psychology*,
Zukunftsfähige Unternehmensführung in Forschung und Praxis,
https://doi.org/10.1007/978-3-658-23562-8

B Stimuli for the attribute categories in the Implicit Association Test

Approach (German: *Annäherung*) words:
Greifen (reach out), nehmen (take), anfassen (grab), berühren (touch), holen (collect), annähern (approach), heranholen (zoom in), fassen (grasp)
Avoidance (*German: Vermeidung*) words:
Vermeiden (avoid), ausweichen (elude), wegschieben (push away), entfernen (remove), flüchten (flee), verschwinden (disappear), weggehen (leave), abweisen (refuse)

Table 16: Stimuli for attribute categories in the Implicit Association Test.

C Answer sheet for the behavioral task

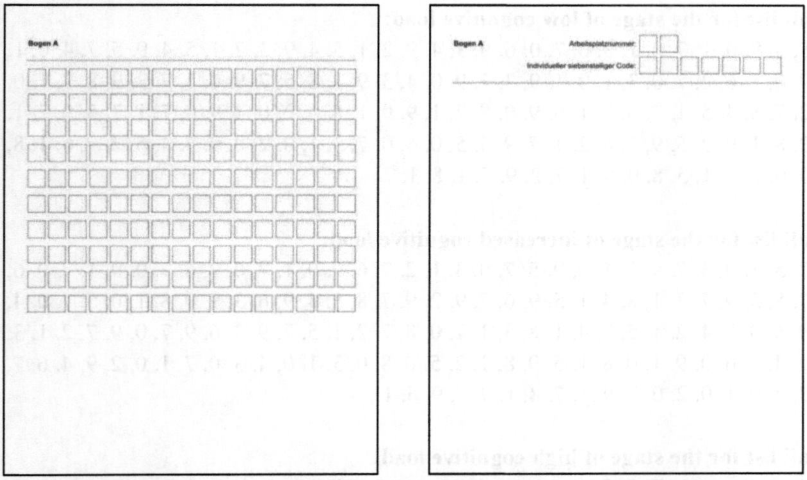

Figure 17: Example of an answer sheet for the behavioral task (face on the left, flipside on the right).

D Stimuli lists for the behavioral task

Stimuli list for the stage of low cognitive load:
0, 1, 5, 3, 9, 0, 1, 7, 0, 1, 3, 0, 7, 0, 6, 9, 3, 4, 9, 2, 1, 5, 4, 9, 3, 7, 1, 5, 4, 9, 5, 7, 4, 0, 1, 0, 7, 9, 0, 1, 6, 2, 7, 0, 3, 1, 0, 1, 9, 3, 7, 9, 0, 4, 3, 9, 1, 8, 5, 7, 9, 0, 4, 7, 2, 9, 8, 7, 1, 0, 9, 6, 2, 7, 8, 4, 5, 1, 7, 0, 7, 1, 6, 9, 0, 8, 7, 1, 9, 0, 1, 8, 6, 2, 0, 4, 9, 0, 7, 1, 7, 5, 9, 2, 1, 7, 9, 0, 8, 1, 9, 7, 5, 9, 3, 8, 2, 1, 7, 9, 4, 5, 0, 6, 0, 7, 3, 1, 0, 2, 0, 9, 7, 4, 6, 2, 9, 6, 1, 8, 6, 9, 0, 6, 3, 7, 1, 5, 8, 0, 9, 1, 7, 2, 9, 7, 1, 8, 1, 7

Stimuli list for the stage of increased cognitive load:
2, 9, 7, 5, 1, 0, 3, 7, 9, 2, 5, 0, 9, 5, 7, 0, 3, 1, 2, 7, 6, 9, 0, 1, 7, 0, 9, 6, 7, 0, 9, 1, 7, 0, 6, 1, 0, 7, 8, 3, 9, 7, 3, 1, 8, 4, 1, 5, 9, 6, 7, 9, 2, 9, 7, 8, 5, 4, 9, 6, 3, 9, 0, 8, 1, 0, 5, 7, 0, 4, 0, 1, 9, 6, 0, 7, 4, 2, 1, 5, 7, 4, 1, 8, 3, 1, 7, 0, 8, 7, 2, 1, 5, 7, 9, 3, 6, 9, 7, 0, 9, 7, 2, 1, 3, 9, 7, 9, 4, 1, 6, 0, 9, 1, 0, 8, 1, 5, 9, 8, 1, 2, 5, 0, 8, 0, 3, 1, 0, 4, 3, 0, 7, 1, 0, 2, 9, 4, 6, 7, 4, 1, 0, 4, 9, 1, 0, 2, 0, 7, 9, 1, 7, 8, 1, 9, 7, 9, 6, 1

Stimuli list for the stage of high cognitive load:
1, 7, 0, 9, Stadt, 0, 7, 9, 0, 1, 2, 9, Samstag, 6, 7, Bild, 1, 9, 8, 3, 5, Mann, 1, 4, 7, 0, Sonntag, 1, Grund, 7, 0, 9, 7, 9, 2, Spiel, 0, 3, 1, 8, 7, 5, Mark, 9, 1, 3, 0, Land, 1, 7, 4, 2, Artikel, 0, 9, 7, 5, Uhr, 8, Platz, 4, 6, Arbeit, 1, 3, 0, 9, Kind, 7, 4, 5, 1, 3, Mai, 8, 6, 0, 1, 7, 9, Jahr, 5, 7, 1, 9, 0, 9, Seite, 0, 1, 7, Freitag, 2, 1, 7, 9, Fall, 4, Euro, 1, Gemeinde, 5, 3, 8, Leben, 9, 1, 2, Haus, 7, 6, 9, 0, Frage, 7, 5, 9, Name, 0, 7, Woche, 2, 8, Zeit, 1, 9, 7, 6, 3, 0, 9, Monat, 5, 6, 0, 7, 1, Tag, 9, 1, 4, 2, 8, 0, Mensch, 4, 9, 0, Straße, 7, 3, 0, Thema, 4, 1, 0, Teil, 9, 7, Welt, 8, 1, 6, Punkt, 3, 6, 2, Frau, 7, 6, 8, 1, 4, Geschichte, 7, 0, 9, 0, 5, Million, 0, 9, 2, 0, 1, 9, Ende, 3, 1, 0, 6, 1, 9, Mitglied, 5, 7, 4, 8, 7, 2

E Questions of the demographic questionnaire

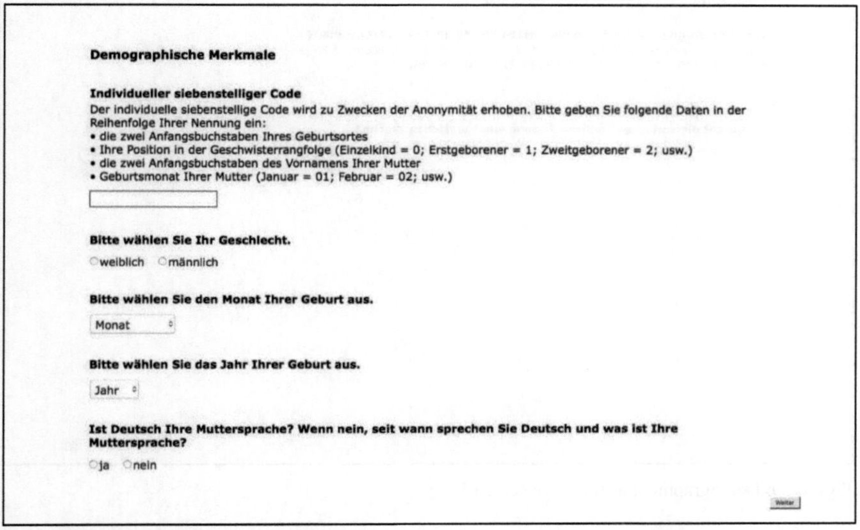

Demographische Merkmale

Individueller siebenstelliger Code
Der individuelle siebenstellige Code wird zu Zwecken der Anonymität erhoben. Bitte geben Sie folgende Daten in der Reihenfolge Ihrer Nennung ein:
- die zwei Anfangsbuchstaben Ihres Geburtsortes
- Ihre Position in der Geschwisterrangfolge (Einzelkind = 0; Erstgeborener = 1; Zweitgeborener = 2; usw.)
- die zwei Anfangsbuchstaben des Vornamens Ihrer Mutter
- Geburtsmonat Ihrer Mutter (Januar = 01; Februar = 02; usw.)

Bitte wählen Sie Ihr Geschlecht.
○weiblich ○männlich

Bitte wählen Sie den Monat Ihrer Geburt aus.
Monat

Bitte wählen Sie das Jahr Ihrer Geburt aus.
Jahr

Ist Deutsch Ihre Muttersprache? Wenn nein, seit wann sprechen Sie Deutsch und was ist Ihre Muttersprache?
○ja ○nein

Weiter

Figure 18: Demographic questionnaire screen 1.

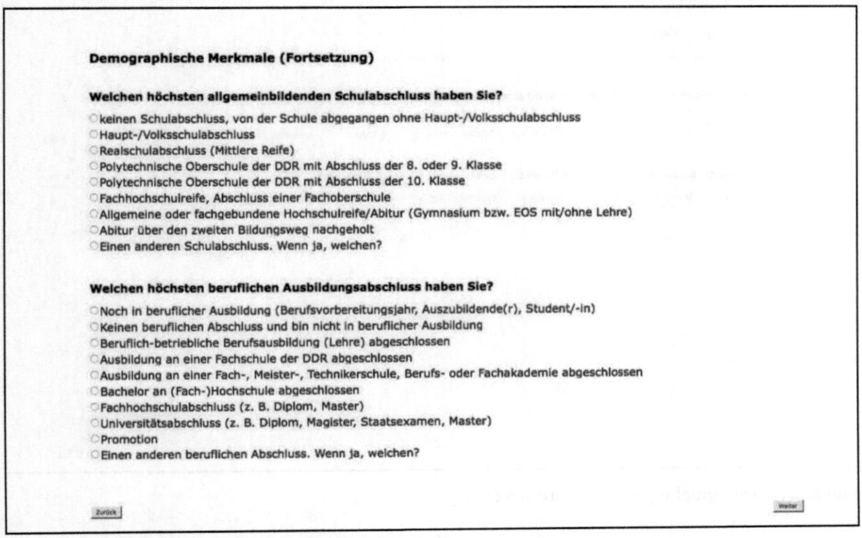

Demographische Merkmale (Fortsetzung)

Welchen höchsten allgemeinbildenden Schulabschluss haben Sie?
○keinen Schulabschluss, von der Schule abgegangen ohne Haupt-/Volksschulabschluss
○Haupt-/Volksschulabschluss
○Realschulabschluss (Mittlere Reife)
○Polytechnische Oberschule der DDR mit Abschluss der 8. oder 9. Klasse
○Polytechnische Oberschule der DDR mit Abschluss der 10. Klasse
○Fachhochschulreife, Abschluss einer Fachoberschule
○Allgemeine oder fachgebundene Hochschulreife/Abitur (Gymnasium bzw. EOS mit/ohne Lehre)
○Abitur über den zweiten Bildungsweg nachgeholt
○Einen anderen Schulabschluss. Wenn ja, welchen?

Welchen höchsten beruflichen Ausbildungsabschluss haben Sie?
○Noch in beruflicher Ausbildung (Berufsvorbereitungsjahr, Auszubildende(r), Student/-in)
○Keinen beruflichen Abschluss und bin nicht in beruflicher Ausbildung
○Beruflich-betriebliche Berufsausbildung (Lehre) abgeschlossen
○Ausbildung an einer Fachschule der DDR abgeschlossen
○Ausbildung an einer Fach-, Meister-, Technikerschule, Berufs- oder Fachakademie abgeschlossen
○Bachelor an (Fach-)Hochschule abgeschlossen
○Fachhochschulabschluss (z. B. Diplom, Master)
○Universitätsabschluss (z. B. Diplom, Magister, Staatsexamen, Master)
○Promotion
○Einen anderen beruflichen Abschluss. Wenn ja, welchen?

Zurück Weiter

Figure 19: Demographic questionnaire screen 2.

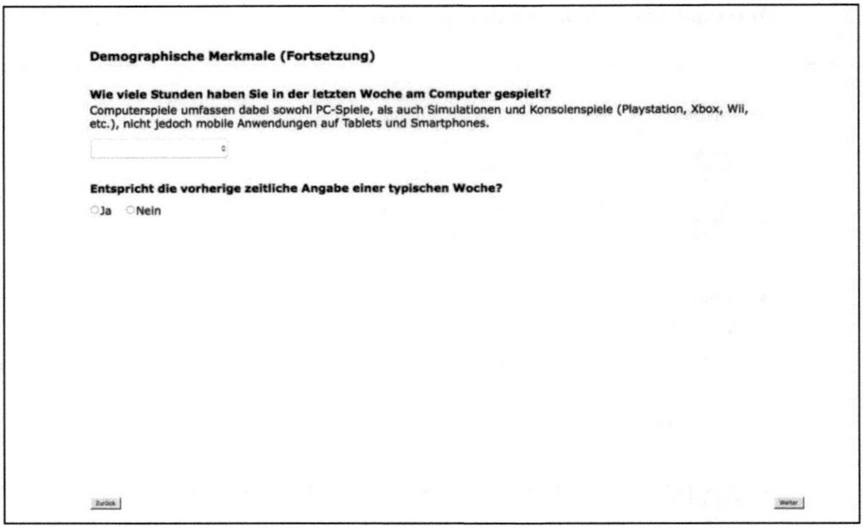

Demographische Merkmale (Fortsetzung)

Wie viele Stunden haben Sie in der letzten Woche am Computer gespielt?
Computerspiele umfassen dabei sowohl PC-Spiele, als auch Simulationen und Konsolenspiele (Playstation, Xbox, Wii, etc.), nicht jedoch mobile Anwendungen auf Tablets und Smartphones.

Entspricht die vorherige zeitliche Angabe einer typischen Woche?
○ Ja ○ Nein

Zurück Weiter

Figure 20: Demographic questionnaire screen 3.

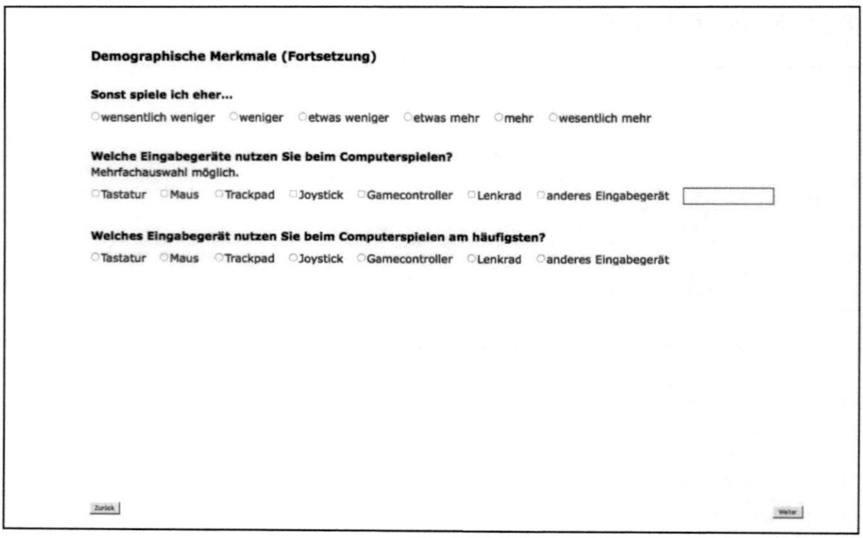

Demographische Merkmale (Fortsetzung)

Sonst spiele ich eher...
○ wensentlich weniger ○ weniger ○ etwas weniger ○ etwas mehr ○ mehr ○ wesentlich mehr

Welche Eingabegeräte nutzen Sie beim Computerspielen?
Mehrfachauswahl möglich.
□ Tastatur □ Maus □ Trackpad □ Joystick □ Gamecontroller □ Lenkrad □ anderes Eingabegerät

Welches Eingabegerät nutzen Sie beim Computerspielen am häufigsten?
○ Tastatur ○ Maus ○ Trackpad ○ Joystick ○ Gamecontroller ○ Lenkrad ○ anderes Eingabegerät

Zurück Weiter

Figure 21: Demographic questionnaire screen 4.

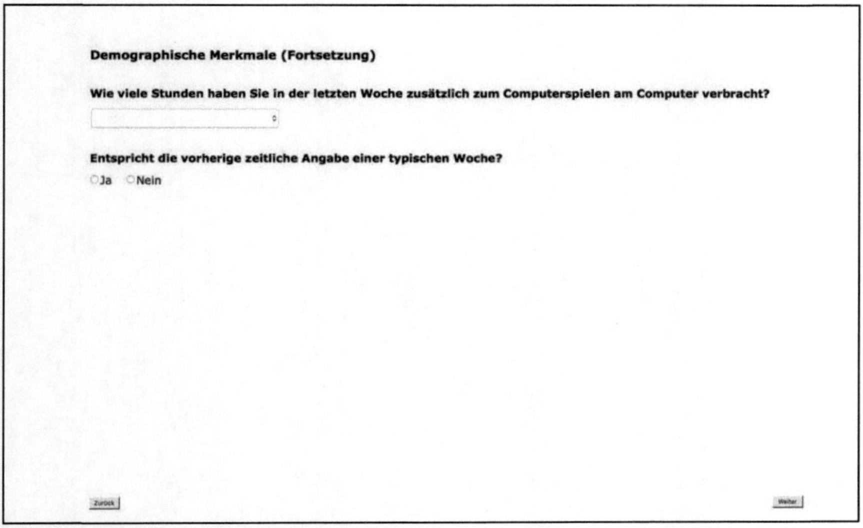

Figure 22: Demographic questionnaire screen 5.

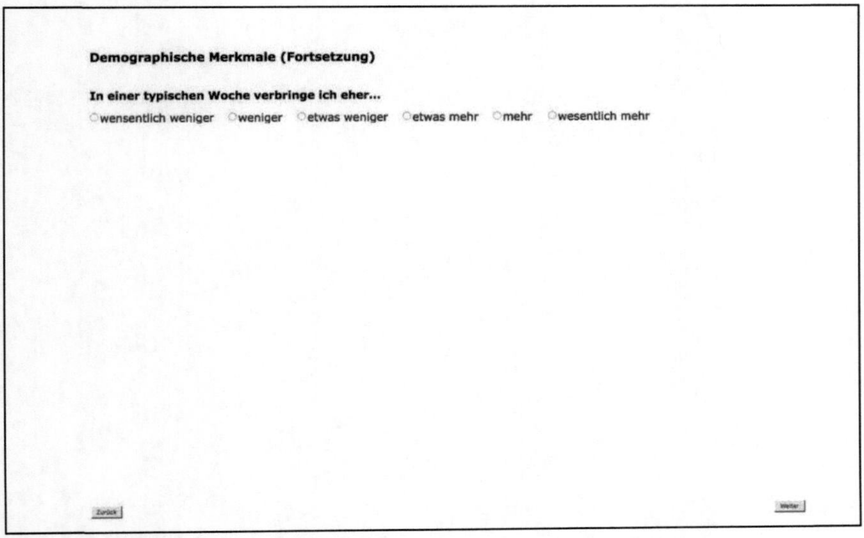

Figure 23: Demographic questionnaire screen 6.

References

Aarts, H. and Dijksterhuis, A., 2000. Habits as knowledge structures: Automaticity in goal-directed behavior. *Journal of Personality and Social Psychology,* 78(1), pp. 53-63.

Abell, P., Felin, T. and Foss, N.J., 2008. Building micro-foundations for the routines, capabilities, and performance links. *Managerial and Decision Economics,* 29(6), pp. 489-502.

Abrahamse, E.L., Jiménez, L., Verwey, W.B. and Clegg, B.A., 2010. Representing serial action and perception. *Psychonomic Bulletin & Review,* 17(5), pp. 603-623.

Adler, P.S., Goldoftas, B. and Levine, D.I., 1999. Flexibility versus efficiency? A case study of model changeovers in the Toyota production system. *Organization Science,* 10(1), pp. 43-68.

Aiken, C. and Keller, S., 2009. The irrational side of change management. *The McKinsey Quarterly,* 2009(2), pp. 101-109.

Aime, F., Johnson, S., Ridge, J.W. and Hill, A.D., 2010. The routine may be stable but the advantage is not: Competitive implications of key employee mobility. *Strategic Management Journal,* 31(1), pp. 75-87.

Aldrich, H.E. and Martinez, M.A., 2010. Entrepreneurship as social construction: A multilevel evolutionary approach. In: Z.J. Acs and D.B. Audretsch (Eds.), *Handbook of entrepreneurship research* (Vol. 5, pp. 387-427). New York: Springer.

Alexander, G., 2001. Institutions, path dependence, and democratic consolidation. *Journal of Theoretical Politics,* 13(3), pp. 249-269.

Amazon.com Inc., (2016). *Annual report 2015.* [PDF]. Available at: Amazon.com Inc., <http://phx.corporate-ir.net/External.File?item=UGFyZW50SUQ9NjI4NTg0fENoaWxkSUQ9MzI5NTMwfFR5cGU9MQ==&t=1> [Accessed Dec 1st, 2016].

Amir, N., Kuckertz, J.M. and Najmi, S., 2013. The effect of modifying automatic action tendencies on overt avoidance behaviors. *Emotion,* 13(3), pp. 478-484.

Amit, R. and Schoemaker, P.J.H., 1993. Strategic assets and organizational rent. *Strategic Management Journal,* 14(1), pp. 33-46.

Amit, R. and Belcourt, M., 1999. Human resources management processes: A value-creating source of competitive advantage. *European Management Journal,* 17(2), pp. 174-181.

Amt für Flugsicherung der Bundeswehr, 2013. *Besondere Anweisung für die Militärische Flugsicherung 2-100*. Frankfurt: Amt für Flugsicherung der Bundeswehr.

Andersen, P.H., 2003. The embeddedness of selfish routines: How routines are replicated in business networks. *Industry & Innovation,* 10(2), pp. 159-177.

Anderson, C.A., 2003. Video games and aggressive behavior. In: D. Ravitch and J.P. Viteritti (Eds.), *Kid stuff: Marketing sex and violence to America's children* (pp. ix, 267 p.). Baltimore: Johns Hopkins University Press.

Anderson, C.A., 2004. An update on the effects of playing violent video games. *Journal of Adolescence,* 27(1), pp. 113-122.

Anderson, J.R., 1995. *Learning and memory: An integrated approach.* New York: Wiley.

Argote, L. and Ingram, P., 2000. Knowledge transfer: A basis for competitive advantage in firms. *Organizational behavior and human decision processes,* 82(1), pp. 150-169.

Arrow, K.J., 2000. Increasing returns: Historiographic issues and path dependence. *The European Journal of the History of Economic Thought,* 7(2), pp. 171-180.

Arthur, W.B., 1989. Competing technologies, increasing returns, and lock-in by historical events. *The Economic Journal,* 99(394), pp. 116-131.

Arthur, W.B., Ermoliev, Y.M. and Kaniovski, Y.M., 1987. Path-dependent processes and the emergence of macro-structure. *European Journal of Operational Research,* 30(3), pp. 294-303.

Asch, S.E., 1952. *Social psychology*. New York: Prentice-Hall.

Ashforth, B.E. and Fried, Y., 1988. The Mindlessness of organizational behaviors. *Human Relations,* 41(4), pp. 305-329.

Baden-Fuller, C. and Winter, S.G. (2007). *Replicating organizational knowledge: Principles or templates?* [Working Paper] DOI: https://doi.org/10.2139/ssrn.1118013 [Accessed Jun 16, 2015].

Banaji, M.R. and Greenwald, A.G., 1995. Implicit gender stereotyping in judgments of fame. *Journal of Personality and Social Psychology,* 68(2), pp. 181-198.

M. Eberl, *Organizational Routines Meet Experimental Psychology*,
Zukunftsfähige Unternehmensführung in Forschung und Praxis,
https://doi.org/10.1007/978-3-658-23562-8

Banaji, M.R. and Greenwald, A.G., 2013. *Blindspot: Hidden biases of good people*. New York: Delacorte Press.

Bandura, A., 1965. Influence of models' reinforcement contingencies on the acquisition of imitative responses. *Journal of Personality and Social Psychology,* 1(6), pp. 589-595.

Bandura, A., 1977a. Self-efficacy: Toward a unifying theory of behavioral change. *Psychological Review,* 84(2), pp. 191-215.

Bandura, A., 1977b. *Social learning theory*. Englewood Cliffs: Prentice Hall.

Bandura, A., 1986. *Social foundations of thought and action: A social cognitive theory*. Englewood Cliffs: Prentice-Hall.

Bandura, A., Ross, D. and Ross, S.A., 1961. Transmission of aggression through imitation of aggressive models. *The Journal of Abnormal and Social Psychology,* 63(3), pp. 575-582.

Bandura, A., Ross, D. and Ross, S.A., 1963a. Vicarious reinforcement and imitative learning. *The Journal of Abnormal and Social Psychology,* 67(6), pp. 601-607.

Bandura, A., Ross, D. and Ross, S.A., 1963b. Imitation of film-mediated aggressive models. *The Journal of Abnormal and Social Psychology,* 66(1), pp. 3-11.

Banse, R., Seise, J. and Zerbes, N., 2001. Implicit attitudes towards homosexuality: Reliability, validity, and controllability of the IAT. *Experimental Psychology,* 48(2), pp. 145-160.

Bapuji, H., Hora, M. and Saeed, A.M., 2012. Intentions, intermediaries, and interaction: Examining the emergence of routines. *Journal of Management Studies,* 49(8), pp. 1586-1607.

Barney, J., 1991. Firm resources and sustained competitive advantage. *Journal of Management,* 17(1), pp. 99-120.

Barreto, I., 2010. Dynamic capabilities: A review of past research and an agenda for the future. *Journal of Management,* 36(1), pp. 256-280.

Barsade, S.G. and Gibson, D.E., 2007. Why does affect matter in organizations? *Academy of Management Perspectives,* 21(1), pp. 36-59.

Bazerman, M.H. and Moore, D.A., 2009. *Judgment in managerial decision making* (7th ed.). Hoboken: John Wiley & Sons.

Becker, D., Jostmann, N.B., Wiers, R.W. and Holland, R.W., 2015. Approach avoidance training in the eating domain: Testing the effectiveness across three single session studies. *Appetite,* 85, pp. 58-65.

Becker, E.S., Wittkowski, M., te Velthuis, S., Kerstholt, M., Woud, M.L., Kampmann, I.L., Telli, S. and Rinck, M., 2013. Training approach-avoidance of smiling faces affects emotional vulnerability in socially anxious individuals. *Frontiers in Human Neuroscience,* 7(481), pp. 1-6.

Becker, M.C. (2003). *The concept of routines twenty years after Nelson and Winter (1982) A review of the literature*. [Working paper] Available at: Danish Research Unit for Industrial Dynamics <http://www3.druid.dk/wp/20030006.pdf> [Accessed June 16, 2015].

Becker, M.C., 2004. Organizational routines: A review of the literature. *Industrial and Corporate Change,* 13(4), pp. 643-678.

Becker, M.C., 2005a. A framework for applying organizational routines in empirical research: Linking antecedents, characteristics and performance outcomes of recurrent interaction patterns. *Industrial and Corporate Change,* 14(5), pp. 817-846.

Becker, M.C., 2005b. The concept of routines: Some clarifications. *Cambridge Journal of Economics,* 29(2), pp. 249-262.

Becker, M.C., 2007. Routines: A brief history of the concept. In: S. Ioannides and K. Nielsen (Eds.), *Economics and the social sciences: Boundaries, interaction and integration* (pp. vii, 302 p.). Cheltenham: Edward Elgar.

Becker, M.C., 2008. The past, present and future of organizational routines: Introduction to the handbook of organizational routines. In: M.C. Becker (Ed.), *Handbook of organizational routines* (pp. 3-14). Cheltenham: Edward Elgar.

Becker, M.C. and Lazaric, N., 2003. The influence of knowledge in the replication of routines. *Economie Appliquée,* LVI(3), pp. 65-94.

Becker, M.C. and Zirpoli, F., 2008. Applying organizational routines in analyzing the behavior of organizations. *Journal of Economic Behavior & Organization,* 66(1), pp. 128-148.

Becker, M.C., Lazaric, N., Nelson, R.R. and Winter, S.G., 2005. Applying organizational routines in understanding organizational change. *Industrial and Corporate Change,* 14(5), pp. 775-791.

Beer, S., 1972. *Brain of the firm: A development in management cybernetics*. New York: Herder and Herder.

Beer, S., 1979. *The heart of enterprise*. Chichester: Wiley.

Beer, S., 1985. *Diagnosing the system for organizations*. Chichester: Wiley.

Benner, M.J. and Tripsas, M., 2012. The influence of prior industry affiliation on framing in nascent industries: The evolution of digital cameras. *Strategic Management Journal,* 33(3), pp. 277-302.

Bergius, R., 2004. Lernen, Lernforschung. In: O. Häcker and K. Stapf (Eds.), *Dorsch: Psychologisches Wörterbuch* (14th ed., pp. 546). Bern: Verlag Hans Huber.

Berman, S., 1998. Path dependency and political action: Reexamining responses to the depression. *Comparative Politics,* 30(4), p. 379.

Berninger, V.W., Mizokawa, D.T. and Bragg, R., 1991. Scientific practitioner: Theory-based diagnosis and remediation of writing disabilities. *Journal of School Psychology,* 29(1), pp. 57-79.

Berry, D.C., 1997. Concluding note: How implicit is implicit learning? In: D. Berry (Ed.), *How implicit is implicit learning?* (pp. 235-240). Oxford: Oxford University Press.

Berry, D.C. and Broadbent, D.E., 1984. On the relationship between task performance and associated verbalizable knowledge. *The Quarterly Journal of Experimental Psychology Section A,* 36(2), pp. 209-231.

Berry, D.C. and Broadbent, D.E., 1987. The combination of explicit and implicit learning processes in task control. *Psychological Research,* 49(1), pp. 7-15.

Berry, D.C. and Broadbent, D.E., 1988. Interactive tasks and the implicit-explicit distinction. *British Journal of Psychology,* 79(2), pp. 251-272.

Berry, D.C. and Dienes, Z., 1993. Towards a working characterisation of implicit learning. In: D.C. Berry and Z. Dienes (Eds.), *Implicit learning: Theoretical and empirical issues*. Hove: Lawrence Erlsbaum.

Bertels, S., Howard-Grenville, J. and Pek, S., 2016. Cultural molding, shielding, and shoring at Oilco: The role of culture in the integration of routines. *Organization Science,* 27(3), pp. 573-593.

Bessant, J., Caffyn, S. and Gallagher, M., 2001. An evolutionary model of continuous improvement behaviour. *Technovation,* 21(2), pp. 67-77.

Betsch, T., Fiedler, K. and Brinkmann, J., 1998. Behavioral routines in decision making: The effects of novelty in task presentation and time pressure on routine maintenance and deviation. *European Journal of Social Psychology,* 28(6), pp. 861-878.

Betsch, T., Brinkmann, B.J., Fiedler, K. and Breining, K., 1999. When prior knowledge overrules new evidence: Adaptive use of decision strategies and the role of behavioral routines. *Swiss Journal of Psychology,* 58(3), pp. 151-160.

Biddle, J.E., 1990. Purpose and evolution in commons's institutionalism. *History of Political Economy,* 22(1), pp. 19-47.

Blau, P.M., 1955. *The dynamics of bureaucracy: A study of interpersonal relations in two government agencies*. Chicago: Chicago University Press.

Bless, H., Fiedler, K. and Strack, F., 2004. *Social cognition: How individuals construct social reality*. Hove: Psychology Press.

BMVg: Bundesministerium der Verteidigung, 1990. Nr.15: Empirische Untersuchungen zur Einstellungs-, Meinungs- und Verhaltensforschung in der Bundeswehr. *Ministerialblatt des Bundesministers der Verteidigung*, pp. 403-404.

Bourdieu, P., 1977. *Outline of a theory of practice*. Cambridge: Cambridge University Press.

Bourdieu, P., 1990. *The logic of practice*. Stanford: Stanford University Press.

Bransford, J., Barron, B., Pea, R., Meltzoff, A., Kuhl, P., Bell, P., Stevens, R., Schwartz, D., Vye, N., Reeves, B., Roschelle, J. and Sabelli, N., 2006. Foundations and opportunities for an interdisciplinary science of learning. In: R.K. Sawyer (Ed.), *The Cambridge handbook of the learning sciences*. Cambridge: Cambridge University Press.

Bredenkamp, J. and Wippich, W., 1977. *Lern- und Gedächtnispsychologie*. Stuttgart: Kohlhammer.

Bresman, H., 2012. Changing routines: A process model of vicarious group learning in pharmaceutical R&D. *Academy of Management Journal,* 56(1), pp. 35-61.

Bright, J.E. and Burton, A.M., 2007. Past midnight: Semantic processing in an implicit learning task. *The Quarterly Journal of Experimental Psychology Section A,* 47(1), pp. 71-89.

Brockmeyer, T., Schmidt, U. and Friederich, H.-C., 2016. The ABBA study – approach bias modification in bulimia nervosa and binge eating disorder: Study protocol for a randomised controlled trial. *Trials,* 17(1), pp. 1-9.

Brockmeyer, T., Hahn, C., Reetz, C., Schmidt, U. and Friederich, H.-C., 2015. Approach bias modification in food craving: A proof-of-concept study. *European Eating Disorders Review,* 23(5), pp. 352-360.

Brooks, S., Prince, A., Stahl, D., Campbell, I.C. and Treasure, J., 2011. A systematic review and meta-analysis of cognitive bias to food stimuli in people with disordered eating behaviour. *Clinical Psychology Review,* 31(1), pp. 37-51.

Brown, A.D. and Lewis, M.A., 2011. Identities, discipline and routines. *Organization Studies,* 32(7), pp. 871-895.

Brown, A.L., 1978. Knowing when, where, and how to remember: A problem of metacognition. In: R. Glaser (Ed.), *Advances in instructional psychology: Educational design and cognitive science* (Vol. 1, pp. 77-165). Hillsdale: Lawrence Erlbaum.

Bruggeman, D., 2002. NASA: A path dependent organization. *Technology in Society,* 24(4), pp. 415-431.

Bruns, H.C., 2009. Leveraging functionality in safety routines: Examining the divergence of rules and performance. *Human Relations,* 62(9), pp. 1399-1426.

Buchner, A. and Wippich, W., 1998. Differences and commonalities between implicit learning and explicit memory. In: M.A. Stadler and P.A. Frensch (Eds.), *Handbook of implicit learning* (pp. 3-45). Thousand Oaks: SAGE.

Bundesdatenschutzgesetz (BDSG), 1990. As amended and promulgated on Sept 1, 2014. Available at <http://www.gesetze-im-internet.de/bdsg_1990> [Accessed June 10th, 2016].

Burns, J., 2000. The dynamics of accounting change inter-play between new practices, routines, institutions, power and politics. *Accounting, Auditing & Accountability Journal,* 13(5), pp. 566-596.

Burns, J. and Scapens, R.W., 2000. Conceptualizing management accounting change: An institutional framework. *Management Accounting Research,* 11(1), pp. 3-25.

Burns, J. and Scapens, R.W., 2008. Organizational routines in accounting. In: M.C. Becker (Ed.), *Handbook of organizational routines* (pp. 87-106). Cheltenham: Edward Elgar.

Burns, J. and Quinn, M., 2011. The routinisation of management controls in software. *Journal of Management Control,* 22(1), pp. 5-24.

Burns, T. and Stalker, G.M., 1961. *The management of innovation.* London: Tavistock.

Cacciatori, E., 2012. Resolving conflict in problem-solving: Systems of artefacts in the development of new routines. *Journal of Management Studies,* 49(8), pp. 1559-1585.

Cacioppo, J.T., Priester, J.R. and Berntson, G.G., 1993. Rudimentary determinants of attitudes. II: Arm flexion and extension have differential effects on attitudes. *Journal of Personality and Social Psychology,* 65(1), pp. 5-17.

Cadsby, C.B., Song, F. and Tapon, F., 2007. Sorting and incentive effects of pay for performance: An experimental investigation. *Academy of Management Journal,* 50(2), pp. 387-405.

Carlile, P.R. and Rebentisch, E.S., 2003. Into the black box: The knowledge transformation cycle. *Management Science,* 49(9), pp. 1180-1195.

Carlsson, B.O. and Eliasson, G., 1994. The nature and importance of economic competence. *Industrial and Corporate Change,* 3(3), pp. 687-711.

Caspar, F., 2004. Verhalten. In: O. Häcker and K. Stapf (Eds.), *Dorsch: psychologisches Wörterbuch* (14th ed.). Bern: Hans Huber.

Cavalcante, S., Kesting, P. and Ulhøi, J., 2011. Business model dynamics and innovation: (Re)establishing the missing linkages. *Management Decision,* 49(8), pp. 1327-1342.

Celen, B., Kariv, S. and Schotter, A., 2010. An experimental test of advice and social learning. *Management Science,* 56(10), pp. 1687-1701.

Chaiken, S. and Trope, Y., 1999. *Dual-process theories in social psychology.* New York: Guilford Press.

Chambers, C., Sharbanee, J.M., Hu, L., Stritzke, W.G.K., Wiers, R.W., Rinck, M. and MacLeod, C., 2014. The effect of approach/avoidance training on alcohol consumption is mediated by change in alcohol action tendency. *PLoS ONE,* 9(1), p. e85855.

Chartrand, T.L. and Bargh, J.A., 1996. Automatic activation of impression formation and memorization goals: Nonconscious goal priming reproduces effects of explicit task instructions. *Journal of Personality and Social Psychology,* 71(3), pp. 464-478.

Chomsky, N., 1955. *The logical structure of linguistic theory*. New York: Plenum Press.

Chomsky, N., 1956. Three models for the description of language. *IRE Transactions on Information Theory,* 2(3), pp. 113-124.

Chomsky, N., 1957. *Syntactic structures*. The Hague: Mouton.

Chomsky, N., 1959. Verbal Behavior by B. F. Skinner: A review. *Language,* 35(1), pp. 26-58.

Chomsky, N., 1988. *Language and problems of knowledge: The Managua lectures*. Cambridge: MIT Press.

Clagett, R.P. (1967). *Receptivity to innovation - overcoming N.I.H.* (Master of Science Thesis), Alfred P. Sloan School of Management; Massachusetts Institute of Technology, Massachusetts.

Cleeremans, A., 1993. *Mechanisms of implicit learning: Connectionist models of sequence processing*. Cambridge: MIT Press.

Cleeremans, A., 2006a. Implicit learning and consciousness: A graded, dynamic perspective. In: Q. Jing, M.R. Rosenzweig, G. D'Ydewalle, H. Zhang, H.-C. Chen and K. Zhang (Eds.), *Progress in psychological science around the world: proceedings of the 28th International Congress of Psychology* (pp. 401-418). New York: Psychology Press.

Cleeremans, A., 2006b. Implicit learning models. In: L. Nadel (Ed.), *Encyclopedia of Cognitive Science* (pp. 415-423). Chichester: Wiley.

Cleeremans, A. and Dienes, Z., 2008. Computational Models of Implicit Learning. In: R. Sun (Ed.), *The Cambridge handbook of computational psychology* (pp. 396-421). Cambridge: Cambridge University Press.

Cleeremans, A., Destrebecqz, A. and Boyer, M., 1998. Implicit learning: News from the front. *Trends in Cognitive Sciences,* 2(10), pp. 406-416.

Clegg, B.A., Digirolamo, G.J. and Keele, S.W., 1998. Sequence learning. *Trends in Cognitive Sciences,* 2(8), pp. 275-281.

Cock, J.J., Berry, D.C. and Gaffan, E.A., 1994. New strings for old: The role of similarity processing in an incidental learning task. *The Quarterly Journal of Experimental Psychology Section A,* 47(4), pp. 1015-1034.

Cockburn, I.M., Henderson, R.M. and Stern, S., 2000. Untangling the origins of competitive advantage. *Strategic Management Journal,* 21(10-11), pp. 1123-1145.

Cohen, M.D., 1991. Individual learning and organizational routine: Emerging connections. *Organization Science,* 2(1), pp. 135-139.

Cohen, M.D., 2007. Reading Dewey: Reflections on the study of routine. *Organization Studies,* 28(5), pp. 773-786.

Cohen, M.D., 2012. Perceiving and remembering routine action: Fundamental micro-level origins. *Journal of Management Studies,* 49(8), pp. 1383-1388.

Cohen, M.D. and Bacdayan, P., 1994. Organizational routines are stored as procedural memory: Evidence from a laboratory study. *Organization Science,* 5(4), pp. 554-568.

Cohen, M.D., Burkhart, R., Dosi, G., Egidi, M., Marengo, L., Warglien, M. and Winter, S.G., 1996. Routines and other recurring action patterns of organizations: Contemporary research issues. *Industrial and Corporate Change,* 5(3), pp. 653-698.

Cohendet, P. and Llerena, P., 2003. Routines and incentives: The role of communities in the firm. *Industrial and Corporate Change,* 12(2), pp. 271-297.

Cohendet, P., Kern, F., Mehmanpazir, B. and Munier, F., 1999. Knowledge coordination, competence creation and integrated networks in globalised firms. *Cambridge Journal of Economics,* 23(2), pp. 225-241.

Collis, D.J., 1994. Research note: How valuable are organizational capabilities? *Strategic Management Journal,* 15(S1), pp. 143-152.

Coriat, B., 1995. Variety, routines and networks: The metamorphosis of fordist firms. *Industrial and Corporate Change,* 4(1), pp. 205-227.

Coriat, B. and Dosi, G., 1998. Learning how to govern and learning how to solve problems: On the co-evolution of competences, conflicts and organizational routines. In: A.D. Chandler, P. Hagström and O. Sölvell (Eds.), *The dynamic firm: The role of technology, strategy, organization and regions*. Oxford: Oxford University Press.

Costello, N., 2000. *Stability and change in high-tech enterprises: Organisational practices and routines*. London: Routledge.

Cournot, A.A., 1838 [1897]. *Researches into the mathematical principles of the theory of wealth* (N.T. Bacon and I. Fisher, Trans.). New York: Macmillan.

Cousijn, J., Luijten, M. and Wiers, R.W., 2014. Mechanisms underlying alcohol-approach action tendencies: The role of emotional primes and drinking motives. *Frontiers in Psychiatry,* 5.

Croskerry, P., 2013. From mindless to mindful practice: Cognitive bias and clinical decision making. *New England Journal of Medicine,* 368(26), pp. 2445-2448.

Cyert, R.M. and March, J.G., 1963. *A behavioral theory of the firm*. Englewood Cliffs: Prentice-Hall.

D'Adderio, L., 2003. Configuring software, reconfiguring memories: The influence of integrated systems on the reproduction of knowledge and routines. *Industrial and Corporate Change,* 12(2), pp. 321-350.

D'Adderio, L., 2008. The performativity of routines: Theorising the influence of artefacts and distributed agencies on routines dynamics. *Research Policy,* 37(5), pp. 769-789.

D'Adderio, L., 2010. Artifacts at the centre of routines: Performing the material turn in routines theory. *Journal of Institutional Economics,* 7(02), pp. 197-230.

D'Adderio, L., 2014. The replication dilemma unravelled: How organizations enact multiple goals in routine transfer. *Organization Science,* 25(5), pp. 1325-1350.

Darwin, C., 1859. *On the origin of species by means of natural selection or the preservation of favoured races in the struggle for life*. London: John Murray.

Darwin, C., 1868. *The variation of animals and plants under domestication* (Vol. 1). London: John Murray.

Dasgupta, N., McGhee, D.E., Greenwald, A.G. and Banaji, M.R., 2000. Automatic preference for white Americans: Eliminating the familiarity explanation. *Journal of Experimental Social Psychology,* 36(3), pp. 316-328.

David, P.A., 1985. Clio and the economics of QWERTY. *The American Economic Review,* 75(2), pp. 332-337.

David, P.A., 2005. Path dependence in economic processes: Implications for policy analysis in dynamical system contexts. In: K. Dopfer (Ed.), *The evolutionary foundations of economics* (pp. 149-194). Cambridge: Cambridge University Press.

David, P.A. and Greenstein, S., 1990. The economics of compatibility standards: An introduction to recent research. *Economics of Innovation and New Technology,* 1(1-2), pp. 3-41.

De Houwer, J., 2006. What are implicit measures and why are we using them? In: R. Wiers and A.W. Stacy (Eds.), *Handbook of implicit cognition and addiction* (pp. 11-28). Thousand Oaks: SAGE.

Delmestri, G., 1998. Do all roads lead to Rome... or Berlin? The evolution of intra- and inter-organizational routines in the machinebuilding industry. *Organization Studies,* 19(4), pp. 639-665.

Descartes, R., 1633 [1985]. Treatise on man (J. Cottingham, R. Stoothoff and D. Murdoch, Trans.). In *The philosophical writings of Descartes* (Vol. I, pp. 99-108). Cambridge: Cambridge University Press.

Dewey, J., 1922. *Human nature and conduct: An introduction to social psychology*. New York: Holt.

Dienes, Z. and Berry, D.C., 1997. Implicit learning: Below the subjective threshold. *Psychonomic Bulletin & Review,* 4(1), pp. 3-23.

Dienes, Z. and Perner, J., 1999. A theory of implicit and explicit knowledge. *Behavioral and Brain Sciences,* 22(5), pp. 735-755; discussion 755-808.

Dionysiou, D.D. and Tsoukas, H., 2013. Understanding the (re)creation of routines from within: A symbolic interactionist perspective. *Academy of Management Review,* 38(2), pp. 181-205.

Domjan, M., Grau, J.W. and Krause, M.A., 2010. *The principles of learning and behavior* (6th ed.). Belmont: Wadsworth.

Dosi, G. and Kaniovski, Y., 1994. On 'badly behaved' dynamics: Some applications of generalized urn schemes to technological and economic change. *Journal of Evolutionary Economics,* 4(2), pp. 93-123.

Dosi, G., Nelson, R.R. and Winter, S.G., 2000. Introduction: The nature and dynamics of organizational capabilities. In: G. Dosi, R.R. Nelson and S.G. Winter (Eds.), *The nature and dynamics of organizational capabilities* (Vol. 1-22). Oxford: Oxford University Press.

Dosi, G., Faillo, M. and Marengo, L., 2008. Problem solving and governance in the capability-based view of the firm: The roles and theoretical representations of organizational routines. In: M.C. Becker (Ed.), *Handbook of organizational routines* (pp. 107-121). Cheltenham: Edward Elgar.

Durkheim, É., 1895 [1982]. *The rules of sociological method* (S. Lukes Ed. 1st American ed.). New York: Free Press.

Durkheim, É., 1897 [2002]. *Suicide: A study in sociology* (2nd ed.). London: Routledge.

Dyer, J.H. and Singh, H., 1998. The relational view: Cooperative strategy and sources of interorganizational competitive advantage. *The Academy of Management Review,* 23(4), pp. 660-679.

Earley, P.C., 1997. *Face, harmony, and social structure: An analysis of organizational behavior across cultures*. New York: Oxford University Press.

Eberl, C. (2014). *Implicit processes in psychopathology: Exploring their relevance for prediction and for treatment improvement.* (Ph.D. Doctoral thesis), Radboud University Nijmegen, Nijmegen.

Eberl, C., Wiers, R.W., Pawelczack, S., Rinck, M., Becker, E.S. and Lindenmeyer, J., 2013. Approach bias modification in alcohol dependence: Do clinical effects replicate and for whom does it work best? *Developmental Cognitive Neuroscience,* 4, pp. 38-51.

Eberl, C., Wiers, R.W., Pawelczack, S., Rinck, M., Becker, E.S. and Lindenmeyer, J., 2014. Implementation of approach bias re-training in alcoholism: How many sessions are needed? *Alcoholism: Clinical and Experimental Research,* 38(2), pp. 587-594.

Edmondson, A.C. and Zuzul, T., 2016. Teaming routines in complex innovation projects. In: J. Howard-Grenville, C. Rerup, A. Langley and H. Tsoukas (Eds.), *Organizational routines: How they are created, maintained, and changed* (pp. 179-202). Oxford: Oxford Scholarship.

Edmondson, A.C., Bohmer, R.M. and Pisano, G.P., 2001. Disrupted routines: Team learning and new technology implementation in hospitals. *Administrative Science Quarterly,* 46(4), pp. 685-716.

Eggers, J.P. and Kaplan, S., 2009. Cognition and renewal: Comparing CEO and organizational effects on incumbent adaptation to technical change. *Organization Science,* 20(2), pp. 461-477.

Eggers, J.P. and Kaplan, S., 2013. Cognition and capabilities: A multi-level perspective. *The Academy of Management Annals,* 7(1), pp. 295-340.

Egidi, M., 1996. Routines, hierarchies of problems, procedural behaviour: Some evidence from experiments. In: K.J. Arrow, E. Colombatto, M. Perlman and C. Schmidt (Eds.), *The rational foundations of economic behaviour: Proceedings of the IEA Conference held in Turin, Italy* (pp. 303-333). Houndmills: Macmillan Press.

Egidi, M. and Narduzzo, A., 1997. The emergence of path-dependent behaviors in cooperative contexts. *International Journal of Industrial Organization,* 15(6), pp. 677-709.

Eisenhardt, K.M. and Martin, J.A., 2000. Dynamic capabilities: What are they? *Strategic Management Journal,* 21(10-11), pp. 1105-1121.

Elam, M., 1993. *Innovation as the craft of combination: Perspectives on technology and economy in the spirit of Schumpeter*. Linköping: Linköping Universitet.

Elam, M. and Arrow, K.J., 1993. Markets, morals and powers of innovation. *Economy and Society,* 22(1), pp. 1-41.

Elfenbein, H.A., 2006. Emotion in organizations: A review and theoretical integration in stages. *The Academy of Management Annals,* 1, pp. 315-386.

Ellis, N., 1993. Rules and instances in foreign language learning: Interactions of explicit and implicit knowledge. *European Journal of Cognitive Psychology,* 5(3), pp. 289-318.

Elster, J., 1982. Marxism, functionalism, and game theory: The case for methodological individualism. *Theory and Society,* 11(4), pp. 453-482.

Elster, J., 1985. *Making sense of Marx*. Cambridge: Cambridge University Press.

Elster, J., 1989. *Nuts and bolts for the social sciences*. Cambridge: Cambridge University Press.

Emery, J.D., 2002. Designing firm integrating processes from the knowledge-based view. *Computational & Mathematical Organization Theory,* 8(3), pp. 243-250.

Epstein, S., 1994. Integration of the cognitive and the psychodynamic unconscious. *American Psychologist,* 49(8), pp. 709-724.

Evans, J., 2002. Logic and human reasoning: An assessment of the deduction paradigm. *Psychological Bulletin,* 128(6), pp. 978-996.

Evans, J., 2008. Dual-processing accounts of reasoning, judgment, and social cognition. *Annual Review of Psychology,* 59(1), pp. 255-278.

Evans, J., 2009. How many dual-process theories do we need? One, two, or many? In: J. Evans and K. Frankish (Eds.), *In two minds: Dual processes and beyond* (pp. 33-54). Oxford: Oxford University Press.

Evans, J., 2010. Intuition and reasoning: A dual-process perspective. *Psychological Inquiry,* 21(4), pp. 313-326.

Evans, J., 2012. Dual-process theories of reasoning: Facts and fallacies. In: K.J. Holyoak and R.G. Morrison (Eds.), *The Oxford handbook of thinking and reasoning* (pp. 115-133). Oxford: Oxford University Press.

Evans, J. and Stanovich, K.E., 2013. Dual-process theories of higher cognition: Advancing the debate. *Perspectives on Psychological Science,* 8(3), pp. 223-241.

Farjoun, M., 2010. Beyond dualism: Stability and change as a duality. *Academy of Management Review,* 35(2), pp. 202-225.

Feldman, M.S., 2000. Organizational routines as a source of continuous change. *Organization Science,* 11(6), pp. 611-629.

Feldman, M.S., 2003. A performative perspective on stability and change in organizational routines. *Industrial and Corporate Change,* 12(4), pp. 727-752.

Feldman, M.S., 2016. Routines as process. In: J. Howard-Grenville, C. Rerup, A. Langly and H. Tsoukas (Eds.), *Organizational routines: How they are created, maintained, and changed* (pp. 23-46). Oxford: Oxford University Press.

Feldman, M.S. and Rafaeli, A., 2002. Organizational routines as sources of connections and understandings. *Journal of Management Studies,* 39(3), pp. 309-331.

Feldman, M.S. and Pentland, B.T., 2003. Reconceptualizing organizational routines as a source of flexibility and change. *Administrative Science Quarterly,* 48(1), pp. 94-118.

Feldman, M.S. and Pentland, B.T., 2008. Routine dynamics. In: D. Barry and H. Hansen (Eds.), *The SAGE handbook of new approaches in management and organization* (pp. 302-317). Los Angeles: SAGE.

Feldman, M.S. and Orlikowski, W.J., 2011. Theorizing practice and practicing theory. *Organization Science,* 22(5), pp. 1240-1253.

Felin, T. and Foss, N.J., 2005. Strategic organization: A field in search of micro-foundations. *Strategic Organization,* 3(4), pp. 441-455.

Felin, T. and Hesterly, W.S., 2007. The knowledge-based view, nested heterogeneity, and new value creation: Philosophical considerations on the locus of knowledge. *Academy of Management Review,* 32(1), pp. 195-218.

Felin, T. and Foss, N.J., 2009. Organizational routines and capabilities: Historical drift and a course-correction toward microfoundations. *Scandinavian Journal of Management,* 25(2), pp. 157-167.

Felin, T. and Foss, N.J., 2010. The endogenous origins of experience, routines, and organizational capabilities: The poverty of stimulus. *Journal of Institutional Economics,* 7(02), pp. 231-256.

Felin, T. and Foss, N.J., 2011. The (proper) microfoundations of routines and capabilities: A response to Winter, Pentland, Hodgson and Knudsen. *Journal of Institutional Economics,* 8(02), pp. 271-288.

Felin, T., Foss, N.J., Heimeriks, K.H. and Madsen, T.L., 2012. Microfoundations of routines and capabilities: Individuals, processes, and structure. *Journal of Management Studies,* 49(8), pp. 1351-1374.

Ferster, C.B. and Skinner, B.F., 1957. *Schedules of reinforcement.* New York: Appleton-Century-Crofts.

Field, A., 2013. *Discovering Statistics Using IBM SPSS Statistics* (4th ed.). London: SAGE.

Fisher, H., 2009. *Self, logic, and figurative thinking.* New York: Columbia University Press.

Flavell, J. and Wellman, H., 1977. Metamemory. In: R.V. Kail and J.W. Hagen (Eds.), *Perspectives on the development of memory and cognition* (pp. 3-33). New York: Lawrence Erlbaum.

Fletcher, J., Maybery, M.T. and Bennett, S., 2000. Implicit learning differences: A question of developmental level? *Journal of Experimental Psychology: Learning, Memory, and Cognition,* 26(1), pp. 246-252.

Foray, D. and Steinmueller, W.E. (2001). *Replication of routine, the domestication of tacit knowledge and the economics of inscription technology: A brave new world?* Paper presented at the Conference in honour of Richard R. Nelson and Sidney G. Winter., Aalborg, Denmark.

Forkstam, C. and Petersson, K.M., 2005. Towards an explicit account of implicit learning. *Current Opinion in Neurology,* 18(4), pp. 435-441.

Foss, N.J., 1993. Theories of the firm: Contractual and competence perspectives. *Journal of Evolutionary Economics,* 3(2), pp. 127-144.

Foss, N.J., Heimeriks, K.H., Winter, S.G. and Zollo, M., 2012. A hegelian dialogue on the micro-foundations of organizational routines and capabilities. *European Management Review,* 9(4), pp. 173-197.

Frankish, K. and Evans, J., 2009. The duality of mind: An historical perspective. In: J. Evans and K. Frankish (Eds.), *In two minds: Dual processes and beyond* (pp. 1-30). Oxford: Oxford University Press.

Fraport AG Frankfurt Airport Services Worldwide. (2015). *Zahlen, Daten, Fakten 2015 zum Flughafen Frankfurt.* <http://www.fraport.de/content/fraport/de/misc/binaer/presse/publikationen/2015/zahlen--daten--fakten-2015/jcr:content.file/zahlen-daten-fakten-2015.pdf> [Accessed Dec 12, 2016].

Frensch, P.A., 1998. One concept, multiple meanings: On how to define the concept of implicit learning. In: M.A. Stadler and P.A. Frensch (Eds.), *Handbook of implicit learning* (pp. 47-104). Thousand Oaks: Sage.

Frensch, P.A. and Rünger, D., 2003. Implicit learning. *Current Directions in Psychological Science,* 12(1), pp. 13-18.

Freud, S., 1915 [2005]. *The Unconscious.* London: Penguin.

Freud, S., 1927. *The ego and the id* (J. Riviere, Trans.). London: Hogarth Press.

Friesl, M. and Larty, J., 2013. Replication of routines in organizations: Existing literature and new perspectives. *International Journal of Management Reviews,* 15(1), pp. 106-122.

Funke, G., 1958. Gewohnheit. *Archiv für Begriffsgeschichte,* 3, pp. 345-546.

Galbraith, C.S., 1990. Transferring core manufacturing technologies in high-technology firms. *California Management Review,* 32(4).

van Galen, G.P., 1991. Handwriting: Issues for a psychomotor theory. *Human Movement Science,* 10(2-3), pp. 165-191.

Galor, O. and Tsiddon, D., 1991. Technological breakthroughs and development traps. *Economics Letters,* 37(1), pp. 11-17.

Garapin, A. and Hollard, M., 1999. Routines and incentives in group tasks. *Journal of Evolutionary Economics,* 9(4), pp. 465-486.

Gasparini, S., 2004. Implicit versus explicit learning: Some implications for L2 teaching. *European Journal of Psychology of Education,* 19(2), pp. 203-219.

Gaulin, S.J. and McBurney, D., 2004. *Evolutionary psychology* (2nd ed.). Upper Saddle River: Prentice Hall.

Gavetti, G., 2005. Cognition and hierarchy: Rethinking the microfoundations of capabilities' development. *Organization Science,* 16(6), pp. 599-617.

Gavetti, G. and Levinthal, D., 2000. Looking forward and looking backward: Cognitive and experiential search. *Administrative Science Quarterly,* 45(1), p. 113.

Gebauer, G.F. and Mackintosh, N.J., 2007. Psychometric intelligence dissociates implicit and explicit learning. *Journal of Experimental Psychology: Learning, Memory, and Cognition,* 33(1), pp. 34-54.

Geiger, D. and Koch, J., 2008. Von der individuellen Routine zur organisationalen Praktik: Ein neues Paradigma für die Organisationsforschung? *Zeitschrift für betriebswirtschaftliche Forschung,* 60(11), pp. 693-712.

Geiger, D. and Schröder, A., 2014. Ever-changing routines? Toward a revised understanding of organizational routines between rule-following and rule-breaking. *Schmalenbach Business Review,* 66(2), pp. 170-190.

Gerrig, R.J., 2013. *Psychology and life* (20th ed.). Boston: Pearson.

Gersick, C.J. and Hackman, J.R., 1990. Habitual routines in task-performing groups. *Organizational behavior and human decision processes,* 47(1), pp. 65-97.

Gibson, J.J. and Gibson, E.J., 1955. Perceptual learning: Differentiation or enrichment? *Psychological Review,* 62(1), pp. 32-41.

Giddens, A., 1984. *The constitution of society: Outline of the theory of structuration.* Cambridge: Polity Press.

Gilbert, C., 2005. Unbundling the structure of inertia: Resource versus routine rigidity. *Academy of Management Journal,* 48(5), pp. 741-763.

Gioia, D.A. and Poole, P.P., 1984. Scripts in organizational behavior. *Academy of Management Review,* 9(3), pp. 449-459.

Gladwin, T.E., Figner, B., Crone, E.A. and Wiers, R.W., 2011. Addiction, adolescence, and the integration of control and motivation. *Developmental Cognitive Neuroscience,* 1(4), pp. 364-376.

Glaser, R., 1963. Instructional technology and the measurement of learing outcomes: Some questions. *American Psychologist,* 18(8), pp. 519-521.

Goh, J.M., Gao, G. and Agarwal, R., 2011. Evolving work routines: Adaptive routinization of information technology in healthcare. *Information Systems Research,* 22(3), pp. 565-585.

Goldstein, E.B., 2008. *Cognitive psychology : Connecting mind, research, and everyday experience* (2nd ed.). Belmont: Wadsworth.

Goschke, T., 1998. Implicit learning of perceptual and motor sequences. In: M.A. Stadler and P.A. Frensch (Eds.), *Handbook of implicit learning* (pp. 401-444). Thousand Oaks: SAGE.

Grant, R.M., 1991. The resource-based theory of competitive advantage: Implications for strategy formulation. *California Management Review,* 33(3), pp. 114-135.

Grant, R.M., 1996. Toward a knowledge-based theory of the firm. *Strategic Management Journal,* 17, pp. 109-122.

Greener, I., 2002. Understanding NHS reform: The policy-transfer, social learning, and path-dependency perspectives. *Governance,* 15(2), pp. 161-183.

Greener, I., 2005. The potential of path dependence in political studies. *Politics,* 25(1), pp. 62-72.

Greenhalgh, T., 2008. Role of routines in collaborative work in healthcare organisations. *BMJ,* 337, pp. a2448-a2448.

Greenhoot, A.F., 2003. Design and analysis of experimental and quasi-experimental investigations. In: M.C. Roberts and S.S. Ilardi (Eds.), *Handbook of research methods in clinical psychology* (pp. 92-114). Malden: Blackwell.

Greenwald, A.G. and Banaji, M.R., 1995. Implicit social cognition: Attitudes, self-esteem, and stereotypes. *Psychological Review,* 102(1), pp. 4-27.

Greenwald, A.G. and Nosek, B.A., 2001. Health of the Implicit Association Test at age 3. *Experimental Psychology,* 48(2), pp. 85-93.

Greenwald, A.G., McGhee, D.E. and Schwartz, J.L.K., 1998. Measuring individual differences in implicit cognition: The Implicit Association Test. *Journal of Personality and Social Psychology,* 74(6), pp. 1464-1480.

Greenwald, A.G., Nosek, B.A. and Banaji, M.R., 2003. Understanding and using the Implicit Association Test: I. An improved scoring algorithm. *Journal of Personality and Social Psychology,* 85(2), pp. 197-216.

Greenwald, A.G., Poehlman, T.A., Uhlmann, E.L. and Banaji, M.R., 2009. Understanding and using the Implicit Association Test: III. Meta-analysis of predictive validity. *Journal of Personality and Social Psychology,* 97(1), pp. 17-41.

Greif, S., 2004. Handlung. In: O. Häcker and K. Stapf (Eds.), *Dorsch: psychologisches Wörterbuch* (14th ed.). Bern: Hans Huber.

Grenard, J.L., Ames, S.L., Wiers, R.W., Thush, C., Sussman, S. and Stacy, A.W., 2008. Working memory capacity moderates the predictive effects of drug-related associations on substance use. *Psychology of Addictive Behaviors,* 22(3), pp. 426-432.

Griffiths, A. and Schabracq, M., 2003. Work and health psychology as a scientific discipline: Facing the limits of the natural science paradigm. In: M. Schabracq, J.A. Winnubst and C.L. Cooper (Eds.), *The handbook of work and health psychology* (2nd ed., pp. 173-189). Chichester: Wiley.

Gross, R.D., 2010. *Psychology: The science of mind and behaviour* (6th ed.). London: Hodder.

Grote, G., Weichbrodt, J.C., Günter, H., Zala-Mezö, E. and Künzle, B., 2008. Coordination in high-risk organizations: The need for flexible routines. *Cognition, Technology & Work,* 11(1), pp. 17-27.

Gureckis, T.M., James, T.W. and Nosofsky, R.M., 2011. Re-evaluating dissociations between implicit and explicit category learning: an event-related fMRI study. *J Cogn Neurosci,* 23(7), pp. 1697-1709.

Hall, C.S., 1957. Stimulus-response theory. In: C.S. Hall and G. Lindzey (Eds.), *Theories of personality* (pp. 572 p.). New York: Wiley.

Hannan, M.T. and Freeman, J., 1977. The Population Ecology of Organizations. *American Journal of Sociology,* 82(5), pp. 929-964.

Hannan, M.T. and Freeman, J., 1989. *Organizational ecology*. Cambridge: Harvard University Press.

Hansen, N.K. and Vogel, R. (2010). *The routine concept in organization theory and strategic management: A co-citation analysis.* Paper presented at the 4th International Conference on Organizational Routines: "Organizational routines between change and stability: Linking empirical research to recent theoretical debates", Nizza.

Hansen, R., 2002. Globalization, embedded realism, and path dependence: The other immigrants to Europe. *Comparative Political Studies,* 35(3), pp. 259-283.

Haselton, M.G., Nettle, D. and Andrews, P.W., 2015. The evolution of cognitive bias. In: D.M. Buss (Ed.), *The handbook of evolutionary psychology* (pp. 724-746). Hoboken: Wiley & Sons.

Hasselhorn, M. and Gold, A., 2009. *Pädagogische Psychologie: Erfolgreiches Lernen und Lehren* (2nd ed.). Stuttgart: Kohlhammer.

Hassin, R.R., 2005. Nonconscious control and implicit working memory. In: R.R. Hassin, J.S. Uleman and J.A. Bargh (Eds.), *The new unconscious* (pp. 196-222). Oxford: Oxford University Press.

Hauknes, J., 2000. Dynamic innovation systems: What is the role of services? In: M. Boden and I. Miles (Eds.), *Services and the knowledge-based economy* (pp. 38-63). London: Continuum.

von Hayek, F.A., 1942. Scientism and the study of society I. *Economica,* 9(35), pp. 267-291.

von Hayek, F.A., 1943. Scientism and the study of society II. *Economica,* 10(37), pp. 34-63.

von Hayek, F.A., 1944. Scientism and the study of society III. *Economica,* 11(41), pp. 27-39.

von Hayek, F.A., 1952. *The counter-revolution of science*. Glencoe: Free Press.

Hayes, A.F. and Preacher, K.J., 2014. Statistical mediation analysis with a multicategorical independent variable. *British Journal of Mathematical and Statistical Psychology,* 67(3), pp. 451-470.

Hayward, D.A., Shore, D.I., Ristic, J., Kovshoff, H., Iarocci, G., Mottron, L. and Burack, J.A., 2012. Flexible visual processing in young adults with autism: The effects of implicit learning on a global–local task. *Journal of Autism and Developmental Disorders,* 42(11), pp. 2383-2392.

Hazeltine, E., Grafton, S.T. and Ivry, R., 1997. Attention and stimulus characteristics determine the locus of motor- sequence encoding: A PET study. *Brain,* 120(1), pp. 123-140.

Heineken, E. and Habermann, T., 1994. *Lernpsychologie für den beruflichen Alltag*. Heidelberg: Sauer.

Helfat, C.E. and Lieberman, M.B., 2002. The birth of capabilities: Market entry and the importance of pre-history. *Industrial and Corporate Change,* 11(4), pp. 725-760.

Helfat, C.E. and Peteraf, M.A., 2003. The dynamic resource-based view: Capability lifecycles. *Strategic Management Journal,* 24(10), pp. 997-1010.

Helfat, C.E., Finkelstein, S., Mitchell, W., Peteraf, M.A., Singh, H., Teece, D.J. and Winter, S.G., 2007. *Dynamic capabilities: Understanding strategic change in organizations.* Malden: Blackwell.

Henderson, R. and Cockburn, I., 1994. Measuring competence? Exploring firm effects in pharmaceutical research. *Strategic Management Journal,* 15(S1), pp. 63-84.

Heron, W.T. and Skinner, B.F., 1940. The rate of extinction in maze-bright and maze-dull rats. *The Psychological Record,* 4, pp. 11-18.

Hilgard, E.R. and Marquis, D.G., 1961. *Conditioning and learning* (2nd ed.). New York: Appleton-Century-Crofts.

Hodgson, G.M., 1993. Institutional Economics: Surveying the 'Old' and the 'New'. *Metroeconomica,* 44(1), pp. 1-28.

Hodgson, G.M., 1997. The ubiquity of habits and rules. *Cambridge Journal of Economics,* 21(6), pp. 663-684.

Hodgson, G.M., 2003. The mystery of the routine: The darwinian destiny of an evolutionary theory of economic change. *Revue économique,* 54(2), pp. 355-384.

Hodgson, G.M., 2007a. Meanings of methodological individualism. *Journal of Economic Methodology,* 14(2), pp. 211-226.

Hodgson, G.M., 2007b. Institutions and individuals: Interaction and evolution. *Organization Studies,* 28(1), pp. 95-116.

Hodgson, G.M., 2008. The concept of a routine. In: M.C. Becker (Ed.), *Handbook of organizational routines* (pp. 15-28). Cheltenham: Edward Elgar.

Hodgson, G.M., 2009. The nature and replication of routines. In: M.C. Becker and N. Lazaric (Eds.), *Organizational routines: Advancing empirical research* (pp. 26-44). Cheltenham: Edward Elgar.

Hodgson, G.M. and Knudsen, T., 2004a. The complex evolution of a simple traffic convention: The functions and implications of habit. *Journal of Economic Behavior & Organization,* 54(1), pp. 19-47.

Hodgson, G.M. and Knudsen, T., 2004b. The firm as an interactor: Firms as vehicles for habits and routines. *Journal of Evolutionary Economics,* 14(3), pp. 281-307.

Hodgson, G.M. and Knudsen, T., 2010. *Darwin's conjecture: The search for general principles of social and economic evolution.* Chicago: University of Chicago Press.

Hoffer Gittell, J., 2002. Coordinating mechanisms in care provider groups: Relational coordination as a mediator and input uncertainty as a moderator of performance effects. *Management Science,* 48(11), pp. 1408-1426.

Hofstede, G., 1986. Cultural differences in teaching and learning. *International Journal of Intercultural Relations,* 10(3), pp. 301-320.

Holzinger, K. and Knill, C., 2002. Path dependencies in European integration: A constructive response to German foreign minister Joschka Fischer. *Public Administration,* 80(1), pp. 125-152.

Houben, K. and Wiers, R.W., 2009. Response inhibition moderates the relationship between implicit associations and drinking behavior. *Alcoholism: Clinical and Experimental Research,* 33(4), pp. 626-633.

Howard-Grenville, J. and Rerup, C., 2016. A process perspective on organizational routines. In: A. Langley and H. Tsoukas (Eds.), *The SAGE Handbook of Process Organization Studies* (pp. 323-337). London: Sage.

Howard-Grenville, J., Rerup, C., Langly, A. and Tsoukas, H., 2016. Advancing a process perspective on routines by zooming out and zooming in. In: J. Howard-Grenville, C. Rerup, A. Langly and H. Tsoukas (Eds.), *Organizational routines: How they are created, maintained, and changed* (pp. 1-18). Oxford: Oxford University Press.

Howard-Grenville, J.A., 2005. The persistence of flexible organizational routines: The role of agency and organizational context. *Organization Science,* 16(6), pp. 618-636.

Huesmann, L.R., Moise-Titus, J., Podolski, C.-L. and Eron, L.D., 2003. Longitudinal relations between children's exposure to TV violence and their aggressive and violent behavior in young adulthood: 1977-1992. *Developmental Psychology,* 39(2), pp. 201-221.

Hutchins, E., 1991. Organizing work by adaptation. *Organization Science,* 2(1), pp. 14-39.

Ise, E., Arnoldi, C.J., Bartling, J. and Schulte-Körne, G., 2012. Implicit learning in children with spelling disability: Evidence from artificial grammar learning. *Journal of Neural Transmission,* 119(9), pp. 999-1010.

Jacoby, L.L. and Brooks, L.R., 1984. Nonanalytic cognition: Memory, perception, and concept learning. *Psychology of Learning and Motivation,* 18(1), pp. 1-47.

Jaffee, D., 2001. *Organization theory: Tension and change*. Boston: McGraw Hill.

James, W., 1892. *Psychology: Briefer course.* New York: Macmillan.

Jarzabkowski, P., 2004. Strategy as practice: Recursiveness, adaptation, and practices-in-use. *Organization Studies,* 25(4), pp. 529-560.

Jarzabkowski, P. and Wilson, D.C., 2002. Top teams and strategy in a UK university. *Journal of Management Studies,* 39(3), pp. 355-381.

Jenkins, J.G., 1933. Instruction as a factor in 'incidental' learning. *The American Journal of Psychology,* 45(3), p. 471.

Jensen, R. and Szulanski, G., 2004. Stickiness and the adaptation of organizational practices in cross-border knowledge transfers. *Journal of International Business Studies,* 35(6), pp. 508-523.

Jiménez, L., 2003. Introduction: Attention and implicit learning. In: L. Jiménez (Ed.), *Attention and implicit learning* (Series 48 pp. 1-7). Amsterdam: John Benjamins.

Johnson-Laird, P.N., Khemlani, S.S. and Goodwin, G.P., 2015. Logic, probability, and human reasoning. *Trends in Cognitive Sciences,* 19(4), pp. 201-214.

Jones, O. and Craven, M., 2001. Beyond the routine: Innovation management and the Teaching Company Scheme. *Technovation,* 21(5), pp. 267-279.

Jonsson, A. and Foss, N.J., 2011. International expansion through flexible replication: Learning from the internationalization experience of IKEA. *Journal of International Business Studies,* 42(9), pp. 1079-1102.

Kahneman, D., 2011. *Thinking, fast and slow*. New York: Farrar, Straus and Giroux.

Kahneman, D. and Tversky, A., 1982. On the study of statistical intuitions. *Cognition,* 11(2), pp. 123-141.

Kahneman, D. and Frederick, S., 2002. Representativeness revisited: Attribute substitution in intuitive judgment. In: T. Gilovich, D. Griffin and D. Kahneman (Eds.), *Heuristics and biases: The psychology of intuitive judgment* (pp. 49-81). Cambridge: Cambridge University Press.

Kaiser, S. and Kozica, A.M., 2013. Organisationale Routinen. *OrganisationsEntwicklung,* (01).

Kakoschke, N., Kemps, E. and Tiggemann, M., 2017. Approach bias modification training and consumption: A review of the literature. *Addictive Behaviors,* 64, pp. 21-28.

Kantabutra, S. and Avery, G.C., 2010. The power of vision: Statements that resonate. *Journal of Business Strategy,* 31(1), pp. 37-45.

Kantowitz, B.H., Roediger, H.L. and Elmes, D.G., 2009. *Experimental psychology* (9th ed.). Belmont: Wadsworth.

Katz, D. and Kahn, R.L., 1978. *The social psychology of organizations* (2nd ed.). New York: Wiley.

Katz, R. and Allen, T.J., 1982. Investigating the Not Invented Here (NIH) syndrome: A look at the performance, tenure, and communication patterns of 50 R&D project groups. *R&D Management,* 12(1), pp. 7-20.

Kaufman, S.B., DeYoung, C.G., Gray, J.R., Jiménez, L., Brown, J. and Mackintosh, N., 2010. Implicit learning as an ability. *Cognition,* 116(3), pp. 321-340.

Kawakami, K., Phills, C.E., Steele, J.R. and Dovidio, J.F., 2007. (Close) distance makes the heart grow fonder: Improving implicit racial attitudes and interracial interactions through approach behaviors. *Journal of Personality and Social Psychology,* 92(6), pp. 957-971.

Kiesel, A. and Koch, I., 2012. *Lernen: Grundlagen der Lernpsychologie*. Wiesbaden: VS.

Kihlstrom, J.F., 2008. The psychological unconscious. In: O.P. John, R.W. Robins and L.A. Pervin (Eds.), *Handbook of personality: Theory and research* (3rd ed., pp. 583-602). New York: Guilford Press.

Kihlstrom, J.F. and Harackiewicz, J.M., 1990. Book review essays on Bandura's social foundations of thought and action: An evolutionary milestone in the psychology of personality. *Psychological Inquiry,* 1(1), pp. 86-92.

Kilduff, M., 1992. Performance and interaction routines in multinational corporation. *Journal of International Business Studies,* 23(1), pp. 133-145.

Kirk, R.E., 1996. Practical significance: A concept whose time has come. *Educational and Psychological Measurement,* 56(5), pp. 746-759.

Klein, A.M., Becker, E.S. and Rinck, M., 2010. Approach and avoidance tendencies in spider fearful children: The approach-avoidance task. *Journal of Child and Family Studies,* 20(2), pp. 224-231.

Knott, A.M., 2001. The dynamic value of hierarchy. *Management Science,* 47(3), pp. 430-448.

Knott, A.M., 2003. The organizational routines factor market paradox. *Strategic Management Journal,* 24(10), pp. 929-943.

Knudsen, T., 2008. Organizational routines in evolutionary theory. In: M.C. Becker (Ed.), *Handbook of organizational routines* (pp. 125-151). Cheltenham: Edward Elgar.

Koch, J., 2009. Innovation, organisationale Routinen und strategische Pfade. *Zeitschrift für Management,* 4(3), pp. 189-208.

Kogut, B. and Zander, U., 1992. Knowledge of the firm, combinative capabilities, and the replication of technology. *Organization Science,* 3(3), pp. 383-397.

Kolers, P.A. and Roediger, H.L., 1984. Procedures of mind. *Journal of Verbal Learning and Verbal Behavior,* 23(4), pp. 425-449.

Konlechner, S., 2011. Spiel's noch einmal, Sam: Wie sich Unternehmen präzise kopieren können, ohne dabei auf das Generieren von Lernerfahrung verzichten zu müssen. *Austrian Management Review,* 1, pp. 34-44.

Konlechner, S. and Güttel, W.H., 2010. Die Evolution von Replikationsstrategien im Spannungsfeld von Exploration und Exploitation. In: M. Stephan and W. Kerber (Eds.), *Ambidextrie: Der unternehmerische Drahtseilakt zwischen Ressourcenexploration und -exploitation* (Jahrbuch Strategisches Kompetenz-Management, Vol. 4, pp. 27-58). Munich: Rainer Hampp.

Kostova, T., 1999. Transnational transfer of strategic organizational practices: A contextual perspective. *Academy of Management Review,* 24(2), pp. 308-324.

Kostova, T. and Roth, K., 2002. Adoption of an organizational practice by subsidiaries of multinational corporations: Institutional and relational effects. *Academy of Management Journal,* 45(1), pp. 215-233.

Kotter, J.P., 1996. *Leading change*. Boston: Harvard Business School Press.

Kozica, A.M.F., Kaiser, S. and Friesl, M., 2014. Organizational routines: Conventions as a source of change and stability. *Schmalenbach Business Review*, 66(3), pp. 334-356.

Krieger, L.H., 1995. The content of our categories: A cognitive bias approach to discrimination and equal employment opportunity. *Stanford Law Review,* 47(6), p. 1161.

Kruglanski, A.W. and Orehek, E., 2007. Partitioning the domain of social inference: Dual mode and systems models and their alternatives. *Annual Review of Psychology,* 58, pp. 291-316.

Kunc, M.H. and Morecroft, J.D., 2010. Managerial decision making and firm performance under a resource-based paradigm. *Strategic Management Journal,* 31(11), pp. 1164-1182.

Langlois, R.N., 1992. Transaction-cost economics in real time. *Industrial and Corporate Change,* 1(1), pp. 99-127.

Langlois, R.N. and Everett, M.J., 1994. What is evolutionary economics? In: L. Magnusson (Ed.), *Evolutionary and Neo-Schumpeterian approaches to economics* (Vol. 36, pp. 11-47). Boston: Kluwer.

Laszlo, E., Masulli, I., Artigiani, R. and Csányi, V. (Eds.). (1993). *The Evolution of cognitive maps: New paradigms for the twenty-first century*. Yverdon: Gordon and Breach.

Latour, B., 1986. The powers of association. In: J. Law (Ed.), *Power, action, and belief: A new sociology of knowledge?* (pp. 264-280). London: Routledge & Kegan Paul.

Lawson, T., 1997. *Economics and reality*. London: Routledge.

Lazaric, N., 2000. The role of routines, rules and habits in collective learning: Some epistemological and ontological considerations. *European Journal of Economic and Social Systems,* 14(2), pp. 157-171.

Lazaric, N., 2008. Routines and routinization: An exploration of some micro-cognitive foundations. In: M.C. Becker (Ed.), *Handbook of organizational routines* (pp. 205-227). Cheltenham: Edward Elgar.

Lazaric, N. (2013). *Are routines reducible to mere cognitive automatisms? Some contributions from cognitive science to help shed light on change in routines*. [Working paper] Available at: Danish research unit for industrial dynamics [Accessed June 16, 2015].

Lazaric, N. and Mangolte, P.-A., 1999. Routines in theory and in practice: A criticism of the cognitive perspective. *Revista de economia contemporânea,* 1999(5), pp. 7-35.

Lazaric, N. and Denis, B., 2005. Routinization and memorization of tasks in a workshop: The case of the introduction of ISO norms. *Industrial and Corporate Change,* 14(5), pp. 873-896.

Lefrançois, G.R., 2006. *Psychologie des Lernens* (4th ed.). Berlin: Springer.

Lefrançois, G.R., 2012. *Theories of human learning* (6th ed.). Belmont: Wadsworth.

Leonard-Barton, D., 1992. Core capabilities and core rigidities: A paradox in managing new product development. *Strategic Management Journal,* 13(S1), pp. 111-125.

Lerner, R.M., 1990. Weaving development into the fabric of personality and social psychology: On the significance of Bandura's social foundation of thought and action. *Psychological Inquiry,* 1(1), pp. 92-96.

Levi, M., 1997. A model, a method, and a map: Rational choice in comparative and historical analysis. In: M.I. Lichbach and A.S. Zuckerman (Eds.), *Comparative politics : rationality, culture, and structure* (pp. 19-41). Cambridge: Cambridge University Press.

Levinthal, D.A., 2001. Organizational capabilities in complex worlds. In *The nature and dynamics of organizational capabilities* (pp. 363-380). Oxford: Oxford University Press.

Levinthal, D.A. and Rerup, C., 2006. Crossing an apparent chasm: Bridging mindful and less-mindful perspectives on organizational learning. *Organization Science,* 17(4), pp. 502-513.

Levitt, B. and March, J.G., 1988. Organizational Learning. *Annual Review of Sociology,* 14(1), pp. 319-338.

Lewicki, P., 1986. Processing information about covariations that cannot be articulated. *Journal of Experimental Psychology: Learning, Memory, and Cognition,* 12(1), pp. 135-146.

Lewicki, P., Czyzewska, M. and Hoffman, H., 1987. Unconscious acquisition of complex procedural knowledge. *Journal of Experimental Psychology: Learning, Memory, and Cognition,* 13(4), pp. 523-530.

Lewin, A.Y., Massini, S. and Peeters, C., 2011. Microfoundations of internal and external absorptive capacity routines. *Organization Science,* 22(1), pp. 81-98.

Lillrank, P., 2003. The quality of standard, routine and nonroutine processes. *Organization Studies,* 24(2), pp. 215-233.

Lipton, M., 1996. Demystifying the development of an organizational vision. *MIT Sloan Management Review,* 37(4), pp. 83-92.

Liu, S. and Vince, R., 1999. The cultural context of learning in international joint ventures. *Journal of Management Development,* 18(8), pp. 666-675.

Loch, C.H., Sengupta, K. and Ahmad, M.G., 2013. The microevolution of routines: How problem solving and social preferences interact. *Organization Science,* 24(1), pp. 99-115.

Lopes, M.C. (2011). *Wirksamkeit von impliziten und expliziten Lernprozessen: Aneignung taktischer Kompetenzen und motorischer Fertigkeiten im Basketball.* (Dr. phil. Dissertation), Universität Heidelberg, Heidelberg.

Lord, R.G. and Kernan, M.C., 1987. Scripts as determinants of purposeful behavior in organizations. *Academy of Management Review,* 12(2), pp. 265-277.

Louis, M.R. and Sutton, R., 1991. Switching cognitive gears: From habits of mind to active thinking. *Human Relations,* 44(1), pp. 55-76.

Love, J.F., 1995. *McDonald's: Behind the arches*. New York: Bantam Books.

Luchins, A.S., 1942. Mechanization in problem solving: The effect of Einstellung. *Psychological Monographs,* 54(6), pp. 1-95.

MacLeod, C., Rutherford, E., Campbell, L., Ebsworthy, G. and Holker, L., 2002. Selective attention and emotional vulnerability: Assessing the causal basis of their association through the experimental manipulation of attentional bias. *Journal of Abnormal Psychology,* 111(1), pp. 107-123.

MacLeod, C.M., 1991. Half a century of research on the Stroop effect: An integrative review. *Psychological Bulletin,* 109(2), pp. 163-203.

MacLeod, C.M. and MacDonald, P.A., 2000. Interdimensional interference in the Stroop effect: uncovering the cognitive and neural anatomy of attention. *Trends in Cognitive Sciences,* 4(10), pp. 383-391.

Madhok, A., 1997. Cost, value and foreign market entry mode: The transaction and the firm. *Strategic Management Journal,* 18(1), pp. 39-61.

Madsen, K.B., 1988. *A history of psychology in metascientific perspective*. Amsterdam: North-Holland.

Mahoney, A., Weetjens, B.J., Cox, C., Beyene, N., Reither, K., Makingi, G., Jubitana, M., Kazwala, R., Mfinanga, G.S., Kahwa, A., Durgin, A. and Poling, A., 2012. Pouched rats' detection of tuberculosis in human sputum: Comparison to culturing and polymerase chain reaction. *Tuberculosis Research and Treatment,* 2012, pp. 1-5.

Malerba, F. and Orsenigo, L., 1996. Technological regimes and firm behaviour. In: G. Dosi and F. Malerba (Eds.), *Organization and strategy in the evolution of the enterprise* (pp. 42-71). Houndmills: Macmillan.

Manning, V., Staiger, P.K., Hall, K., Garfield, J.B.B., Flaks, G., Leung, D., Hughes, L.K., Lum, J.A.G., Lubman, D.I. and Verdejo-Garcia, A., 2016. Cognitive bias modification training during inpatient alcohol detoxification reduces early relapse: A randomized controlled trial. *Alcoholism: Clinical and Experimental Research,* 40(9), pp. 2011-2019.

Manza, L., Zizak, D. and Reber, A.S., 1998. Artificial grammar learning and the mere exposure effect: Emotional preference tasks and the implicit learning process. In: M.A. Stadler and P.A. Frensch (Eds.), *Handbook of implicit learning* (pp. 201-222). Thousand Oaks: SAGE.

March, J.G., 1988. Variable risk preferences and adaptive aspirations. *Journal of Economic Behavior & Organization,* 9(1), pp. 5-24.

March, J.G., 1991. Exploration and exploitation in organizational learning. *Organization Science,* 2(1), pp. 71-87.

March, J.G., 1994. The evolution of evolution. In: J.A. Baum and J.V. Singh (Eds.), *Evolutionary dynamics of organizations* (pp. 39-49). New York: Oxford University Press.

March, J.G., 1996. Learning to be risk averse. *Psychological Review,* 103(2), pp. 309-319.

March, J.G., 2006. Rationality, foolishness, and adaptive intelligence. *Strategic Management Journal,* 27(3), pp. 201-214.

March, J.G. and Simon, H.A., 1958. *Organizations.* New York: Wiley.

March, J.G. and Olsen, J.P., 1989. *Rediscovering institutions: The organizational basis of politics.* New York: The Free Press.

Matsumoto, D.R., 2009. *The Cambridge dictionary of psychology.* Cambridge: Cambridge University Press.

McDougall, W.F.R.S., 1908. *An introduction to social psychology.* London: Methuen.

McKeown, T.J., 2001. Plans and routines, bureaucratic bargaining, and the cuban missile crisis. *The Journal of Politics,* 63(4), pp. 1163-1190.

McLeod, A.N. and Hahn, F.H., 1949. Proportionality, divisibility, and economies of scale: Comment. *The Quarterly Journal of Economics,* 63(1), pp. 131-137.

Medwell, J. and Wray, D., 2007. Handwriting: What do we know and what do we need to know? *Literacy,* 41(1), pp. 10-15.

Mensen, H., 2014. *Moderne Flugsicherung: Organisation, Verfahren, Technik.* Berlin: Springer.

Mgode, G.F., Weetjens, B.J., Nawrath, T., Cox, C., Jubitana, M., Machang'u, R.S., Cohen-Bacrie, S., Bedotto, M., Drancourt, M., Schulz, S. and Kaufmann, S.H.E., 2011. Diagnosis of tuberculosis by trained african giant pouched rats and confounding impact of pathogens and microflora of the respiratory tract. *Journal of Clinical Microbiology,* 50(2), pp. 274-280.

Michas, I.C. and Berry, D.C., 1994. Implicit and explicit processes in a second-language learning task. *European Journal of Cognitive Psychology,* 6(4), pp. 357-381.

Miller, G.A., 1956. The magical number seven, plus or minus two: Some limits on our capacity for processing information. *Psychological Review,* 63(2), pp. 81-97.

Miller, G.A., 2003. The cognitive revolution: A historical perspective. *Trends in Cognitive Sciences,* 7(3), pp. 141-144.

Miller, K.D., Pentland, B.T. and Choi, S., 2012. Dynamics of performing and remembering organizational routines. *Journal of Management Studies,* 49(8), pp. 1536-1558.

Miner, A.S., Ciuchta, M.P. and Gong, Y., 2008. Organizational routines and organizational learning. In: M.C. Becker (Ed.), *Handbook of organizational routines* (pp. 152-186). Northampton: Edward Elger.

Mintzberg, H., Ahlstrand, B.W. and Lampel, J., 1998. *Strategy safari: A guided tour through the wilds of strategic management.* New York: Free Press.

Mitchell, C.J., De Houwer, J. and Lovibond, P.F., 2009. The propositional nature of human associative learning. *Behavioral and Brain Sciences,* 32(02), p. 183.

Morgan, G., 2006. *Images of organization.* Thousand Oaks: Sage Publications.

Moss-Racusin, C.A., Dovidio, J.F., Brescoll, V.L., Graham, M.J. and Handelsman, J., 2012. Science faculty's subtle gender biases favor male students. *Proceedings of the National Academy of Sciences,* 109(41), pp. 16474-16479.

Murphy, J.B., 1994. The kinds of order in society. In: P. Mirowski (Ed.), *Natural images in economic thought: Markets read in tooth and claw* (pp. 536-582). Cambridge: Cambridge University Press.

Musen, G. and Treisman, A., 1990. Implicit and explicit memory for visual patterns. *Journal of experimental psychology. Learning, memory, and cognition,* 16(1), pp. 127-137.

Myers, D.G., 2010. *Psychology* (9th ed.). New York: Worth.

Narduzzo, A. and Warglien, M., 2008. Conducting experimental research on organizational routines. In: M.C. Becker (Ed.), *Handbook of organizational routines* (pp. 301-324). Cheltenham: Edward Elgar.

Narduzzo, A., Rocco, E. and Warglien, M., 2001. Talking about routines in the field: The emergence of organizational capabilities in a new cellular phone network company. In: G. Dosi, R.R. Nelson and S.G. Winter (Eds.), *The nature and dynamics of organizational capabilities* (pp. 27-50). Oxford: Oxford University Press.

Neisser, U., 1967. *Cognitive psychology*. New York: Appleton-Century-Crofts.

Nelson, R.R., 1995. Recent evolutionary theorizing about economic change. *Journal of economic literature*, pp. 48-90.

Nelson, R.R. and Winter, S.G., 1982. *An evolutionary theory of economic change*. Cambridge: Belknap Press of Harvard University Press.

Neumann, R. and Strack, F., 2000. Approach and avoidance: The influence of proprioceptive and exteroceptive cues on encoding of affective information. *Journal of Personality and Social Psychology,* 79(1), pp. 39-48.

Nissen, M.J. and Bullemer, P., 1987. Attentional requirements of learning: Evidence from performance measures. *Cognitive Psychology,* 19(1), pp. 1-32.

Norman, D., 1978. Notes toward a theory of complex learning. In: A. Lesgold and S. Pellegrino (Eds.), *Cognitive psychology and instruction* (Series 5 NATO conference series : III, Human factors, pp. 39-48). New York: Plenum Press.

North, D.C., 1991. Towards a theory of institutional change. *Quarterly Review of Economics and Business,* 31(4), pp. 61-69.

Nosek, B.A., 2005. Moderators of the Relationship Between Implicit and Explicit Evaluation. *Journal of Experimental Psychology: General,* 134(4), pp. 565-584.

Nosek, B.A., Banaji, M.R. and Greenwald, A.G., 2002a. Harvesting implicit group attitudes and beliefs from a demonstration web site. *Group Dynamics: Theory, Research, and Practice,* 6(1), pp. 101-115.

Nosek, B.A., Banaji, M.R. and Greenwald, A.G., 2002b. Math = male, me = female, therefore math ≠ me. *Journal of Personality and Social Psychology,* 83(1), pp. 44-59.

Nosek, B.A., Greenwald, A.G. and Banaji, M.R., 2006. The Implicit Association Test at age 7: A methodological and conceptual review. In: J.A. Bargh (Ed.), *Social psychology and the unconscious: The automaticity of higher mental processes* (pp. 265-292). New York: Psychology Press.

Novick, L. and Bassok, M., 2005. Problem solving. In: K.J. Holyoak and R.G. Morrison (Eds.), *The Cambridge handbook of thinking and reasoning*. New York: Cambridge University Press.

O'Brien, F. and Meadows, M., 2001. How to develop visions: A literature review, and a revised choices approach for an uncertain world. *Systemic Practice and Action Research,* 14(4), pp. 495-515.

Obstfeld, D., 2012. Creative projects: A less routine approach toward getting new things done. *Organization Science,* 23(6), pp. 1571-1592.

Ochsner, K.N. and Gross, J.J., 2005. The cognitive control of emotion. *Trends in Cognitive Sciences,* 9(5), pp. 242-249.

Ochsner, K.N. and Gross, J.J., 2008. Cognitive emotion regulation: Insights from social cognitive and affective neuroscience. *Current Directions in Psychological Science,* 17(2), pp. 153-158.

Okano, H., Hirano, T. and Balaban, E., 2000. Learning and memory. *Proceedings of the National Academy of Sciences,* 97(23), pp. 12403-12404.

Orlikowski, W.J., 2000. Using technology and constituting structures: A practice lens for studying technology in organizations. *Organization Science,* 11(4), pp. 404-428.

Orlikowski, W.J., 2002. Knowing in practice: Enacting a collective capability in distributed organizing. *Organization Science,* 13(3), pp. 249-273.

Ouellette, J.A. and Wood, W., 1998. Habit and intention in everyday life: The multiple processes by which past behavior predicts future behavior. *Psychological Bulletin,* 124(1), pp. 54-74.

Parmigiani, A. and Howard-Grenville, J., 2011. Routines revisited: Exploring the capabilities and practice perspectives. *The Academy of Management Annals,* 5(1), pp. 413-453.

Pavlov, I.P., 1927. *Conditioned reflexes: An investigation of the physiological activity of the cerebral cortex*. London: Oxford University Press.

Pentland, B.T., 1995. Grammatical models of organizational processes. *Organization Science,* 6(5), pp. 541-556.

Pentland, B.T., 2010. The foundation is solid, if you know where to look: Comment on Felin and Foss. *Journal of Institutional Economics,* 7(2), pp. 279-293.

Pentland, B.T. and Rueter, H.H., 1994. Organizational routines as grammars of action. *Administrative Science Quarterly,* 39(3), p. 484.

Pentland, B.T. and Feldman, M.S., 2005. Organizational routines as a unit of analysis. *Industrial and Corporate Change,* 14(5), pp. 793-815.

Pentland, B.T. and Feldman, M.S., 2008. Designing routines: On the folly of designing artifacts, while hoping for patterns of action. *Information and Organization,* 18(4), pp. 235-250.

Pentland, B.T. and Hærem, T., 2015. Organizational routines as patterns of action: Implications for organizational behavior. *Annual Review of Organizational Psychology and Organizational Behavior,* 2(1), pp. 465-487.

Pentland, B.T., Haerem, T. and Hillison, D., 2010. Comparing organizational routines as recurrent patterns of action. *Organization Studies,* 31(7), pp. 917-940.

Pentland, B.T., Feldman, M.S., Becker, M.C. and Liu, P., 2012. Dynamics of organizational routines: A generative model. *Journal of Management Studies,* 49(8), pp. 1484-1508.

Perren, L. and Grant, P., 2000. The evolution of management accounting routines in small businesses: A social construction perspective. *Management Accounting Research,* 11(4), pp. 391-411.

Perrig, W.J., 1996. Implitzites Lernen. In: J. Hoffmann and W. Kintsch (Eds.), *Enzyklopädie der Psychologie* (Series C, II Kognition, Vol. 7: Lernen). Göttingen: Hogrefe.

Perruchet, P. and Vinter, A., 1998. Learning and development: The implicit knowledge assumption reconsidered. In: M.A. Stadler and P.A. Frensch (Eds.), *Handbook of implicit learning* (pp. 495-531). Thousand Oaks: SAGE.

Phillips, D.J., 2005. Organizational genealogies and the persistence of gender inequality: The case of Silicon Valley law firms. *Administrative Science Quarterly,* 50(3), pp. 440-472.

Piaget, J., 1954. *The construction of reality in the child.* New York: Basic Books.

Piening, E.P., 2011. *Prozessdynamiken der Implementierung von Innovationen: Eine empirische Analyse dynamischer Fähigkeiten und ihrer Wirkung in Krankenhäusern.* Wiesbaden: Gabler.

Pierson, P., 2000. Increasing returns, path dependence, and the study of politics. *The American Political Science Review,* 94(2), pp. 251-267.

Plato, 1993. *Republic* (R. Waterfield, Trans.). Oxford: Oxford University Press.

Polanyi, M., 1958. *Personal knowledge: Towards a post-critical philosophy.* Chicago: University of Chicago Press.

Polanyi, M., 1966. *The tacit dimension.* Garden City: Doubleday.

Poling, A., Weetjens, B., Cox, C., Beyene, N. and Sully, A., 2010a. Using giant African pouched rats (Cricetomys Gambianus) to detect landmines. *The Psychological Record,* 60(4), pp. 715-728.

Poling, A., Weetjens, B., Cox, C., Beyene, N., Bach, H. and Sully, A., 2010b. Teaching giant African pouched rats to find landmines: operant conditioning with real consequences. *Behavior analysis in practice,* 3(2), pp. 19-25.

Poling, A., Weetjens, B., Cox, C., Beyene, N.W., Bach, H., Sully, A. and Dallery, J., 2011. Using trained pouched rats to detect land mines: Another victory for operant conditioning. *Journal of Applied Behavior Analysis,* 44(2), pp. 351-355.

Popper, K., 1944a. The poverty of historicism I. *Economica,* 11(42), pp. 86-103.

Popper, K., 1944b. The poverty of historicism II. *Economica,* 11(43), pp. 119-137.

Popper, K., 1945. The poverty of historicism III. *Economica,* 12(46), pp. 69-89.

Popper, K.R., 1945 [1947]. *The open society and its enemies: The high tide of prophecy: Hegel, Marx, and the aftermath* (2nd ed. Vol. 1). London: Routledge.

Porter, M.E., 1991. Towards a dynamic theory of strategy. *Strategic Management Journal,* 12(S2), pp. 95-117.

Postrel, S. and Rumelt, R.P., 1992. Incentives, Routines, and Self-Command. *Industrial and Corporate Change,* 1(3), pp. 397-425.

Prahalad, C.K. and Hamel, G., 1990. The core competence of the corporation. *Harvard Business Review,* 1990(May-June), pp. 79-90.

Projekt Deutscher Wortschatz, (2014). *Liste der Top 1000 deutschen Wörter.* [online]. Available at: Universität Leipzig, Institut für Informatik, Abteilung Automatische Sprachverarbeitung <wortschatz.uni-leipzig.de/Papers/top1000de.txt> [Accessed April 24, 2014].

Quinn, M., 2011. Routines in management accounting research: Further exploration. *Journal of Accounting & Organizational Change,* 7(4), pp. 337-357.

Radwan, L. and Kinder, S., 2013. Practising the diffusion of organizational routines. *Environment and Planning A,* 45(10), pp. 2442-2458.

Raub, S. (1998). *Towards a knowledge-based view of organizational capability.* (Ph.D. Doctoral thesis), Université de Genève, Genève.

Rauch, S.L., Savage, C.R., Brown, H.D., Curran, T., Alpert, N.M., Kendrick, A., Fischman, A.J. and Kosslyn, S.M., 1995. A PET investigation of implicit and explicit sequence learning. *Human Brain Mapping,* 3(4), pp. 271-286.

Ray, G., Barney, J.B. and Muhanna, W.A., 2004. Capabilities, business processes, and competitive advantage: choosing the dependent variable in empirical tests of the resource-based view. *Strategic Management Journal,* 25(1), pp. 23-37.

Reason, J.T., 1990. *Human error*. Cambridge: Cambridge University Press.

Reason, J.T., 2000. Human error: Models and management. *The BMJ,* 320(7237), pp. 768-770.

Reber, A.S., 1967. Implicit learning of artificial grammars. *Journal of Verbal Learning and Verbal Behavior,* 6(6), pp. 855-863.

Reber, A.S., 1989. Implicit learning and tacit knowledge. *Journal of Experimental Psychology: General,* 118(3), pp. 219-235.

Reber, A.S., 1993. *Implicit learning and tacit knowledge: An essay on the cognitive unconscious.* Oxford: Oxford University Press.

Reber, A.S. and Millward, R.B., 1968. Event observation in probability learning. *Journal of Experimental Psychology,* 77(2), pp. 317-327.

Reber, A.S. and Millward, R.B., 1971. Event tracking in probability learning. *The American Journal of Psychology,* 84(1), p. 85.

Reber, A.S., Walkenfeld, F.F. and Hernstadt, R., 1991. Implicit and explicit learning: individual differences and IQ. *Journal of experimental psychology. Learning, memory, and cognition,* 17(5), pp. 888-896.

Reber, A.S., Allen, R. and Reber, P., 1999. Implicit versus explicit learning. In: R.J. Sternberg (Ed.), *The nature of cognition* (pp. 475-513). Cambridge: MIT Press.

Reimer, T., Opwis, K. and Bornstein, A.-L., 2002. Routine problem solving in groups. In: W.D. Gray and C.D. Schunn (Eds.), *Proceedings of the Twenty-fourth Annual Conference of the Cognitive Science Society.* Fairfax: Erlbaum. pp. 780-785.

Reinecke, A., Becker, E.S. and Rinck, M., 2010. Three indirect tasks assessing implicit threat associations and behavioral response tendencies. *Journal of Psychology,* 218(1), pp. 4-11.

Rerup, C. and Feldman, M.S., 2011. Routines as a source of change in organizational schemata: The role of trial-and-error learning. *Academy of Management Journal,* 54(3), pp. 577-610.

Reynaud, B., 1996. Types of rules, interpretation and colletive dynamics: Reflections on the introduction of a salary rule in a maintenance workshop. *Industrial and Corporate Change,* 5(3), pp. 699-721.

Reynaud, B., 1998. Les propriétés des routines: Outils pragmatiques de décision et modes de coordination collective. *Sociologie du Travail,* 40(4), pp. 465-477.

Reynaud, B., 2005. The void at the heart of rules: Routines in the context of rule-following. The case of the Paris Metro Workshop. *Industrial and Corporate Change,* 14(5), pp. 847-871.

Reynolds-Keefer, L. and Johnson, R., 2011. Is a picture is worth a thousand words? Creating effective questionnaires with pictures. *Practical Assessment, Research & Evaluation,* 16(8), pp. 1-7.

Rice, R.E. and Cooper, S.D., 2010. *Organizations and unusual routines: A systems analysis of dysfunctional feedback processes.* Cambridge: Cambridge University Press.

Rinck, M. and Becker, E.S., 2007. Approach and avoidance in fear of spiders. *Journal of Behavior Therapy and Experimental Psychiatry,* 38(2), pp. 105-120.

Rivkin, J.W., 2001. Reproducing knowledge: Replication without imitation at moderate complexity. *Organization Science,* 12(3), pp. 274-293.

Rose, N., 2007. Genomic susceptibility as an emergent form of life? Genetic testing, identity and the remit of medicine. In: R.V. Burri and J. Dumit (Eds.), *Biomedicine as culture: Instrumental practices, technoscientific knowledge, and new modes of life* (Series 6 pp. 141-150). New York: Routledge.

Rozin, P. and Fallon, A.E., 1987. A perspective on disgust. *Psychological Review,* 94(1), pp. 23-41.

Rumelt, R.P., 1995. Inertia and transformation. In: C.A. Montgomery (Ed.), *Resource-based and evolutionary theories of the firm: Towards a synthesis* (pp. 101-132). Boston: Kluwer Academic.

Rycroft, R.W. and Kash, D.E., 2002. Path dependence in the innovation of complex technologies. *Technology Analysis & Strategic Management,* 14(1), pp. 21-35.

Ryle, G., 1949. *The concept of mind.* London: Hutchinson's University Library.

Sætrevik, B., Reber, R. and Sannum, P., 2006. The utility of implicit learning in the teaching of rules. *Learning and Instruction,* 16(4), pp. 363-373.

Salancik, G. and Leblebici, H., 1988. Variety and form in organizing transactions: A generative grammar of organization. In: N. Ditomaso and B. Bacharach (Eds.), *Research in the sociology of organizations* (pp. 1-31). Greenwich: JAI Press.

Salvato, C., 2003. The role of micro-strategies in the engineering of firm evolution. *Journal of Management Studies,* 40(1), pp. 83-108.

Salvato, C., 2009. Capabilities unveiled: The role of ordinary activities in the evolution of product development processes. *Organization Science,* 20(2), pp. 384-409.

Salvato, C. and Rerup, C., 2010. Beyond collective entities: Multilevel research on organizational routines and capabilities. *Journal of Management,* 37(2), pp. 468-490.

Sanchez, D.J. and Reber, P.J., 2013. Explicit pre-training instruction does not improve implicit perceptual-motor sequence learning. *Cognition,* 126(3), pp. 341-351.

Schank, R.C. and Abelson, R.P., 1977. *Scripts, plans, goals, and understanding: An inquiry into human knowledge structures.* New York: Erlbaum.

Schegloff, E.A., 1982. Discourse as an interactional achievement: Some uses of 'uh huh' and other things that come between sentences. In: D. Tannen (Ed.), *Georgetown University roundtable on languages and linguistics 1981* (pp. 71-93). Georgetown: Georgetown University Press.

Schein, E.H., 1985 [2004]. *Organizational culture and leadership* (3rd ed.). San Francisco: Jossey-Bass.

Schendan, H.E., Searl, M.M., Melrose, R.J. and Stern, C.E., 2003. An fMRI study of the role of the medial temporal lobe in implicit and explicit sequence learning. *Neuron,* 37(6), pp. 1013-1025.

Schoenmakers, T., Wiers, R.W., Jones, B.T., Bruce, G. and Jansen, A.T., 2007. Attentional re-training decreases attentional bias in heavy drinkers without generalization. *Addiction,* 102(3), pp. 399-405.

Schreyogg, G. and Sydow, J., 2011. Organizational path dependence: A process view. *Organization Studies,* 32(3), pp. 321-335.

Schreyögg, G., 2013. In der Sackgasse. *OrganisationsEntwicklung*(01).

Schuck, K., Keijsers, G. and Rinck, M., 2012. Implicit processes in pathological skin picking: Responses to skin irregularities predict symptom severity and treatment susceptibility. *Journal of Behavior Therapy and Experimental Psychiatry,* 43(1), pp. 685-691.

Schultz, D.P. and Schultz, S.E., 2011. *A history of modern psychology* (10th ed.). Belmont: Wadsworth.

Schulz, M., 2008. Staying on track: A voyage to the internal mechanisms of routine reproduction. In: M.C. Becker (Ed.), *Handbook of organizational routines* (pp. 228-255). Cheltenham: Edward Elgar Publishing.

Schumpeter, J.A., 1908. *Das Wesen und der Hauptinhalt der theoretischen Nationalökonomie.* Leipzig: Duncker & Humblot.

Schumpeter, J.A., 1908 [2010]. *The nature and essence of economic theory.* New Brunswick: Transaction.

Schumpeter, J.A., 1909. On the concept of social value. *The Quarterly Journal of Economics,* 23(2), pp. 213-232.

Scott, D., Scott, L. and Goldwater, B., 1997. A performance improvement program for an international-level track and field athlete. *Journal of Applied Behavior Analysis,* 30(3), pp. 573-575.

Seger, C., 1998. Multiple forms of implicit learning. In: M.A. Stadler and P.A. Frensch (Eds.), *Handbook of implicit learning* (pp. 295-320). Thousand Oaks: SAGE.

Senge, P.M., 1990. *The fifth discipline: The art and practice of the learning organization.* New York: Doubleday.

Shamsie, J. and Mannor, M.J., 2013. Looking inside the dream team: Probing into the contributions of tacit knowledge as an organizational resource. *Organization Science,* 24(2), pp. 513-529.

Shanks, D.R., 2005. Implicit learning. In: K. Lamberts and R.L. Goldstone (Eds.), *Handbook of cognition* (pp. 202-220). London: SAGE.

Shanks, D.R., 2010. Learning: From association to cognition. *Annual Review of Psychology,* 61(1), pp. 273-301.

Shanks, D.R. and St. John, M.F., 1994. Characteristics of dissociable human learning systems. *Behavioral and Brain Sciences,* 17(03), pp. 367-395.

Shapira, Z., 1994. Commentary: Evolution, externalities, and managerial action. In: J.A. Baum and J.V. Singh (Eds.), *Evolutionary dynamics of organizations* (pp. 117-124). New York: Oxford University Press.

Sharbanee, J.M., Stritzke, W.G., Jamalludin, M.E. and Wiers, R.W., 2013. Approach-alcohol action tendencies can be inhibited by cognitive load. *Psychopharmacology,* 231(5), pp. 967-975.

Shaughnessy, J.J., Zechmeister, E.B. and Zechmeister, J.S., 2011. *Research methods in psychology* (9th ed.). New York: McGraw-Hill.

Shuell, T.J., 1986. Cognitive conceptions of learning. *Review of Educational Research,* 56(4), pp. 411-436.

Siegel, S., 1984. Pavlovian conditioning and heroin overdose: Reports by overdose victims. *Bulletin of the Psychonomic Society,* 22(5), pp. 428-430.

Siegel, S., 2001. Pavlovian conditioning and drug overdose: When tolerance fails. *Addiction Research & Theory,* 9(5), pp. 503-513.

Siegel, S. and Ellsworth, D.W., 1986. Pavlovian conditioning and death from apparent overdose of medically prescribed morphine: A case report. *Bulletin of the Psychonomic Society,* 24(4), pp. 278-280.

Siegel, S., Hinson, R.E., Krank, M.D. and McCully, J., 1982. Heroin 'overdose' death: Contribution of drug-associated environmental cues. *Science,* 216(4544), pp. 436-437.

Simmel, G., 1908 [2009]. *Sociology: Inquiries into the construction of social forms* (A.J. Blasi, A.K. Jacobs and M.J. Kanjirathinkal Eds.). Leiden: Brill.

Simon, H.A., 1947. *Administrative behavior: A study of decision-making processes in administrative organization.* New York: Macmillan.

Simon, H.A., 1955. A behavioral model of rational choice. *The Quarterly Journal of Economics,* 69(1), p. 99.

Simon, H.A., 1967. Motivational and emotional controls of cognition. *Psychological Review,* 74(1), pp. 29-39.

Simon, H.A., 1972. Theories of bounded rationality. In: J. Marschak, C.B. McGuire, R. Radner and K.J. Arrow (Eds.), *Decision and organization* (pp. 161-176). Amsterdam: North-Holland.

Simon, H.A., 1985. Human nature in politics: The dialogue of psychology with political science. *American Political Science Review,* 79(02), pp. 293-304.

Simon, H.A., 1991. Bounded rationality and organizational learning. *Organization Science,* 2(1), pp. 125-134.

Simpson, B. and Lorino, P., 2016. Re-viewing routines through a pragmatist lens. In: J. Howard-Grenville, C. Rerup, A. Langly and H. Tsoukas (Eds.), *Organizational routines: How they are created, maintained, and changed* (pp. 47-70). Oxford: Oxford University Press.

Singley, M.K. and Anderson, J.R., 1989. *The transfer of cognitive skill.* Cambridge: Harvard University Press.

Skinner, B.F., 1938. *The behavior of organisms: An experimental analysis.* New York: Appleton-Century.

Skinner, B.F., 1953. *Science and human behavior.* New York: The Free Press.

Skinner, B.F., 1957. *Verbal behavior.* New York: Appleton-Century-Crofts.

Sloman, S.A., 1996. The empirical case for two systems of reasoning. *Psychological Bulletin,* 119(1), pp. 3-22.

Smith, A., 1776 [1982]. *An inquiry into the nature and causes of the wealth of nations* (R.H. Cambell, A.S. Skinner and W.B. Todd Eds.). Indianapolis: Liberty Fund.

Smith, E.R. and DeCoster, J., 2000. Dual-process models in social and cognitive psychology: Conceptual integration and links to underlying memory systems. *Personality and Social Psychology Review,* 4(2), pp. 108-131.

Spender, J.-C., 2002. Knowledge management uncertainty, and an emergent theory of the firm. In: C.W. Choo and N. Bontis (Eds.), *The strategic management of intellectual capital and organizational knowledge* (pp. 149-162). Oxford: Oxford University Press.

Spunt, R., 2015. Dual-process theories in social cognitive neuroscience. In: A.W. Toga (Ed.), *Brain mapping: An encyclopedic reference* (pp. 211-215). Amsterdam: Elsevier.

Squire, L.R., 1987. *Memory and brain.* New York: Oxford University Press.

Stadler, M.A. and Frensch, P.A., 1994. Whither learning, whither memory? *Behavioral and Brain Sciences,* 17(3), pp. 423-424.

Stanley, W.B., Mathews, R.C., Buss, R.R. and Kotler-Cope, S., 1989. Insight without awareness: On the interaction of verbalization, instruction and practice in a simulated process control task. *The Quarterly Journal of Experimental Psychology Section A,* 41(3), pp. 553-577.

Stanovich, K.E., 1999. *Who is rational? Studies of individual differences in reasoning.* Mahwah: Lawrence Erlbaum Associates.

Stanovich, K.E., 2004. *The robot's rebellion : finding meaning in the age of Darwin.* Chicago: University of Chicago Press.

Statistisches Bundesamt, Hoffmeyer-Zlotnik, J.H.P., Glemser, A., Heckel, C., Heyde, C.v.d. and Quitt, H., 2010. *Demographische Standards: Eine gemeinsame Empfehlung des ADM Arbeitskreis Deutscher Markt- und Sozialforschungsinstitute e.V., der Arbeitsgemeinschaft Sozialwissenschaftlicher Institute e.V. (ASI) und des Statistischen Bundesamtes* (5th ed.). Wiesbaden: Statistisches Bundesamt.

Stene, E.O., 1940. An approach to a science of administration. *The American Political Science Review,* 34(6), pp. 1124-1137.

Stinchcombe, A.L., 1990. *Information and organizations.* Berkeley: University of California Press.

Strack, F. and Deutsch, R., 2004. Reflective and impulsive determinants of social behavior. *Personality and Social Psychology Review,* 8(3), pp. 220-247.

Strauss, E., Sherman, E.M.S. and Spreen, O., 2006. *A compendium of neuropsychological tests: Administration, norms, and commentary* (3rd ed.). Oxford: Oxford University Press.

Stroop, J.R., 1935. Studies of interference in serial verbal reactions. *Journal of Experimental Psychology,* 18(6), pp. 643-662.

Suchman, L.A., 1983. Office procedure as practical action: Models of work and system design. *ACM Transactions on Information Systems,* 1(4), pp. 320-328.

Sun, R., 2002. *Duality of the mind: A bottom-up approach toward cognition.* Mahwah: Erlbaum.

Sun, R., Slusarz, P. and Terry, C., 2005. The interaction of the explicit and the implicit in skill learning: A dual-process approach. *Psychological Review,* 112(1), pp. 159-192.

Sydow, J., Schreyögg, G. and Koch, J., 2009. Organizational path dependence: Opening the black box. *Academy of Management Review,* 34(4), pp. 689-709.

Szulanski, G., 1996. Exploring internal stickiness: Impediments to the transfer of best practice within the firm. *Strategic Management Journal,* 17(WINTER), pp. 27-43.

Szulanski, G. and Winter, S., 2002. Getting it right the second time. *Harvard Business Review,* 80(1), pp. 62-69, 125.

Szulanski, G. and Jensen, R.J., 2004. Overcoming stickiness: An empirical investigation of the role of the template in the replication of organizational routines. *Managerial and Decision Economics,* 25(67), pp. 347-363.

Taatgen, N. and Anderson, J., 2008. Constraints in cognitive architectures. In: R. Sun (Ed.), *The Cambridge handbook of computational psychology* (pp. 170-185). Cambridge: Cambridge University Press.

Taylor, F.W., 1911. *The principles of scientific management.* New York: Harper & Brothers.

Teece, D. and Pisano, G., 1994. The dynamic capabilities of firms: An introduction. *Industrial and Corporate Change,* 3(3), pp. 537-556.

Teece, D.J., 1982. Towards an economic theory of the multiproduct firm. *Journal of Economic Behavior & Organization,* 3(1), pp. 39-63.

Teece, D.J., 2009. *Dynamic capabilities and strategic management: Organizing for innovation and growth.* Oxford: Oxford University Press.

Teece, D.J., Pisano, G. and Shuen, A., 1997. Dynamic capabilities and strategic management. *Strategic Management Journal,* 18(7), pp. 509-533.

Thompson, V.A., 2009. Dual-process theories: A metacognitive perspective. In: J. Evans and K. Frankish (Eds.), *In two minds: Dual processes and beyond* (pp. 171-196). Oxford: Oxford University Press.

Thorndike, E.L., 1898. *Animal intelligence: An experimental study of the associative processes in animals.* New York: Macmillan.

Thorndike, E.L. and Rock, R.T., 1934. Learning without awareness of what is being learned or intent to learn it. *Journal of Experimental Psychology,* 17(1), pp. 1-19.

Tinbergen, N., 1951. *The study of instinct.* Oxford: Clarendon Press.

Todorovic, D., 2011. What Is The Origin Of The Gestalt Principles? *Humana Mente,* 17(July), pp. 1-19.

Tolman, E.C., 1948. Cognitive maps in rats and men. *Psychological Review,* 55(4), pp. 189-208.

Turner, S.F. and Rindova, V., 2012. A balancing act: How organizations pursue consistency in routine functioning in the face of ongoing change. *Organization Science,* 23(1), pp. 24-46.

Turner, S.F. and Fern, M.J., 2012. Examining the stability and variability of routine performances: The effects of experience and context change. *Journal of Management Studies,* 49(8), pp. 1407-1434.

Turner, S.F. and Cacciatori, E., 2016. The multiplicity of habit: Implications for routines research. In: J. Howard-Grenville, C. Rerup, A. Langly and H. Tsoukas (Eds.), *Organizational routines: How they are created, maintained, and changed* (pp. 71-95). Oxford: Oxford University Press.

Tversky, A. and Kahneman, D., 1974. Judgment under uncertainty: Heuristics and biases. *Science,* 185(4157), pp. 1124-1131.

Tyre, M.J. and Orlikowski, W.J., 1996. The episodic process of learning by using. *International Journal of Technology Management,* 11(7-8), pp. 790-798.

Udehn, L., 2001. *Methodological individualism: Background, history, and meaning.* London: Routledge.

Udehn, L., 2002. The Changing Face of Methodological Individualism. *Annual Review of Sociology,* 28(1), pp. 479-507.

VandenBos, G.R. (Ed.). (2015). *APA dictionary of psychology* (2nd ed.). Washington: American Psychological Association.

Veblen, T., 1915. *Imperial Germany and the industrial revolution.* New York: Macmillan.

van de Ven, A.H. and Poole, M.S., 1995. Explaining development and change in organizations. *Academy of Management Review,* 20(3), pp. 510-540.

Verburgh, L., Scherder, E.J.A., van Lange, P.A.M. and Oosterlaan, J., 2016. The key to success in elite athletes? Explicit and implicit motor learning in youth elite and non-elite soccer players. *Journal of Sports Sciences,* 34(18), pp. 1782-1790.

Vergne, J.-P. and Durand, R., 2010. The missing link between the theory and empirics of path dependence: Conceptual clarification, testability issue, and methodological implications. *Journal of Management Studies,* 47(4), pp. 736-759.

Verneau, M., van der Kamp, J., Savelsbergh, G.J.P. and de Looze, M.P., 2014. Age and time effects on implicit and explicit learning. *Experimental Aging Research,* 40(4), pp. 477-511.

Volpert, W., 1974. *Handlungsstrukturanalyse als Beitrag zur Qualifikationsforschung.* Köln: Pahl-Rugenstein.

Vrijsen, J.N., Oostrom, I., Speckens, A., Becker, E.S. and Rinck, M., 2012. Approach and avoidance of emotional faces in happy and sad mood. *Cognitive Therapy and Research,* 37(1), pp. 1-6.

Vromen, J.J., 2006. Routines, genes and program-based behavior. *Journal of Evolutionary Economics,* 16(5), pp. 543-560.

Vromen, J.J., 2011. Routines as multilevel mechanisms. *Journal of Institutional Economics,* 7(02), pp. 175-196.

Wallach, D. and Lebiere, C., 2003. Implicit and explicit learning in a unified architecture of cognition. In: L. Jiménez (Ed.), *Attention and implicit learning* (pp. 215-250). Amsterdam: John Benjamins Publishing.

Wallas, G., 1926. *The art of thought*. New York: Harcourt.

Waller, W.T., 1988. The concept of habit in economic analysis. *Journal of Economic Issues,* 22(1), pp. 113-126.

Watson, J.B., 1913. Psychology as the behaviorist views it. *Psychological Review,* 20(2), pp. 158-177.

Watson, P., de Wit, S., Cousijn, J., Hommel, B. and Wiers, R.W., 2013. Motivational mechanisms underlying the approach bias to cigarettes. *Journal of Experimental Psychopathology,* 4(3), pp. 250-262.

Weber, M., 1913 [1981]. Some categories of interpretive sociology. *The Sociological Quarterly,* 22(2), pp. 151-180.

Weber, M., 1922. *Wirtschaft und Gesellschaft*. Tübingen: Mohr.

Weber, M., 1922 [1978]. *Economy and society: An outline of interpretive sociology* (G. Roth and C. Wittich Eds.). Berkeley: University of California Press.

Weick, K.E., 1990. The vulnerable system: An analysis of the Tenerife air disaster. *Journal of Management,* 16(3), pp. 571-593.

Weick, K.E., 1993. The collapse of sensemaking in organizations: The mann gulch disaster. *Administrative Science Quarterly,* 38(4), p. 628.

Weick, K.E., 1995. *Sensemaking in organizations*. Thousand Oaks: SAGE.

Weick, K.E. and Roberts, K.H., 1993. Collective mind in organizations: Heedful interrelating on flight decks. *Administrative Science Quarterly,* 38(3), p. 357.

Weiss, H.M. and Ilgen, D.R., 1985. Routinized behavior in organizations. *Journal of Behavioral Economics,* 14(1), pp. 57-67.

Wentura, D., Rothermund, K. and Bak, P., 2000. Automatic vigilance: The attention-grabbing power of approach- and avoidance-related social information. *Journal of Personality and Social Psychology,* 78(6), pp. 1024-1037.

Wertheimer, M., 1925. Über Gestalttheorie. Lecture at the Kant Society, Berlin, Dec. 17, 1924. *Philosophische Zeitschrift für Forschung und Aussprache,* 1, pp. 39-60.

Wertheimer, M., 1938. Gestalt theory. In: W.D. Ellis (Ed.), *A source book of gestalt psychology* (pp. 1-11). London: K. Paul, Trench, Trubner & Co.

Wertheimer, M., 1945. *Productive thinking*. New York: Harper.

Wiers, R.W., van Woerden, N., Smulders, F.T. and de Jong, P.J., 2002. Implicit and explicit alcohol-related cognitions in heavy and light drinkers. *Journal of Abnormal Psychology,* 111(4), pp. 648-658.

Wiers, R.W., Beckers, L., Houben, K. and Hofmann, W., 2009a. A short fuse after alcohol: Implicit power associations predict aggressiveness after alcohol consumption in young heavy drinkers with limited executive control. *Pharmacology Biochemistry and Behavior,* 93(3), pp. 300-305.

Wiers, R.W., Rinck, M., Dictus, M. and van den Wildenberg, E., 2009b. Relatively strong automatic appetitive action-tendencies in male carriers of the OPRM1 G-allele. *Genes, Brain and Behavior,* 8(1), pp. 101-106.

Wiers, R.W., Rinck, M., Kordts, R., Houben, K. and Strack, F., 2010. Retraining automatic action-tendencies to approach alcohol in hazardous drinkers. *Addiction,* 105(2), pp. 279-287.

Wiers, R.W., Eberl, C., Rinck, M., Becker, E.S. and Lindenmeyer, J., 2011. Retraining automatic action tendencies changes alcoholic patients' approach bias for alcohol and improves treatment outcome. *Psychological Science,* 22(4), pp. 490-497.

Wiers, R.W., Gladwin, T.E., Hofmann, W., Salemink, E. and Ridderinkhof, K.R., 2013. Cognitive bias modification and cognitive control training in addiction and related psychopathology: Mechanisms, clinical perspectives, and ways forward. *Clinical Psychological Science,* 1(2), pp. 192-212.

Wiers, R.W., Houben, K., Fadardi, J.S., van Beek, P., Rhemtulla, M. and Cox, W.M., 2015. Alcohol Cognitive Bias Modification training for problem drinkers over the web. *Addictive Behaviors,* 40, pp. 21-26.

Winkel, S., Petermann, F. and Petermann, U., 2006. *Lernpsychologie*. Paderborn: Ferdinand Schöningh.

Winter, S.G., 1964. Economic 'natural selection' and the theory of the firm. *Yale Economic Essays,* 4(1), pp. 225-272.

Winter, S.G., 1975. Optimization and evolution in the theory of the firm. In: R.H. Day and T. Groves (Eds.), *Adaptive economic models* (pp. 73-118). New York: Academic Press.

Winter, S.G., 1986. The research program of the behavioral theory of the firm: Orthodox critique and evolutionary perspective. In: B. Gilad and S. Kaish (Eds.), *Handbook of behavioral economics* (Vol. A, pp. 151-188). Greenwich: JAI Press.

Winter, S.G., 1987. Natural selection and evolution. In: J. Eatwell, M. Murray and P. Newman (Eds.), *The new Palgrave: A dictionary of economics* (Vol. 3, pp. 614-617). London: Palgrave Macmillan.

Winter, S.G., 1990. Survival, selection, and inheritance in evolutionary theories of organization. In: J. Singh (Ed.), *Organizational evolution: New directions* (pp. 269-297). Newbury Park: SAGE.

Winter, S.G., 1994. Organizing for continuous improvement: Evolutionary theory meets the quality revolution. In: J.A. Baum and J.V. Singh (Eds.), *Evolutionary dynamics of organizations* (pp. 90-108). New York: Oxford University Press.

Winter, S.G., 1995. Four Rs of profitability: Rents, resources, routines, and replication. In: C.A. Montgomery (Ed.), *Resource-based and evolutionary theories of the firm: Towards a synthesis* (pp. 147-178). Boston: Kluwer Academic.

Winter, S.G., 2000. The satisficing principle in capability learning. *Strategic Management Journal,* 21(10-11), pp. 981-996.

Winter, S.G., 2003. Understanding dynamic capabilities. *Strategic Management Journal,* 24(10), pp. 991-995.

Winter, S.G., 2013. Habit, deliberation, and action: Strengthening the microfoundations of routines and capabilities. *Academy of Management Perspectives,* 27(2), pp. 120-137.

Winter, S.G. and Szulanski, G., 2001. Replication as strategy. *Organization Science,* 12(6), pp. 730-743.

Winter, S.G. and Szulanski, G., 2002. Replication of organizational routines: conceptualizing the exploitation of knowledge assets. In: C.W. Choo and N. Bontis (Eds.), *The strategic management of intellectual capital and organizational knowledge* (pp. 207-221). Oxford: Oxford University Press.

Witt, U., 2010. Emergence and functionality of organizational routines: An individualistic approach. *Journal of Institutional Economics,* 7(02), pp. 157-174.

Wittgenstein, L., 1953 [1958]. *Philosophical investigations* (G.E.M. Anscombe, Trans.). Oxford: Blackwell.

Wittgenstein, L., 1956. *Remarks on the foundations of mathematics*. Oxford: Blackwell.

Wittig, A.F., 2001. *Schaum's outline of theory and problems of introduction to psychology* (2nd ed.). New York: McGraw-Hill.

Wood, W. and Neal, D.T., 2009. The habitual consumer. *Journal of Consumer Psychology,* 19(4), pp. 579-592.

Woud, M.L., Becker, E.S. and Rinck, M., 2008. Implicit evaluation bias induced by approach and avoidance. *Cognition & Emotion,* 22(6), pp. 1187-1197.

Woud, M.L., Becker, E.S. and Rinck, M., 2011. Induction of implicit evaluation biases by approach–avoidance training: A commentary on Vandenbosch and De Houwer. *Cognition & Emotion,* 25(7), pp. 1331-1338.

Woud, M.L., Maas, J., Becker, E.S. and Rinck, M., 2013a. Make the manikin move: Symbolic approach–avoidance responses affect implicit and explicit face evaluations. *Journal of Cognitive Psychology,* 25(6), pp. 738-744.

Woud, M.L., Becker, E.S., Lange, W.-G. and Rinck, M., 2013b. Effects of approach-avoidance training on implicit and explicit evaluations of neutral, angry, and smiling face stimuli. *Psychological Reports,* 113(1), pp. 199-216.

Wright, A., 2016. Organizational routines as embodied performatives: A communication as constitutive of organization perspective. *Organization,* 23(2), pp. 147-163.

Xie, Q., Gao, X. and King, R.B., 2013. Thinking styles in implicit and explicit learning. *Learning and Individual Differences,* 23, pp. 267-271.

Zahra, S.A., Sapienza, H.J. and Davidsson, P., 2006. Entrepreneurship and dynamic capabilities: A review, model and research agenda. *Journal of Management Studies,* 43(4), pp. 917-955.

Zbaracki, M.J. and Bergen, M., 2010. When truces collapse: A longitudinal study of price-adjustment routines. *Organization Science,* 21(5), pp. 955-972.

Zellmer-Bruhn, M.E., 2003. Interruptive events and team knowledge acquisition. *Management Science,* 49(4), pp. 514-528.

Zervos-Kopp, J., 2013. *Anatomie, Biologie und Physiologie* (3rd ed.). Stuttgart: Thieme.

Zhou, X., 1993. The dynamics of organizational rules. *American Journal of Sociology,* 98(5), pp. 1134-1166.

Zhuang, P., Dang, N., Warzeri, A., Gerloff, C., Cohen, L.G. and Hallett, M., 2009. Implicit and explicit learning in an auditory serial reaction time task. *Acta Neurologica Scandinavica,* 97(2), pp. 131-137.

Zimmerman, B.J. and Schunk, D.H., 2003. *Educational psychology: A century of contributions.* Mahwah: Erlbaum.

Zimmerman, D.H., 1970. The practicalities of rule use. In: J.D. Douglas (Ed.), *Understanding everyday life: Toward the reconstruction of sociological knowledge* (pp. 221-238). Chicago: Aldine.

Zollo, M. and Winter, S.G., 2002. Deliberate learning and the evolution of dynamic capabilities. *Organization Science,* 13(3), pp. 339-351.

Zollo, M., Reuer, J.J. and Singh, H., 2002. Interorganizational routines and performance in strategic alliances. *Organization Science,* 13(6), pp. 701-713.

Zott, C., 2003. Dynamic capabilities and the emergence of intraindustry differential firm performance: Insights from a simulation study. *Strategic Management Journal,* 24(2), pp. 97-125.

MIX
Papier aus verantwortungsvollen Quellen
Paper from responsible sources
FSC® C105338
FSC
www.fsc.org

If you have any concerns about our products,
you can contact us on
ProductSafety@springernature.com

In case Publisher is established outside the EU,
the EU authorized representative is:
Springer Nature Customer Service Center GmbH
Europaplatz 3, 69115 Heidelberg, Germany

Printed by Libri Plureos GmbH
in Hamburg, Germany